The Conservation of Conservation

The Conservation of Conservation

The Child's
Acquisition
of a
Fundamental
Concept

Adrien Pinard

Translated by
Helga Feider

University of Chicago Press
Chicago and London

The University of Chicago Press, Chicago 60637
The University of Chicago Press, Ltd., London

©1981 by The University of Chicago
All rights reserved. Published 1981
Printed in the United States of America

85 84 83 82 81   5 4 3 2 1

Library of Congress Cataloging in Publication Data

Pinard, Adrien.
    The conservation of conservation.

    Translation of La conservation de la conserva-
tion.
    Bibliography: p.
    Includes index.
    1. Conservation (Psychology)   2. Cognition in
children.   3. Piaget, Jean, 1896–1980   I. Title.
BF723.C68P5613   155.4'13   80-26339
ISBN 0-226-66834-7

ADRIEN PINARD is professor of psychology at the University of Montreal.

Le réel se démontre, il
ne se montre pas.
Bachelard

Contents

Introduction

The reader will certainly ask himself, Why dedicate an entire book to the special problem of mental conservations? The literature on the subject is already overly abundant, both concerning the nature and meaning of the conservation concept, and also specifically the factors that are responsible for the spontaneous acquisition or experimentally induced learning of conservation in the child. Our motivation to add further to this literature is related not only to our conviction that the development of conservation constitutes a cornerstone for the acquisition of each and every notion the child needs to construct in the course of cognitive development, but also to our wish to meet a number of particular needs which have not been adequately responded to by the countless writings on the subject.

There is, in the first place, a need to systematize in some way, by trying to bring together in a single comprehensive structure, all the various elements Piaget has contributed toward a solution of the problem of mental conservation throughout his numerous writings on the child's cognitive development. Certainly, psychology owes to Piaget the discovery of the role of conservation in cognitive development, many ingenious techniques for describing the way it functions and evolves in the child, and the inspiration for a multitude of normative and experimental studies on factors responsible for both spontaneous and induced acquisition of conservation. Nevertheless, Piaget himself has never offered a systematic and general exposition of the processes mediating the acquisition of conservation. This is probably due to the fact that conservation problems are usually treated by him only in the context of each of the concepts to be constructed by the child. One can find a brief description of the child's successive strategies in the construction of conservations in general within Piaget's first model of the equilibration of cognitive structures (see Apostel, Mandelbrot, & Piaget 1957). But this model deals directly with the evolution of the general process of equilibration, where the problems of conservation are used only as examples characteristic of this process. Even the revised, most recent version (Piaget [1975] 1977) maintains the same general perspective with no specific or systematic application to the acquisition of conservation. Therefore, one of the aims of the present text is to respond to this need for systematization. This will be done by tracing the main features of a model applied to conservation in its most inclusive sense—that can accommodate the fact that conservation is at the heart of everyone of the particular notions the child needs to build up.

Beyond this first aim, there are two additional goals. The first is to identify, more explicitly than is done in Piaget's theory, the essential role played by the processes involved in the progressive structuring of objects (e.g., the construction of the object itself, the discrimination of its various properties) upon which the child acts. A host of studies, both recent and not so recent, which we shall have occasion to discuss below, have increasingly stressed the importance of these processes. Piaget himself, although he attributes an important place to physical experience and abstraction in his equilibration model, particularly in his rather late studies concerning physical causality, still may have neglected these processes to some extent in favor of orienting his system on the basis of the coordination of actions the child performs upon objects (logical experience and reflective abstraction). Therefore, what is needed is a more general model that indicates more clearly—while recognizing the crucial role of logical experience as a frame necessary for physical experience—the complementarity and necessary integration of these two aspects, both essential to the acquisition of conservation. The third aim, even more ambitious, is to try to go beyond the purely descriptive level to which Piaget is commonly accused of having limited himself. He is aware of this objection and has recently made an effort to respond to it (Piaget [1975] 1977) by invoking a set of functional and structural arguments or rationales that could be construed to provide his equilibration model with explanatory power. It appears in no way obvious, however, that Piaget's arguments suffice to dissipate the stubborn impression one has of a system which offers an extremely rich and detailed description of each successive level in the construction of particular concepts, but where it is very difficult to identify the mechanisms that could explain the observed developmental sequences in the evolution of the general equilibration process. Thus, it seems worthwhile to try—limiting ourselves to the particular domain of mental conservations—at least to suggest a number of elements toward explanation, by first considering the way physical experience leads the child to progressively structure objects, then proceeding to systematically analyze the processes involved in the transition from empirical necessity to logical necessity (from induction to deduction) in the acquisition of conservation.

Finally, the model sketched in this text of the nature and origin of conservation will be compared to certain other models, which are often very different from the present one, models proposed previously and which are most often quite far removed from Piaget's perspective. The discussion of these alternative models will be concerned with delimiting their true theoretical and empirical scope by pointing to three interrelated facts, that is, these models are almost always concerned with the induced learning of the most traditional forms of conservation; further, these models are incapable of explaining the emergence of logical necessity in children; and, finally, frequently they contain errors of interpretation of various kinds concerning the nature of mental conservation, the critical factors involved in the spontaneous learning of conservation, or the authenticity of the induced learning.

These are, then, the principal aims of this work, as seen within the framework of Piaget's cognitive approach. Its title already indicates the main concerns that have led to the problems as formulated in this study and to the structure of the model proposed. To conclude this Introduction with a brief allegorical and vaguely humoristic excursion, the fact that mental conservations constitute a kind of universe by their omnipresence in children's acquisition of each and every concept (see Chap. 1) reminds us of a distribution of roles similar to that found in Brahman trinity, wherein Brahma is thought of as being the creator of the universe, Vishnu its conserver, and Civa its destructor. If, just for fun, we transpose this distribution of roles and apply it to the universe of conservation, evidently the role of Brahma himself is no longer to be attributed, while the pretenders to the throne of Civa are getting ever more numerous. It is for the role of Vishnu that I somewhat pretentiously pose his candidacy, but hoping that this role will not be simply that of custodian, however noble that may be, to be entrusted only with the care of treasures of the past.

It remains for me the pleasant task of expressing my gratitude to all those who in one way or another have contributed to the publication of this volume. First, I wish to thank the Canada Council for awarding me a Leave Fellowship during my sabbatical year when this book was written. I also wish to thank the Ministère de l'Education du Québec whose continuing financial support to our research team has helped in the collection of the data reported in this book.

I want to express my gratitude to (*a*) Dr. Monique Lefebvre-Pinard, my wife, for her incisive criticisms and stimulating suggestions and her enduring patience all the while this book was written; (*b*) my colleague Dr. Helga Feider for having performed the arduous task of translating without error or distortion this exceedingly abstract text, which was thought out and written in French; (*c*) my student Luc Doré for having kindly agreed to carry out an exhaustive and tiresome search of all of Piaget's publications already available in English translations and to find the exact references as they appear in the text; (*d*) the two outside advisors of the University of Chicago Press for their competent criticism and comments which I have tried to take into account in the final version of my book; (*e*) the editorial staff of the University of Chicago Press for their understanding, their efficiency, and their expediency in the study and edition of the text; (*f*) and all the others—colleagues, research assistants, school board authorities, secretaries, experimental subjects, etc.—for their generous cooperation.

November 1979

1   On the Concept of Conservation

Before approaching the main topic of this book, it is useful to consider briefly two preliminary questions related to the nature of the conservation concept. Two specific problems will be discussed. The first concerns the polymorphic character of the conservation concept, and the second the décalages between different kinds of conservation.

The Polymorphic Character of Conservation

The term "conservation" is usually employed to refer to the invariance of certain logical or spatiotemporal properties such as number, length, surface, quantity of matter, etc., in spite of the transformations that can be performed on the material involved. The examples cited are certainly among the most typical ones— perhaps because of their proximity to the etymological sense of the word "conservation"—which is also the reason why the current literature, rich as it is, has come to delimit the meaning of the term in so narrow a fashion. Even a cursory examination of Piaget's writings, however, reveals that conservation is not any particular operation, nor even a "principle" (as, e.g., Gagné 1968 has Piaget assert), but that actually it is the invariant necessary in the coordination of mental operations; more specifically, it follows from one particular property of these operations, which is reversibility.

There is, in fact, no such thing as a "conservative" operation: conservation is but one of several aspects of any operational system, all of which call for a combination of transformations (of the characteristics a, b, c, etc.) with the conservation of some of their interconnections (sum or product, etc.). (Piaget & Inhelder [1968] 1973, p. 310)

It is precisely the reversibility which brings about the conservation, as can easily be demonstrated in the psychological field;

1

reversibility is the very process from which conservation is produced. (Piaget [1967a] 1971, p. 209).

Now the conservation of matter is a structure—or at least the index of a structure, which, of course, rests on a whole operational group of greater complexity—whose reversibility is manifested by the compensations exercised by the operations. (Piaget [1964] 1967, p. 153)

Looked at in this way, the meaning of the conservation concept becomes considerably extended, since it appears implicated in the way all concepts are constructed by children. If this is true, it may be interesting (a) to describe briefly the various aspects in which the conservation phenomenon appears and, related to that, (b) to review the various kinds of pseudoconservation which may sometimes be observed.

The Different Types of Conservation

Consider as beyond the scope of the present discussion the more primitive forms of conservation which gradually evolve during the sensorimotor period (see especially Mounoud 1973 and Mounoud & Bower 1974 for very interesting work on weight conservation at the sensorimotor level). Also exclude from consideration the more advanced forms of conservation which are treated within physics (e.g., conservation of matter, of energy, of inert motion, etc.) which, as Piaget notes (Inhelder & Piaget [1955] 1958; Piaget 1950b, 1967c), cannot be verified by experience, since this would require transformations and spatiotemporal divisions to be carried out ad infinitum. Limiting the discussion to just those kinds of conservation which are constructed at the level of representational thinking and which are amenable to verification by experience, an important distinction concerns that between conservations of the logicoarithmetical kind and conservations of the infralogical kind (to be taken in the most general sense), depending on whether they concern the logicoarithmetical properties that characterize a collection of discrete objects or the spatiotemporal properties that characterize a continuum.[1]

1. It is well known, according to Piaget, that corresponding to the logicoarithmetical operations of classes, relations, and number are the equivalent infralogical or spatiotemporal operations: i.e., partition and reconstitution of an object, the relations of position and change of position existing between its parts, and the operations of measurement applied to it.

I. The first group includes: (*a*) conservation of a class *B* of objects in spite of its division into subclasses *A* and *A'* (e.g., the class inclusion problem), (*b*) conservation (seldom studied) of an asymmetric order relation in spite of changes performed on the elements of the ordered series (e.g., inequality of differences in size or in spacing, reduction in the number of elements), (*c*) conservation (very popular) of the number of elements in a collection in spite of changes in the spatial arrangement within the collection.

II. The second group consists of three subgroups: one for conservation with respect to spatial, another for temporal, and the third for spatiotemporal properties of objects.

1. To begin with the *spatial* properties, a distinction can be made between conservations with respect to the geometrical properties of the objects (mathematical space) and conservations regarding their physical properties (physical space). As for geometrical properties, one may cite (*a*) the conservation of topological entities (e.g., conservation of a line in spite of its decomposition into adjacent parts, a conservation implied in the notion of point and continuum), of projective sets (e.g., conservation of the whole of a cone when its shadow is projected onto a screen in spite of the apparent disappearance of some of its parts), or of Euclidean objects (e.g., conservation of a surface in spite of variable arrangements of its parts); (*b*) the conservation of topological relations (e.g., conservation of neighborhood and order relations within a series, in spite of variable dispositions such as linear or circular arrangements, etc.), of projective relations (conservation of relative locations within a landscape, in spite of differences in perspective), or of Euclidean relations (e.g., conservation of distances between elements of a village to be reconstructed on a different scale); (*c*) the conservation of the metric properties of an object (e.g., conservation of geometrical volume). As for the physical properties of objects, there are the classical conservations of quantity of matter, of weight, of volume. One might also mention conservation of the shape of a living entity, in spite of all the changes taking place during its growth (cited by Piaget but not having been studied by him: cf. Piaget & Voyat 1968), and, finally, the many different conservations, studied by Piaget more recently, pertaining to the domain of physical causality (Piaget [1971] 1974, 1972a, 1972b, 1973a, 1973b).

2. Considering next the *temporal* properties of objects, which involve in each case some form of compensation between two complementary aspects of a nontemporal nature such as space and velocity (Piaget [1946a] 1970, [1946b] 1970), one might refer to (*a*) the conservation of physical duration (e.g., conservation of a total time span in spite of its being divided into a sequence of partial durations, conservation of age differences in spite of changes in size differences or termination of height increases) as well as conservation of psychological duration (conservation of the time of action in spite of differences in speed, difficulty, interest, productiveness, etc.), (*b*) the conservation of physical time relations (e.g., conservation of temporal order of events in the case of mobiles covering different distances at different speeds, conservation of the order of births between children in spite of cancellation of size differences) and of psychological time relations (e.g., conservation of the order of succession of life experiences in spite of interference deriving from diversity of contents), (*c*) the conservation of metric time (e.g., conservation of time measured by a chronometer in spite of differences in speed and work output).

3. Finally, with respect to object properties that are *spatial and temporal* at once, suffice it to point to (*a*) the conservation of the speed of moving bodies in spite of inequalities of distance and time; (*b*) the conservation of distance covered in spite of differences in speed, time, or the spatial disposition of partial distances, etc.; (*c*) the conservation of order relations between various moving bodies (e.g., conservation of the order of marbles entering a tunnel in spite of rotations performed on the system); (*d*) the conservation of a kinetic quantity per unit of time (e.g., the conservation of flow, that is, of a quantity of water circulating in a duct, where a reduction in diameter is to be compensated by an increase in velocity, a situation recently studied by Blanchet 1974).

In sum, it can be seen that the conservation concept extends far beyond the few privileged domains to which it is customarily restricted. Without loss to its essential meaning, which is the invariance of physical and logical properties of objects in the face of apparent changes brought about by the actions the subject performs on these objects, or by the interactions arising between various objects, conservation is the very heart of all concepts the child constructs. As shown below, conservation is in fact the result of the reversible character of mental operations which need to be brought into coordination in order for any concept to be acquired by the child.

Types of Pseudoconservation

The wide range of phenomena encompassed by the conservation concept doubtlessly accounts for a similar variety of types of pseudoconservations which have been found in children, either in the normal course of development, that is, as evolving naturally and spontaneously, or as a result of the numerous experiments performed to provoke the learning of certain concepts.

To begin with those that can be observed in the course of spontaneous development, one might first mention the many varieties of pseudoconservation which are due to the young child's inability to overcome certain limitations of a topological nature (e.g., order relations, relations of neighborhood, enclosure). These pseudoconservations, which essentially consist in wrongly conserving topological relations and which, therefore, Piaget (Piaget & Inhelder [1966] 1971, p. 262) has designated as "primary" pseudoconservations, offer a major obstacle to the operational acquisition of a host of concepts. For instance, when a child is asked to draw the line that would result from straightening the arc of a circle, he might refuse to draw a line extending beyond the limits of the arc (conservation of order relations). Such pseudoconservation can also be observed when a child, questioned about the conservation of substances, predicts, for example, that transforming a ball of clay into a sausage will change its length without affecting its height, or that pouring water from a large into a narrow container will neither change the amount of the water nor the water level (false conservation of order relations). Similarly, a child, who believes that a square (or circle, etc.) can never lose its rectangular (or circular) shape to become a point following an infinite number of reductions, conserves inappropriately the elementary topological relations of neighborhood, continuity, etc., which he uses as criteria differentiating the various geometrical shapes. On the other hand, the inappropriate conservation of the relation of enclosure or being inside will lead a child to think that a perimeter included within another is necessarily shorter and takes up less space to travel through. The studies by Piaget and Inhelder ([1966] 1971) about mental images abound in such examples. In addition to these primary pseudoconservations, there are more advanced forms which Piaget (Piaget & Inhelder [1966] 1971, p. 262) designates as "operational" or advanced, since they are the result of an inappropriate extension of the correct operational conservation of one property to the incorrect conservation of another property of the same object, due to inadequate differentiation between the two properties. A typical example of this type of pseudoconservation is provided in Lunzer's elegant study (1965), in which children before the onset of formal thought are led to falsely conserve the surface of a shape ("still the same amount of grass to eat in the field") while correctly conserving the perimeter ("still the same distance walk around the field") when, for example, a 12×12-inch square is transformed into a 9×15-inch rectangle; or, inversely, these children correctly conserve the surface but incorrectly the perimeter, when the lower left corner of a square is cut off and joined at the upper left side of the same square. One may also cite the examples of pseudoconservation of surface and volume observed by Pinard and Chassé (1977) when one of these properties is varied and the other invariant.

Examining next the voluminous literature concerning certain experimentally induced forms of conservation, one could cite a large number of examples—tedious to analyze here in detail (for an extensive review of these, see Beilin 1971, 1978)—where the acquisitions observed in children do not necessarily pertain to conservation, even though they may appear to exhibit all its characteristic features. There are many reasons which may justify using the term "pseudoconservation" in these cases. Among the more important ones, one may point to the lack of sufficiently rigorous and operational criteria as seen, for example, in (a) inadequate control measures: oversimplified pre- and posttests, including, for example, only situations of initial inequality; (b) the kind of training methods used, which often resemble the control measures too closely, or at times are extremely didactic or verbal; (c) a great number of confusions in interpretation, as (i) confusion between mental reversibility and physical revertibility; (ii) confusion between simple covariation and multiplicative compensation of two aspects of some physical entity; (iii) confusion between empirical necessity as manifested in the blind application of a rule, drilled into the subject by means of a series of direct reinforcements, and logical necessity as manifested in the flexible, coherent, and generalized application of a new form of reasoning resulting from the need to achieve internal consistency; (iv) confusion between qualitative (e.g., "it is still the same water") and quantitative (e.g., "there is still the same amount of water to drink") identity—the former, acquired earlier, presupposes nothing but the ability to synthetize a certain number of unchanged attributes in an object, while the latter, acquired later, presupposes additive and multiplicative operations (of a logical or numerical character), which are necessary for conservation; (v) confusion between perceptual illusion and conceptual inference at the preoperational level, as evident in most of the experiments where a perceptual illusion paradigm is used to study logical conservation—in fact, it is one thing to learn or to *know* that what one *sees* and *continues to see* is an illusion, and it is quite another matter to substitute an operational inference (a knowledge based on compensation, e.g.) for a preoperational inference, a knowledge derived from figurative aspects only which, by being replaced, ceases to exist (see Gillieron 1974, e.g., who offers a clear analysis of this difference); etc. It would be easy to find more instances of pseudoconservations, especially since they often contaminate or alter in one way or another the nature of the many and various forms of conservation described above. The examples cited, however, should suffice to illustrate the dangers attendant upon hasty and oversimplified interpretations of the conservation concept.

Décalages between Conservations   *Horoz.*

Given, then, the extremely polymorphic character of the conservation concept, it is hardly surprising to find that the acquisition of these various types of conservation is subject to a considerable amount of chronological variation. The sources of these décalages and their nature are to date not well understood. Before approaching this problem, one should first draw a certain number of preliminary distinctions.

The décalages to be considered here have nothing to do with the *vertical décalages*, by virtue of which, according to Piaget, one and the same conceptual content (e.g., causality, space) needs to be structured at different successive levels so that, though already structured at the sensorimotor level, for example, it will have to be restructured again at the level of concrete operational thinking in terms of a new group of operations (e.g., conservation of weight). Rather, when speaking of décalages between different conservations, the reference here is to *horizontal décalages*, which denote the chronological variation in the emergence of a particular class of operations as a function of different contents (e.g., conservation of substance and of weight). It should be pointed out that for Piaget—and this is true of even his earliest theoretical writings (1941)—a décalage proper must involve in principle, and always involves in fact, when empirically observed, different concepts (or content areas) that become structured at different rates but through analogous operational groupings. The *analogy* between the operations concerned may be more or less manifest, nor is it necessarily accompanied by successive implications (such as the conservation of weight, which implies that of matter, etc.). Yet one always finds at least a dual process of progressive differentiation and complementation as well as structural parallelism, essential characteristics of horizontal décalages proper. On the other hand, no décalage should be observed, at least not at the operational level, when the operations in question are applied to the same concept and are connected to each other by means of the *identity* relation inherent in a single object (e.g., conservation of a quantity of liquid which is subject to deformations in varying degrees of intensity), by means of *substitution* relations obtaining between different but homogeneous objects (such as conservation of the quantity of liquid independent of its initial amount, its color, etc.), or, finally, by means of the relation of *correspondence* inherent in different heterogenous objects (e.g., conservation of a liquid or of a solid quantity).

Factors of Décalages

Any effort to find a systematic analysis of the various factors that influence the appearance of décalages in Piaget's writings would be in vain. In his introduction to the publication by Laurendeau and Pinard ([1968] 1970) on the development of spatial representation in the child, Piaget openly acknowledges his conviction that it would be premature to propose a theory of décalages before the outcomes are known of the many studies in progress concerning experimentally provoked learning of logical structures and concerning the development of causality in children. He states there that "décalages derive . . . from the object's resistances" (p. 4) to the subject's operational activity. He singles out the various obstacles to logical operations of the figurative characteristics of the data with which the child's logic has to deal. This brings to mind "the difference in the perceptual and intuitive conditions" by which he had once before (Piaget 1941, p. 266) explained the slight décalages observed within a single concept in the emergence of operations carried out on heterogeneous objects. He further insists, in the same text, that children experience varying degrees of difficulty due to the fact that objects exist independently of the subject and produce causal effects which are more or less easy to understand, and this may interfere, sometimes to a considerable extent, with the formation of the operational structures involved in such concepts. Thus, to explain the well-known décalages between the conservation of substance, of weight, and of volume—which Piaget had earlier attributed to the resistance offered by "perceptual or representational obstacles" (Piaget 1941, p. 270) as well as to the implicational relations existing between the three concepts (that weight presupposes substance as weighing presupposes retrieval, etc.)—Piaget now particularly stresses the fact that the weight of an object produces a far greater number of and more varied effects (according to position, form, physical state, etc., of the object) than does quantity of matter and that analogous causal factors render the conservation of volume more difficult than that of weight.

In any event, in trying to categorize the possible sources of the décalages to be found in the acquisition of different types of conservation, one would have to cite at least the following, specifying however that any one décalage may depend on more than one of the factors mentioned and that, inversely, any one factor may account for more than one type of décalage.

a) *Differential strength of perceptual or intuitional delusions.* It is this first factor that is undoubtedly responsible for the oscillations typical of the intermediate stages where—if one may still legitimately use the term "décalage" in situations of this kind— the child at first accepts conservation of substance only for the slighter changes in form, for example, and only later comes to accept it in the case of more extensive deformations. Another case is that of the relative lag in the acquisition of conservation of length as compared to that of substance, for example, which is probably in large part attributable to the exceptionally strong influence of the intuitions of topological order relations (order change, the action of overtaking another mobile, etc.) characterizing the child's first concepts of space.

b) *Different levels of structuring (or of quantification).* This factor may be illustrated with reference to the kind of décalage which is sometimes observed (e.g., Piaget & Inhelder [1968] 1973, pp. 317 ff.) between (i) conservations which take the form of addition and which mainly involve the grouping of such additive operations as partitioning and reuniting (substitutability of parts)—for example, recognize the equality of two surfaces after subtraction of equal areas differently distributed over the two surfaces; and (ii) conservations which take the form of multiplication and which involve mainly the grouping of the multiplicative operations of position and change of position—for example, recognize the equality of two surfaces by compensation of dimensions after changing the form of one of the two surfaces by repositioning its parts. Even more delayed are conservations implied in measuring areas (or lengths, or volumes), because these kinds of conservation are of a properly quantitative form requiring, with the repeated application of the measurement unit, an operational fusion of the operations of partition and repositioning.

c) *Different degrees of familiarity with a particular content (or domain).* It is well known, for example, that the conservation implied in hierarchical class inclusion is mastered earlier if it is applied to a content of limited extent and one which is not far removed from the subjects' experience (e.g., a child knows fairly early that there are more children than boys in his school "because the girls are children too")[2] than if it is applied to content of a wider scope and one less readily imagined by a global intuitive view (e.g., the same child may not readily admit that there are more animals than flies in the world "because there are flies everywhere"). Or, to take an example used by Piaget (Beth &

2. Bresson (1967) reports in this connection the rather amusing case of a subject who admitted that there were more students than boys in his school, but who refused to make a decision with respect to the neighboring school "because he had not been gone to see in the other school, if there were more boys or more students" (p. 297).

Piaget [1961] 1966, pp. 221–222), a child may affirm that there are more flowers than primroses in a collection before admitting that there are more birds than swallows, because a collection of flowers is spatially more intuitive and practically easier to assemble than a collection of birds. It is also partly in terms of this factor of customary experience that Bovet (1968), for example, in her study of the learning of certain types of conservation by unschooled Algerian subjects, explains why the conservation of quantity is more accessible to these subjects than that of length: limited stocks of consumer goods in conjunction with the diversity of types of containers to be found in that region make the former conservation much more indispensable and thus more familiar than the latter.

d) Different degrees of resistance offered by objects. Under this general title, one might include two important subcategories, both of which result from difficulties related to the differentiation of certain properties of objects. The first concerns the resistance offered by certain physical properties of objects to their being operationally manipulated. This is probably what Piaget (Piaget & Garcia [1971] 1974, p. 115) refers to in speaking of "illegitimate intrusions" of physical causality in operational logic. For example, the fact that children experience a great deal of difficulty in conserving a class B (e.g., 20 wooden beads), in the classical problem of operational inclusion of A (e.g., 18 blue beads) and of A' (e.g., 12 red beads) within B, is largely due to the fact that it is physically impossible to make at the same time a necklace A of 18 blue beads and a necklace B of 20 wooden beads comprising the same 18 blue beads and the remaining 12 red beads. Similarly, in the classical task of area conservation—where the subject is asked to decide whether two surfaces are of equal extension after subtraction of equal-sized part surfaces, where in one case the subareas cut off from the total surfaces are arranged in a closed rectangle and in the other in an open figure—quite a number of children deny equality by arguing that the closed perimeter of the rectangle blocks off access to the partial areas within so that these can no longer be used. One final example: the reason that conservation of substance, weight, and volume appear later in the case of the dissolution of sugar in water than in the case of modeling of clay is probably related to the fact, as already noted by Piaget (1941), that a substance which simply changes its form without becoming imperceptible must be easier to conserve than one which does become imperceptible in the course of the transformation; but it may also be that the nonreversibility of the causal relations operating in physical mixtures singularly impedes the access to mental reversibility necessary for conservation. In sum, to the extent that a conservation problem involves physical causality or is subject to interference of a causal nature, it is likely to offer obstacles to the logical coordination of activities necessary for conservation. This explains the particular difficulty of certain physical conservations (conservation of inert movement, of causal impetus, etc.) which in fact do not emerge before the level of formal thinking, that is, the period in which physical causality and logical operation become clearly differentiated.

The second factor related to the resistance of objects has to do with the particular difficulty that may arise from the necessity to dissociate certain physical attributes. The notion of "relevant attributes" is currently of great appeal, since it was made popular by certain authors (e.g., Gelman 1969; Trabasso 1968) who see the difficulty of conservation problems as resulting from the child's inclination to attend to those features of the object that are irrelevant to the concept examined. For instance, the child's denial of numerical equality with respect to two rows of identical numbers of tokens of different linear spread is said to be a consequence of paying attention to density or length in the two rows instead of to number of objects. Similarly, the child's belief that two equal quantities of liquid will cease being equal when one is poured into a differently shaped container is said to be due to the fact that he reasons in terms of height or width of the vessels rather than in terms of quantity. This interpretation seems appealing by its simplicity, yet it raises more problems than it solves. First of all, let us remember that quantity does not constitute a perceptible dimension like shape, height, content, etc., but rather presupposes compositions of an additive or multiplicative nature—even before the introduction of any kind of metric—which the child for a long time remains incapable of carrying out, and which he cannot be made to know how to do by simply being told to attend to them. Second, it is not so that in order to solve a conservation problem the child has to ignore the so-called irrelevant perceptual attributes, but it is precisely to these figurative aspects that the mental coordinations and inferences required for conservation must be applied so that they may be linked to the perceptual transformations themselves. Finally, and most important, if one wishes to attribute nonconservation simply to a failure to attend to the attributes relevant to the concept at hand, it is presupposed that the child is already capable of discriminating the relevant from the irrelevant attributes and to understand why they are either relevant or irrelevant. But it appears—see in this regard the studies by Piaget and his co-workers (Piaget, Sinclair, & Vinh Bang 1968; Piaget & Garcia [1971] 1974) on the notions of identity and causality—that the child's difficulty derives precisely from the fact that he confuses the different properties of objects and that the acquisition of conservation requires a long process of dissociation between these various properties, a process that is inseparable from and closely associated with the processes involved in the construction of the concepts in question. For this reason, as long as the child confuses, for example, length with protrusion, shape with quantity, or again density with number in a collection of elements, it would be quite useless to imagine that all the child would have to do is to ignore the dimensions of spatial protrusion, of deformation, or of change in density in order to acquire conservation of length, of quantity, or of number. The development of weight conservation, recently studied again by Piaget (Piaget & Garcia [1971] 1974), is a good illustration of the many ways in which décalages may be introduced, within a single concept, by varying degrees of difficulty in the dissociations demanded of the child. In this way, we have been able to observe (see Pierre-Joly 1974; Pinard & Pierre-Joly 1979) that, in the initial stages, the child denies the conservation of weight as soon as such attributes as color, size, texture, temperature, etc., are changed (just as Murray & Johnson 1969 and 1975, and Nummedal & Murray 1969 have been able to demonstrate before with respect to certain transformations, even without physical deformation, which were simply verbally proposed to the subject), as a result of his inability to dissociate the quantity as such from these different attributes. At a more advanced level, the child no longer gets troubled by such simple dissociations but denies conservation depending on whether the object is in motion or not, suspended from a stiff rod or from an elastic, in vertical or in horizontal position, etc., as a result of an incapacity to dissociate, this time, the static weight of an object (which Piaget calls the weight-quantity of matter) from the action exerted by the weight (weight-action or dynamic weight) in particular situations. Even later perhaps is the dissociation of form and quantity due to the fact that the child has to coordinate the changes in form effected upon the object in order to infer the quantitative invariance of weight. Finally, in the last stage, which involves formal thought, weight conservation becomes more difficult still when it requires the dissociation of absolute and relative weight each time the weight of an object has to be coordinated with other spatial dimensions such as volume (concept of density), surface (concept of pressure), and length or distance (concept of momentum).

e) Varying degrees of difficulty in the coordination of actions necessary for conservation. This last factor is both associated with and complementary to the preceding one, from which it can be distinguished by the fact that it relates to actions performed by the subject rather than to properties of objects; thus, it concerns the subject's (logical) experience of his own actions rather than his (physical) experience with the object. The order of difficulty observed in the conservation of substance, weight, and of volume thus can be explained partly (see Piaget 1950b) by the fact that the activities involved in the first case (add, take away, recover, deform, etc.) are easier to coordinate among each other than those involved in the conservation of weight (e.g., testing the weight of an object implies the action of recovering, and the control action often requires a decentration from the subject's own activities); more difficult still is the coordination of activities related to volume (e.g., the action of enclosing an object requires even more decentering when it is left to the surrounding medium, and also presupposes the simpler activities of recovering the substance and of feeling its resistance). Similarly, the fact that the discrimination of the elementary topological properties of space may antedate that of its projective and Euclidean attributes can be explained with reference to the fact that actions related to elementary topology (e.g., open or close, juxtapose or separate, exclude or include, etc.) are easier to coordinate than those related to projective space (e.g., focus, line up, conserve a direction) or to Euclidean space (e.g., equalize, conserve a distance). The conservation of rate of flow, which has been studied by Blanchet (1974), represents another example of a décalage due to difficulties in coordinating the activities entailed in this kind of conservation. Its late acquisition may be explained with reference to the fact that the variables to be compensated are not homogeneous, since it is easier to perceive differences in the diameter of the water ducts than those in the rate of flow. One last example may be cited: the particular difficulty involved in the conservations observed at the level of formal thought (e.g., conservation of inert movement, conservation of balance equilibrium). This difficulty is largely due to the fact that the coordination of the actions or operations required in these kinds of conservation involves combinatorial analysis and demands merging the two forms of reversibility (inversion and reciprocity), characterizing concrete operational logic.

Theoretical Problems Arising from the Existence of Décalages

The diversity of the décalages resulting from the combined effects of the various factors just mentioned raises two main problems. The first concerns the question of how to reconcile the notion of décalage with the general notion of stage in mental development. The second deals with the more specific notion of intermediate stage in the acquisition of a particular mental structure.

I. *Décalage and the general notion of stage.* We know that it is possible to reduce to five the number of criteria that define the Piagetian notion of stage of mental development (see the analysis by Pinard & Laurendeau 1969, 1971): (1) *hierarchization*—the stages or periods of development have to follow a constant, invariant order; (2) *integration*—the behaviors characteristic of an earlier stage become transformed into those of the subsequent stage by a process of reconstruction or coordination rather than simply being added to or replaced by these; (3) *consolidation*—a stage always includes a period where what is characteristically acquired during that stage is completed and a period during which the acquisitions characteristic of the following stage are being prepared; (4) *structuring*—the operations and activities typical of a given level of development are not simply juxtaposed but are functionally interdependent and organically interrelated in one *structure d'ensemble;* (5) *equilibration*—a developmental scale of stages consists of a sequence of levels of equilibrium of operations and actions. Now, it is clear that, among these criteria, the notion of horizontal décalage is most associated with that of consolidation, since a stage is never quite completed or achieved before the horizontal décalages finally disappear, which separate the acquisitions characteristic of a given stage of mental functioning. Therefore, the question whether the notion of décalage may be reconciled with the stage notion really comes down to asking to what extent this aspect of consolidation of a stage jeopardizes the validity of the remaining criteria for the stage concept. There is no simple and unique answer to this question, since it depends upon the kind of décalage one has in mind. With reference to the décalages proper separating the acquisition of different concepts, there is hardly any doubt that the consolidation criterion, whose very definition implies the notion of horizontal décalage, in no way jeopardizes the realization of the other four criteria, since one can still observe (*a*) invariance in the acquisition order of the various concepts as well as a regular order of acquisition for the levels appropriate to each (*hierarchical* aspect); (*b*) a restructuring or progressive coordination of the various behaviors characteristic of the successive levels marking the evolution of each of these concepts, in spite of differences in the rate of acquisition between different concepts (*integrative* aspect); (*c*) a synchronic appearance of the total set of grouping operations constituting each concept (*structural* aspect); and (*d*) a sequence of levels of equilibrium in the evolution of each concept (the *equilibrium* aspect). On the other hand, with respect to the décalages found in the evolution of a single concept—that is, the décalages existing between operations related to each other by correspondence, substitution, or identity—the question becomes much more difficult, since these kinds of décalages are located at an intermediate level between the operational and the preoperational (a substage within the same sequence of development) and thus should disappear at the operational level. It is at this point that the complementary problem arises of the relations between décalages and the notion of intermediate stage.

II. *Décalage and the specific notion of intermediate stage.* This problem is much more difficult, since it implicates directly the notion of logical necessity, which characterizes the operational level of thinking. When a child of an intermediate level denies conservation in the case of a particular deformation but asserts it in the case of another, the reasons he invokes for denying it are in no way different from those invoked by children of a lower level (who deny consistently), while the reasons invoked for the affirmative response are exactly the same as those given by children of an upper level (who conserve consistently). When posed in this way,[3] the question addresses itself directly to the exact interpretation that should be given to the notion of intermediate stage and thus becomes the question of whether an intermediate stage constitutes a unified and homogeneous level of thinking or whether it should not be considered rather a heterogeneous mixture of preoperational and operational thought. The problem is all the more thorny as the child's conservation responses, where they are given, appear to be of the same logical necessity as those of children who are evidently at the operational level. This means, essentially, that the question to be asked is how authentic this kind of logical necessity really is.

Even though a definite answer to this question must await more conclusive empirical evidence, an admittedly speculative and tentative answer appears to be that, in spite of its apparent inconsistencies, the thinking of a child at an intermediate stage does have its own internal logic, but it does not go beyond the preoperational level, never really achieving true operational necessity even in those cases where responses appear to be operational. This lack of authenticity derives from two complementary sources: failure to carry out operational compositions, and absence of a self-critical attitude. In fact, both are expressions of the same incapacity to handle reversibility which, as will be shown later, is the source of internal necessity, mediating the transition from successive to simultaneous modes of reasoning.

a) Absence of operational composition. In his first epistemological studies of the notion of "causality," Piaget (1950b, pp. 292–293, 345–346) distinguished two kinds of generalizations.[4] One, which he calls *purely formal generalization* or *generalization by inclusion,* proceeds from particular cases to the general

3. The example given is a case of a décalage of the identity type. It would have been just as easy to cite cases of décalage of the substitution or the correspondence types.

4. The same distinction is made again in somewhat different terms later on (Piaget 1974a, [1975] 1977) and, more systematically, in his research on generalization (Piaget et al. 1978).

law by means of a progressive accumulation of successive empirical observations, each expressing the same relationship between events; yet the generalization captured in the law (or function) always remains tied to the observed facts or observable phenomena upon which it is based; in and by itself it is incapable of going beyond this purely descriptive level, nor can it attain explanatory value if not complemented by a constructive or deductive process operating on several laws. This latter process leads to the second kind of generalization, which is *generalization by operational composition*, that is, one resulting from the composition of operations as these are applied to the laws or functions derived from empirical observations. The logical necessity inherent in the composition of operations is what makes it possible for this kind of generalization to go beyond the domain of observables and to extend to that purely virtual relations; it also gives it its explanatory value—instead of simply a legal one—and its logical necessity.

This distinction between the two kinds of generalization may help explain the fact that the inconsistency shown by the children at intermediate levels,[5] in their responses to a conservation problem, for instance, is indeed more apparent than real: even though these children are far more flexible than those at earlier stages in intuitively focusing on different aspects of the problem, in actual fact the thinking of these children is strictly preoperational, still being limited to a mode of generalization which proceeds by successive inclusion of new exemplars while formulating a general law. A process of this kind still takes the form of a legal or empirical generalization, devoid of any kind of logical necessity; the child considers each new transformation carried out in front of him, *one after the other*, and then decides each time whether or not it can be included in the general law which he is trying to elaborate. The observed inconsistency between responses accepting and denying conservation[6] is probably a re-

5. It may be maintained that this restriction also applied to the reasoning of children who have only recently attained the operational stage (either spontaneously or through training), as can be seen from the instability of these new acquisitions (e.g., little resistance to extinction), which perhaps do not yet possess generality by operational composition.

6. Charbonneau (1971) gave children of intermediate levels a conservation task involving 33 transformations of substance (12 divisions and 21 changes of shape), but found no correlation whatsoever between nonconservation responses and degree of transformation or of spatial disposition of the transformed elements.

flection of the willful and arbitrary character of the equivalence classes (or preclassifications) typical of the preoperational stage. There is then nothing surprising in the child's changing responses in accordance with each intuitive centration he happens to adopt: at one time being struck by a particular perceptual aspect (e.g., length, height, numerosity) he might deny conservation for one transformation, while at another time he might be impressed by certain rules or empirical facts (e.g., initial identity, absence of addition or subtraction) and thus affirm conservation with a conviction that has all the appearances of logical necessity. On the other hand, a child who is capable of generalization by operational composition will incorporate all actual and virtual transformations *simultaneously* within a single integrated structure (where the actual transformations are only particular cases within the total set of possible transformations). It is this certainty inherent in operational composition that guarantees the logical necessity of reasoning. In other words, to take a concrete example, if a ball of plasticene a gets transformed into a cylinder b, and then into a string c, etc., and conserves its quantity if nothing is added or taken away (i.e., $a \rightarrow b \pm 0 = a; a \rightarrow c \pm 0 = a;$ etc.), it is not because of such and such a transformation in particular but because a direct operation a is *cancelled* by the inverse operation $- a$ (i.e., $+ a - a = 0$, and therefore $a \pm 0 = a$) for any transformation possible. Observationally, this kind of generalization can frequently appear in the form of certain kinds of verbalizations made by children who are given the conservation task (e.g., "if I close my eyes, you can do whatever you want, if you don't cheat, I am sure in my head that it will always be the same amount to eat"; "it has to be the same, or else it would be magic," etc.). In studies of conservation training (see, e.g., Lefebvre & Pinard 1972, 1974), such verbalizations are the most easily accessible evidence one can have of the success of training.

b) Lack of self-criticism. A second reason for thinking that an intermediate stage cannot be a combination of operational and preoperational thought is the absence of a critical attitude with regard to one's own reasoning. This lack of self-criticism is characteristic of children who are still at this intermediate stage. As will be seen later, it constitutes one of the characteristics of preoperational thinking, which remains even though a child at the intermediate level or by the end of a still earlier stage may already have developed a certain coherence and logic in his thinking.

In one of his very early works on judgment and reasoning in the child, Piaget ([1924] 1976) already characterized transductive reasoning in terms of its insensitivity to contradiction. This can be seen in the behavior of a child who offers an explanation for an event just observed without seeking to verify if its converse is also true. Such a child may, for instance, assert that "a nail sinks in the water, because it is heavy"; but if he were sensitive to the need to test the truth of his statement, he should perhaps ask himself (either by means of empirical observation or by mental experimentation) whether the converse of this cause-effect relation is also true, that is, ask if it is true that heavy things will always sink in water. This simple reversal of the relation might keep him from overt self-contradiction such as asserting with utmost confidence only a few minutes later that "a big boat floats, because it is heavy." Similarly, in the task on the concept of life (see, e.g., Laurendeau & Pinard [1962] 1968), a child might affirm that "a dog is alive, because he has legs" or "because it can walk"; but, since he cannot as yet distinguish between "all" and "some," he does not question his affirmations to see if their converse holds, for example, by asking himself if only things that have legs (e.g., by comparing a fish and a table) or that can move (e.g., comparing a car and a tree) are alive.

Much more recently, in their studies concerning the epistemology and the psychology of functions, Piaget and his co-workers (Piaget et al. [1968] 1977) have given particular attention to the problem of preoperational logic. They were able to demonstrate, by means of numerous experiments, that the thinking of a child at this level conforms to a kind of logic which remains within the limits of the logic of functions known to be unidirectional and therefore not reversible. An elegant study done by Van Den Bogaert-Rombouts (1966) illustrates well the unidirectional nature of preoperational thought. A truck drives past a number of toy figures of various colors positioned in a predetermined spatial array; the experimenter places a token of the same color as the figure visited in the back of the truck in the order of the visits to serve as memory aids. It is indeed striking to observe that the preoperational child, who is perfectly able to understand that the order of the tokens is a function of the order of events (e.g., if the yellow token is placed after the blue in the back of the truck, it is because the truck passed by the yellow figure after it had passed by the blue one), is quite incapable of establishing the correspondence in the reversed order, that is, reconstruct the order of events from that of the tokens (e.g., the same child is unable to tell when asked whether the truck had first visited the yellow or the blue figure). Sinclair and Ferreiro (1970) also observed this unidirectional character of preoperational thinking, in this case with respect to the syntactic structures of language. They indicate, for instance, the inability of preoperational children to conserve the idea conveyed by an action as viewed from the perspective of the agent as well as from that of the patient (e.g., express the idea of "John washes Paul" with "Paul" as subject; or, an even more difficult task, since the action is irreversible, describe the idea of "John washes the car" by beginning the sentence with "car").

It is evident that this functional logic, which is both unidirectional and irreversible, can explain the lack of a self-critical attitude on the part of the children at the preoperational level as well as their insensitivity to contradiction. It is also this form of logic which gives to preoperational thought its homogeneity and inner consistency, in spite of the existence of certain apparently operational behaviors which, in actual fact, still lack the true logical necessity imparted by reversibility. This is why, for instance, in a task like conservation of substance, the same child may alternately deny and affirm conservation from one transformation to the next. At one time he denies conservation, basing himself on the fact that the transformed object is longer (or shorter) than the original object, without considering the opposite relation (such as, "if an object is longer than another, does it always contain more substance?") which might enable him to check out his first assertion (e.g., could some of the substance have been taken away, taking thickness into consideration, etc.). A few moments later, he might do the opposite and affirm conservation, arguing this time on the basis of the initial identity of the objects (e.g., "because they were the same before"), but again not thinking of the converse of his assertion (as, "if there are two things that are equal in the beginning, are they always the same afterwards?"), which might lead the child to check his inferences (e.g., the possibility that the experimenter might have taken away from or added something to the substance in the course of the transformation). In sum, the children of intermediate stages remain attached to a form of reasoning that is unidirectional; in the absence of reversibility they are insensitive to contradiction. Proceeding from one instance to the next, each considered separately by itself only, they are just as likely to affirm as to deny conservation in going from one transformation to the next, depending on the intuitively based attentional orientation that they happen to have at any given moment, while forgetting each time their answers to preceding transformations. In a task concerned with the learning of conservation of liquids by a method based on cognitive conflict, Lefebvre and Pinard (1974) were able to show that the initial level of cognitive consistency, as evaluated by means of tasks involving the logic of functions, can predict subjects' ability—all subjects being initially unambiguously classified as preoperational—to profit from the training exercises based on cognitive conflict provided by the method. Specifically, it was observed that those subjects who were unable to go beyond the intermediate stage at the end of their learning experience had, on the predictive measures, shown the kind of unidirectionality typical of the logic of functions (lack of mental retroactivity, successive modes of reasoning, etc.).

In brief, summing up the preceding considerations concerning the horizontal décalages separating the acquisition of the various types of cognitive structures, let us simply recall that these décalages have multiple origins which, in the final analysis, all reduce to a form of interaction between various amounts of resistance associated with different objects and the equally variable degrees of difficulty inherent in different kinds of cognitive coordinations to be performed by the subject. The fact that such décalages exist is not incompatible with the general notion of stage of cognitive development, since the consolidation of a stage—the aspect to which the décalages are related—in no way prevents the remaining conditions defining the stage concept from being fulfilled (i.e., hierarchization, integration, structuring, and equilibration). Certain kinds of décalage, however, raise the problem of whether one should consider the thinking of an intermediate-level child as a heterogeneous mixture of operational and preoperational reasoning, or whether its apparently operational manifestations still remain within the level of preoperational thinking. It appears that the latter solution is the more correct one to be adopted. The thinking of the intermediate-level child possesses its own consistency, but fundamentally of a preoperational character still lacking operational composition and self-critical attitude, characteristics which only cognitive reversibility can impart.

2   On the General Principles Governing the Acquisition of Conservations

The main problem to be covered in this book, the child's acquisition of conservation, will be introduced in this chapter by a systematic discussion of the general principles, or the guidelines, followed in the analysis of the components at work in the acquisition of conservation. After an introductory passage serving to situate the problem in its general perspective, the following two sections will attempt to establish what may be called the cornerstones of the model to be proposed in the next chapter. In the first of these two sections, it will be maintained that the passage from nonconservation to conservation is, in essence, a passage from physical revertibility to mental reversibility. In the second section, it will be argued that this passage is mainly the result of the child's experience; the different types of experience available to the child as he progresses toward conservation will also be described.

The Search for an Explanation

Attempting to explain the origin of conservation in the child means trying to explain how a child, after having denied conservation of a particular property more or less systematically (conservation of length, surface, etc.), often for a considerable period of time, comes to affirm conservation with as much confidence as he had before in denying it. It is well known that Piaget has repeatedly described (e.g., Apostel, Mandelbrot, & Piaget 1957; Piaget [1975] 1977) in minute detail how one stage evolves from the other, proceeding from nonconservation to conservation, and what strategies the child uses successively in this transition. However, to find in Piaget's numerous publications a similarly comprehensive and systematic description of the mechanisms responsible for these successive shifts in strategy seems rather impossible. No doubt, in his more recent publication concerning equilibration of cognitive structures, Piaget ([1975] 1977) gives additions and even corrections to his earlier model (Apostel, Mandelbrot, & Piaget 1957) by paying particular attention to the coordinations the subject establishes in acting upon objects and to the essentially progressive nature of the forms of equilibrium successively attained by the subject (Piaget speaks here of "advancing equilibration" to indicate this constructive aspect of the equilibration mechanism); yet, it is somewhat difficult to grasp concretely what factors are responsible for this progressive advance toward new forms of equilibrium that are never definitive and are constantly left behind. In an effort not to limit himself to a mere descriptive account, as his critics will frequently affirm, Piaget ([1975] 1977) begins by making a distinction between three forms of equilibration that have to get established in the course of development: (*a*) a basic form of equilibration to be established between the subject's schemata and the external objects within a single cognitive system (e.g., the concept of length, of number, etc.); (*b*) a form of equilibration to be established between two or more subsystems developing at different rates, as witnessed in the numerous temporal décalages that have been observed; (*c*) and a form of equilibration to be established between the differentiation of these many subsystems and their integration within a general higher level system with its own laws (e.g., integration of the classificatory systems of concrete operational logic within the combinatorial logic at the formal level). These various forms of equilibration, where each may manifest itself in mutual assimilations and accommodations, may come about only through interactions, and these necessarily involve conditions of disequilibrium, that is, of perturbations and conflicts: resistance from objects, difficulties in assimilations, gaps to bridge, etc. For Piaget ([1975] 1977), p. 17), there is a systematic reason for these states of disequilibrium, and this is the asymmetry between affirmation and negation. Piaget derives this from his recent research (Piaget et al. 1974a, 1974b), which shows that subjects spontaneously focus their attention on the positive characteristics of objects and of their actions upon these objects (e.g., the rising of the water level in a conservation of liquids problem), while neglecting the negative characteristics (e.g, the corresponding decrease in diameter in the same problem). But each of the three forms of equilibration mentioned above requires for its constitution that affirmations be compensated with negations. Thus, in the first form of equilibrium, a distinction must be made between relevant and irrelevant properties of objects and between relevant and irrelevant conceptual schemata available to the subject in each interaction; the second form of equilibration requires a compensation between the aspects that are common and those that are specific to each of the interacting subsystems; and for the third form, equilibration requires a compensation between common and specific properties in the various subsystems to be integrated in the general system. Piaget further explains that the states of disequilibrium produced by this initial asymmetry between affirmations and negations initiate a process of reequilibration, and that this process determines cognitive advances by leading the subject to go beyond this momentary level of equilibrium in order to meet new demands. So, cognitive progress is to be explained by the reactions the subject makes to disturbances. In the complex network of interactions between observed facts (pertaining to empirical abstraction) and the coordination of actions applied or attributed to the objects (pertaining to logical or reflective abstraction), the subject's reactions first take the form of simple regulations (due to the positive and negative feedbacks implied by the latter), later that of true compositions, which in the end cancel or neutralize the disturbances and thus give rise to a more stable form of equilibrium.

There can be no doubt that the experiments designed by Piaget to illustrate the asymmetry between affirmations and negations in the child (Piaget et al. 1974a, 1974b) as well as the new interpretations proposed by him (Piaget [1975] 1977) of some of his earlier observations or experiments in terms of what he calls his new "explanatory scheme" (p. 42) of a reequilibration mechanism, do furnish more concrete descriptions of the steps leading to operational compensation; but, as far as the particular subject matter of conservation is concerned, the question remains how to explain the transition from a stage marked by the primacy of affirmations (this primacy being the source of conflict) to a stage at which the corresponding negations become established and, concurrently, what explains the passage from preoperational regulations to operational compensations (which resolve the conflict). It is precisely with respect to this transitional mechanism that serious questions have to be asked, since it is here that the most difficult problem lies and where the "mystery" of conservations really gets thick. As is generally known, interesting but limited attempts have been made by Gagné (1968), Wallach

(1969), and Halford (1970a, 1970b, 1971) to explain the origin and the emergence of certain forms of conservation in the child. While postponing our evaluation of these isolated attempts until later (Chap. 4), it seems more interesting first to elaborate somewhat on the debate—without necessarily going into as extensive a model as that proposed by Piaget ([1975] 1977)—concerning the equilibration of cognitive structures just reviewed. The aim is rather to propose an explanation that can apply to all of the types of conservation, irrespective of the distinctions made in the previous chapter, and independent also of the various décalages in the progressive structuring of the various forms of conservation, yet remaining conscious of possible and real interactions that are likely to interrelate these various aspects and in this way exert an influence on the acquisitions concerned.

In view of the generality of perspective adopted, which requires that consideration be restricted to only those mechanisms that are common to all forms of conservation, we propose to derive an overall synthesis from Piaget concerning this problem by reducing to two basic solutions all the diverse components of a solution to be found in going through his many publications. The first formulates the *principle* involved in the transition from non-conservation to conservation, stating that this transition is essentially one from a successive to a simultaneous processing or, in other words, from empirical reversion to true reversibility. The second concerns the *how* of this transition and may be described briefly as asserting that the most important factor operating in this transition is the subject's experience (logical and/or physical) with the objects concerned.

Physical Reversion and Mental Reversibility

To illustrate the first of the two principles, let us introduce the simple example of the conservation of liquids in a form that implicates only an additive grouping of parts (or substitution of parts) and, therefore, reversibility by inversion.[1] Let us imagine

1. It would have been just as possible to use a different example without changing the basic logic of the argument (demonstration). I.e., it would have been possible to choose the transferral of a content from a container *A* into another container *B* with a different diameter. In that case, the example would have implicated the multiplicative grouping of relations and reversibility by compensation.

that a content a of a container A is transferred to two other containers B_1 and B_2 (either similar or dissimilar to each other), so that one obtains two contents b_1 and b_2, respectively (either equal or unequal to one another). The subject is then asked to say whether a is conserved. The subject is in a position to *see*, to *note* that $a = b_1 + b_2$, that is, that all of a disappears when it is poured into B_1 and B_2 and one obtains b_1 and b_2. The subject can further note that $b_1 + b_2 = a$, when the contents of B_1 and B_2 are poured back into A. The subject can even note that $a - b_1 = b_2$, or that $a - b_2 = b_1$ (i.e., that only b_2 (or b_1) are left if one takes away first b_1 (or b_2) from a. In spite of all these different kinds of information, there is nothing that can prove to a child that a is conserved when one transfers it to $B_1 + B_2$, or when $b_1 + b_2$ are poured back into A, nor that b_2 (or b_1) is conserved when it is poured back into A, unless he already knows what he has to learn in this situation, that is, that a simple transformation cannot change the quantity of a substance if nothing is added or taken away in the process. For this reason, at the level of the simple registration of facts with no inferences involved, it would be more precise to change the notation of the above equations so that the symbol $=$ is replaced by the symbol $\rightarrow$ in order to emphasize the fact that, as a result of the transfers of liquid between containers, the contents a yields or becomes $(\rightarrow) b_1 + b_2$, that $a - b_1$ yields $(\rightarrow) b_2$, that $b_1 + b_2$ yields again a, etc.

Taking note of these various observations is a necessary condition for the child to acquire conservation, but not a sufficient one. These observations are necessary because, as will be seen later, they form the substance to which the child can apply the coordinations he needs to establish between his various actions; they furnish the framework to his physical experience. But they are not sufficient, because they only concern physical actions and transformations, and these are of necessity different and successive, each being unidirectional and depending on its proper spatiotemporal conditions. Since these actions can also take place in the opposite direction (e.g., pour in and then pour out again, separate and then reunite, fold and then unfold, mix together and then take apart, heat and then cool down), it is legitimate to speak of revertible actions; but this kind of reversion cannot bring about conservation of the objects to which the actions are applied, because there is nothing that allows the subject to be sure that the changes in form (in location, etc.) produced by the successive actions have not brought about concurrent changes in quantity (or in length, etc.). Thus, it is conceivable that the action of dividing the content a of a container A into two contents $b_1 + b_2$ could increase or decrease the amount a and that the action of reuniting $b_1 + b_2$ in a might have the opposite effect.

It is clear that unlike physical actions and transformations which pertain to physical causality, mental operations, which are governed by logical implications, have as their essential characteristic that they are fully reversible. And it is just this characteristic that guarantees the conservation of the objects to which particular actions are applied. In fact, a particular mental operation (e.g., $a = b_1 + b_2$), inasmuch as it is not the simple internal representation of a physical action observed beforehand (internalized preoperational action), lends itself to internal transformations by means of logical implication. These transformations liberate completely such complementary operations from the spatiotemporal restrictions that characterize physical actions and transformations. In more concerte terms, when thinking (or carrying out mentally) the operation $a = b_1 + b_2$, one thinks without having to actually be aware of it, ipso facto, the same thing as if one thought (or carried out mentally) the associated operations such as $b_1 + b_2 = a$ (which affirms the conservation of a), or operations such as $a - b_1 = b_2$ (conservation of b_2), or $a - b_2 = b_1$ (conservation of b_1). The reason for this is evidently that each of these operations is nothing but an internal transformation of the others and that these all imply each other of necessity by virtue of the fact that they constitute a single structure closed upon itself. In sum, reversibility, a property of mental operations, guarantees conservation for two complementary reasons. First, mental operations are related to each other by logical implication, which makes them reversible and thereby gives them simultaneity (necessarily lacking in physical actions and transformations). It is this simultaneity which excludes the possibility that something can be lost and then gained again (or vice versa) in the course of transformations.[2] The second reason, in solidarity with the first, is that this kind of mutual implication of the opera-

2. For this reason, the symbol $=$, as used in the equations above, no longer denotes mere factual succession, which is expressed by the symbol $\rightarrow$; rather, it comes to convey its proper sense, that of equality.

tions thus grouped in a system enables the subject (*a*) to go beyond the level of simple statements of fact where each is not necessarily conserving (or, if so, only after a verification check, e.g., count five elements of a series from left to right and recount them from right to left to discover that the sum has not changed); and (*b*) to reach the level of deduction at which the subject is able to infer, for example, that $b_1 + b_2 = a$ (conservation of *a*) if $a = b_1 + b_2$, without having to carry out each time those slow mental coordinations by means of which the various successive transformations performed previously, and which are not necessarily all conserving, can ultimately constitute a system of operations and transformations related to each other by logic and, therefore, finally reversible.

It appears that in the passage from the successive to the simultaneous, which, in fact, reduces to that of empirical revertibility to reversibility, resides the essential nature of conservation. Before approaching the more difficult problem of what factors are responsible for this change, it seems appropriate to first remove certain ambiguities concerning this distinction between empirical reversion and reversibility. It is generally known that a good number of researchers see no difference between these two notions, that some even confuse the two, while others (e.g., Murray & Johnson 1969, 1975; Gladstone & Palazzo 1974) explicitly rule out such a distinction by even trying to show, by otherwise ingenuously designed experiments, that very young children are capable of mastering consistently what the authors call "reversibility" of operations, even in a situation of nonconservation (e.g., a ball of modeling clay is seen as becoming heavier after cooling off and lighter again when it gets heated). Against the possible objection that these are instances of empirical revertibility rather than of true reversibility, Murray and Johnson (1969) simply answer that they cannot see any difference between the pair "heat-cool off," which Piaget would consider as an example of empirical revertibility, and the pair "add-subtract," which Piaget always cites as an example of the reversibility relation. In any event, goes the argument, if there really is a distinction to be made along the dimension physical reversion-reversibility, then the burden of proof rests with Piaget.

To relieve Piaget somewhat of so heavy a burden, one might immediately point out that the authors are actually quite right in not seeing a difference of this kind between the two pairs of opposites, for the simple reason that both pairs can, in fact, be either instances of physical revertibility as well as of reversibility. The essential difference, if one really does want to make a difference between revertibility and reversibility, is that between an action carried out *physically* and the same action carried out *mentally*. The former is never reversible, even if actions like add-subtract are involved. It is true that a physical subtraction may sometimes be followed by the corresponding physical addition, but one does not necessarily imply the other. It is always possible to perform one action without performing the opposite one, and it happens unfortunately quite often that a physical subtraction cannot be inverted: a decapitation, a chirurgical ablation, a fire, a murder, a suicide, those are the most striking examples. And what is true of the pair addition-subtraction is also true of all other pairs denoting physical actions like heat-cool down, mix up-sort out, plant-dig out, fill-empty, etc. On the other hand, the same actions, when performed mentally, are all reversible, since any mental operation implies simultaneously its inverse by simple internal transformation, so that it is really not possible to assert one without also implicitly asserting the inverse operation. To heat cold water by bringing it near a heat source, and then making it cool down by removing it from the heat, is to carry out two successive physical actions, where the latter one, which is, incidentally, not always executed, inverts the effect of the former; on the other hand, to think or assert mentally that cold water will warm up if heat is applied to it, is to think and simultaneously affirm implicitly that hot water will cool down if one takes the heat away. And it is precisely this simultaneity that prevents gains and losses (both real or possible ones) which are part of the sequential physical actions. Even actions that are nonrevertible, as those cited above—to which one might add such inexorable phenomena as the passage of time or aging—remain mentally reversible. In sum, reversibility is integrated within a system of mental operations, which constitute a self-contained atemporal structure, while reversion implies sequential actions that are independent of one another: one can heat without cooling down, mix without sorting out, etc., but one cannot think $A + B = C$ without also thinking implicitly $C - A = B$, $C - B = A$, etc. In the experimental setting of a conservation task, the difference between the two can be recognized by more than one index. For example, children give evidence of it when they assert that a quantity has increased (or decreased) following a change in form (transformation proper), in location, in temperature, color, etc., but then affirm correspondingly that the quantity has decreased (or increased) once the opposite changes are noted or imagined. Another type of evidence is provided by nonconserving children, who, when asked "what should one do to make it the same amount?" answer simply, "you have to put it back the same way it was," etc. In our opinion, it would be presumptuous to interpret such behaviors as genuine manifestations of reversibility (in the manner of Murray & Johnson 1969, 1975; Gladstone & Palazzo 1974), and, a fortiori, to conclude on the basis of this (in the manner of Murray 1977) that nonconservation is no more a criterion of preoperational thought than conservation is a criterion of operational reasoning, even if the child makes errors in estimating the effects a transformation has upon the quantity of a substance or of weight.[3] It seems fairly obvious that one reason why children fail to conserve is that they fail to dissociate the change in quantity from a change in form (or temperature, etc.), so that a gain or a loss in length, height, temperature, etc., is seen as equivalent to a gain or a loss in material substance or in weight; but the main reason is the fact that these children reason about successive physical actions, which are not necessarily always conserving. If, on the other hand, these same actions are carried out mentally, they take on a simultaneous character (where successive gains and losses are excluded) due to the fact that they constitute a group of mutually related operations such that each is the internal transformation of the other, and the conserving reversible operation is an integral part of this group. In sum, the consistency in the behavior of nonconserving children represents

3. Murray (1977) goes so far as to interpret this as representing the group INRC, which combines the two forms of reversibility (inversion: add-subtract and heat–cool down; reciprocity: add-heat and subtract–cool down). But it seems obvious that this INRC group exists in the psychologist's mind rather than in that of the child: the INRC group disintegrates as soon as it is admitted that the child *does not distinguish a change in quantity from a change in form* (or temperature, position, etc.) and becomes reduced to a simple reversion of sequential physical actions: e.g., heat-add vs. cool down–remove. See also the summary of a report by Hrybyk and Murray (1978), which reiterates the same oddity.

not an early form of reversibility but only the kind of consistency characteristic of preoperational children in the manipulation of physical actions (noted or imagined). The sequential and re-vertible character of these actions thus can lead to two successive responses of nonconservation ("when you add something, there is going to be more and when you take something away, there is going to be less"; "when you make it long, there is more, and when you crowd it together, there is less"; "when you heat it up, there is more, and when you cool it down, there is going to be less," etc.).

Physical and Logical Experience

If it is accepted that the acquisition of conservation reduces to the transition from reversion to reversibility (or from a sequential to a simultaneous mode), one is still faced with the critical prob-lem asking by what mechanism this transition comes about, or, in other words, the problem of the nature of the processes im-plicated in the transition. In spite of the dominant position the conservation problem occupies in Piaget's work, it does not seem possible to find in his writings a clear and precise explanation of the origin of conservations. It is certainly true that one finds a very large number of experiments and very detailed descriptions of the sequence of stages leading up to conservation; but if one is more specifically interested in the factors responsible for this evolution, and especially in their modes of operation and their interactions, it is not easy to separate out which aspects pertain to observations of facts, which to their interpretation. In his most recent paper on equilibration of cognitive structures, Piaget ([1975] 1977) corrects and modifies considerably his earlier prob-abilistic model (Apostel, Mandelbrot, & Piaget 1957), which was based on the notion of strategy; similarly, his equally recent re-searches concerning contradiction (Piaget et al. 1974a, 1974b) and reflective abstraction (Piaget et al. 1977a, 1977b) have yielded a rich crop of new facts and reinterpretations of old facts, furnish-ing a basis for his new model of equilibration. However, the reader who is particularly interested in the specific problem posed by the origin of conservations has a hard time trying to spot, among the complex network of concepts and their vast range of applications, the element that could lead toward the solution of his problem. It appears that the key concept capable of serving as a lead element in this research is the concept of experience, which, if given the encompassing sense it has for Piaget in all of his writings, will be shown to be at the base of each of the main components involved in the acquisition of conservations (see Chap. 3). Therefore, before approaching the main problem of identifying these components, it is necessary to introduce certain fundamental distinctions concerning the concept of experience in Piaget's theory.

To avoid attributing to Piaget an empiricist epistemological position, against which he is known to have taken a firm stance consistently everywhere in his work, it is necessary to draw attention to the important distinction Piaget has made many times between physical and logical experience (or logicoarithmetic experience). Its earliest formulation can be found in his first treatise on epistemology (Piaget 1950a, pp. 72–73), where he introduces for the first time a fundamental distinction between what he already termed at the time a kind of "physical" abstraction and a "reflective" one. This distinction he has resumed several times since in a more systematic form and in greater detail (e.g., Beth & Piaget [1961] 1966, passim; Piaget 1974a, pp. 81 ff.; Piaget et al. 1977a, 1977b). Physical experience deals with objects or the material aspects of actions performed with objects (proprioception, kinetic aspects, etc.) and seeks to discover a physical property already present in the object (or action). An example of this is when a child tries to find out which of two objects is heavier, or more extended, etc. Logical experience, on the other hand, concerns the actions themselves as far as they are structured (e.g., schematization, coordination, reciprocal interaction). It consists, essentially, not in discovering a preexisting property of objects but rather in conferring upon them new characteristics (classification, seriation, numeration, etc.). Thus, to use one of Piaget's favorite examples, when a child discovers that counting a row of five tokens from left to right and from right to left results in the same number, what he experiences is not an attempt to identify, or to recognize an inherent property of the tokens (the number is not in the tokens, it is the child who attributes it to them), but to control and to verify the result of his counting, and the new knowledge derived from this experience is a result precisely of the coordination the child establishes between his different counting actions.

To each of these two kinds of experience there corresponds a particular mode of abstracting. First, in the case of physical experience, Piaget speaks of *empirical abstraction* to indicate that the subject takes his information from the observable aspects noted on the object (or in his own actions) and that the generalization to which it leads is only of the "inductive" or extensional type (Piaget et al. 1978, pp. 51, 61; 1977b, p. 318), because it does not go beyond the discovery that the new objects also possess the property that had already been abstracted and identified on other objects examined before. In the case of logical experience, Piaget speaks rather of a *reflective abstraction* (e.g, Piaget 1974a, pp. 83 ff.; [1975] 1977, pp. 43 ff.; Piaget et al. 1977a, pp. 5–6; 1977b, pp. 303 ff.) to indicate first the fact that the new knowledge the subject derives from these experiences comes directly from the coordination of his actions (actions or operations performed on objects, or attributed to objects in the domain of causal thinking), where this coordination is characterized in terms of the explicit and implicit inferences (be it at the operational, preoperational or even sensorimotor level) the subject makes from and above the observable phenomena. The term further indicates the fact that the generalization corresponding to this type of abstracting is of a "constructive" and a "reflective" nature (Piaget [1975] 1977, pp. 43ff.; Piaget et al. 1978), because it introduces new properties and relations into the objects and includes both a mental projection (a reflecting action) and a reorganization (a reflection) on a higher level of relations already structured at a lower level.[4]

Four additional remarks are in order before we can proceed, in the following chapter, to indicate the role played by these two kinds of experiences in the acquisition of conservation. First, it needs to be specified (see Piaget et al. 1977b, pp. 319–320) that the two processes are not to be interpreted as being absolutely opposed to one another, for the simple reason that, especially at the most elementary levels of cognitive development (sensorimotor period and even concrete operational), the difference is not yet very well established between the actions the subject performs

4. It is in his very early writings (Piaget 1941, pp. 276–277) and in his first studies in the field of genetic epistemology (1950b, pp. 292–293, and 345–348) that Piaget introduces this important distinction between two forms of generalization, one labeled "simple formal generalization" or "generalization by inclusion," the other "generalization by operational composition."

upon external objects (the source of empirical abstraction and of generalization by induction) and the coordinations the subject effects between these actions (source of reflective abstraction and generalization by construction). Thus, the "classifications" at the sensorimotor level express nothing but the logic of the child's physical actions; preoperational "classifications" remain tied to the figural and the functional aspects of objects; even the concrete operational classifications, however logical they are in their structure, still remain bound to a concrete content and become in turn a new kind of content for the classifications at the formal operational level (combinatorial logic is a classification of classifications, etc.). The second remark concerning the distinction between empirical and logical experience or abstraction is to underscore the essential fact that the former necessarily requires the latter (Piaget 1974a, p. 82; [1975] 1977, pp. 44–45).[5] In fact, it is logical experience which furnishes the framework within which empirical abstraction can read empirical data and construct physical laws, since no action performed on objects can lead to new knowledge if it is not coordinated with other actions. Now, it is true, in any kind of physical experience—whether it is a child trying to determine the difference in weight between two or three objects, or whether it is an adult attempting to discover or rediscover a law of physics—that what is new knowledge concerns properties already present in objects and in that respect pertains to empirical abstraction. But whatever actions are deployed in this physical experience necessarily imply—in terms of planning ahead, sequencing, as well as the interpretation of the actions— that relations be established and the actions coordinated which necessarily bring into play logical experience (e.g., identifying the problem, ordering the sequence of motor acts involved, anticipating, comparing, drawing inferences, interpreting facts, formulating laws). A third remark to be made concerns the different forms in which reflective abstraction can manifest itself. In order to give emphasis to the fact that, before the level of formal thinking, reflective abstraction only operates on physical objects,

5. It is, on the other hand, quite plausible to assume that logical abstraction can, at least in its most advanced stages, operate without intervention of empirical abstraction, and in certain cases only operates without such intervention. Logical abstraction then attains purely atemporal forms (see, e.g., Piaget 1950a, pp. 113–114, on the discovery of the number zero and the negative numbers; Piaget et al. 1977b, p. 324).

whereas at the highest formal level it can liberate itself entirely from any kind of material support, Piaget (1974a, pp. 83–84; [1975] 1977, pp. 46; Piaget et al. 1977a, pp. 6–7) likes to use the term "pseudoempirical" for its more elementary manifestations. Even these are still to be considered as forms of logical abstraction or reflective abstraction because, although the subject is able to note or to read off a new property in an object (e.g., a classification, a seriation, numeration, or the infralogical equivalents of such logical properties), it is clear that such property does not exist in the objects independent of the subject and his coordination of actions or operations, which in fact confers the property upon the external objects; the term "pseudoempirical" thus refers to these elementary forms of reflective abstraction. Finally, a fourth remark: to remove certain ambiguities the term "reflective abstraction" may create on a first rapid and cursory reading, it should be pointed out (see Piaget 1974a, pp. 83–84; Piaget et al. 1977a, p. 6; 1977b, pp. 304, 318–319) that this form of abstraction is to be found not only at the level of representational thought but that it can already be recognized in its essential characteristics in the course of the sensorimotor period, when the child comes to discover new knowledge through new, higher level coordinations of actions (or coordinations) already accomplished at the preceding level(s). In his book on reflective abstraction, Piaget (Piaget et al. 1977b, chap. 18) describes a clear case from the sensorimotor period where certain previously established coordinations are projected or reflected onto a more advanced level in the solution of a new problem. One might even go as far as Piaget (e.g., 1974a, pp. 83–84; Piaget et al. 1977b, pp. 318–319) in claiming that the distinction between empirical and reflective abstraction already has its equivalent or analogue at the level of biological, organic functions in contemporary genetic theories, in that these consider both exogenous environmental factors (which would correspond to "empirical abstractions") and factors of endogenous reconstructions or syntheses within the genome (corresponding to "reflective abstractions").[6] Given this wide a scope,

6. The analogy Piaget sees himself between biology and knowledge should at least serve to dispel certain misinterpretations and criticisms such as those advanced by MacNamara (1975, 1978), according to which the notion of reflective abstraction is said to mark the essential distinction between the biological and the cognitive domains.

it need hardly be emphasized that the constructive activity of such a process, operating within the more general mechanism of equilibration, includes of necessity a similarly wide range of levels of consciousness. Evidently absent on the purely biological, organic level, consciousness or awareness still has to be defined for the sensorimotor stage, if it can be explicated at this level in its beginnings; it is clearly observable at the representational level (preoperational or concrete operational levels); it reaches its culmination in formal thought where reflective abstraction becomes eminently conscious when the subject reflects upon his own mental constructions. At this level, reflective abstraction assumes the form of what Piaget calls either "reflective thought" or "reflected abstraction" (e.g., Piaget 1974a, pp. 83–84; Piaget et al. 1977a, p. 6).

To briefly summarize the basic principles of conservation acquisition, it may be said that this acquisition reduces to a change from reversion to reversibility and that this change is the result of the child's logical and physical experience. The following chapter will describe the different components that are operative in the acquisition of conservations and thereby specify more concretely the sense of this change from reversion to reversibility and the type of experience implicated in this evolution.

3   Specific Components
Implicated in the
Acquisition of Conservations

Having established the main principles or guidelines
in the preceding chapter, we are now in a position to approach
the core of the problem, which consists in identifying the
significant components of the complex process leading from nonconservation to conservation, and to indicate for each of the
components the role played by either logical or physical experience in the child's acquisition of conservation. In attempting to
analyze the global activity involved in conservation, one arrives
at three main component processes implicated in the acquisition
of conservation: the discrimination of different physical attributes
of an object; a growing awareness of action schemata operating in
the subject; and, finally, a coordination or integration of the
physical attributes with the subject's schemata, now conscious.
The first two of these components seem to develop together in
close association. They constitute the basic material upon which
are then exercised the activities of coordination, leading the child
toward an inductive recognition of conservation as a fact from
which the subject finally deduces the logical necessity of conservation.

Dissociation of Physical Properties of Objects

Before specifying the nature and mode of functioning of the
first of these components, it may be useful to dispel a certain
ambiguity that may result from the fact that this component is
essentially concentrated around physical properties of objects. It
will be recalled (see Chap. 2, pp. 32 ff.) that there is a distinction,
often mentioned by Piaget, between *physical* experience, which
strives to discover properties preexisting in objects, and *logical*
experience, which essentially introduces into objects certain new
properties not already present in the object. This incidentally
leads Piaget to characterize as pseudoempirical the elementary

form of reflective abstraction implicated in logical experience; it is pseudoempirical in the sense that it involves properties introduced into objects by the subject's actions, not properties preexisting in objects, as is the case with abstraction operating in physical experience. Accepting this distinction and keeping in mind these characteristics of the two kinds of experience, it is not at all inappropriate to speak of physical and of logical (or infralogical) properties present in objects. It is, then, quite indisputable that the child needs to learn to conserve both types of properties, as seen in the wide range of types of conservations, of both logical and spatiotemporal character described in the beginning of Chapter 1.

On the other hand, the distinction made between physical and logical experience ought not to obliterate two related facts (cf. our remarks at the end of the preceding chapter): (1) that logical experience always provides the framework necessary for physical experience; and (2) that the logical and infralogical properties (classifications, relations, number, or their infralogical equivalents) that are introduced into the object imply in turn, necessarily and concurrently, the dissociation of the preexisting physical properties of the object. This is true both at the concrete level (e.g., in order to classify or seriate objects according to color, form, weight, etc., one has to be able to dissociate these properties from each other) and even at the level of formal thought when it is directed at physical objects (e.g., the equilibrium of scales, weight conservation in composition with other spatial properties).

The decision to center the description of the first component in our model around physical properties is motivated by a number of considerations. Not only are the conservations of a spatiotemporal character by far the most frequent; not only has the dissociation of physical properties been relegated to a secondary level in Piaget's model; not only has research but recently begun to be directed at an analysis of children's confusions between different physical properties; but, mainly, the reason for this decision is related to the fact that, before the operational stage of thinking is reached, the two domains—the logicoarithmetical and the spatiotemporal—are not yet differentiated for the child. As already shown by Piaget (1941) in one of the very first versions of his theory, where he described the phenomenon of vertical décalages, and as was also argued in Pinard and Laurendeau (1969) in relation to the integrative nature of the stage concept, the sensorimotor period has no distinction between the domain of praxis (centered upon success in action) and the speculative domain (centered upon simple statements of facts), where the latter encompasses both logical and spatiotemporal aspects (e.g., the classifications made by the infant involve schemata of indiscernibly practical, logical, and spatiotemporal character). Similarly, at the preoperational stage, where a distinction is already made between practical and speculative actions, that between logical and spatiotemporal characteristics is still nonexistent, as shown most eloquently by the figural or functional character of the first classifications, relations, and counting activities made by the child. For this reason it would seem to us as superficial to give separate treatments to the two domains for the preoperational as it would be for the sensorimotor period, particularly when we consider that the two types of conservation involve development of the same operations and grouping structures.

In any case, the reader will quickly become aware of the fact, as he reads this chapter, that our model directly reflects this inevitable lack of differentiation between the logical and the spatiotemporal domains as well as the inevitable dependence on spatiotemporal constraints inherent in any action at the sensorimotor and preoperational levels. For example, even though the description of the first component is centered upon the dissociation of physical properties of objects, our examples are taken just as much from the logicoarithmetical (e.g., conservation of number) as from the spatiotemporal domains (e.g., conservation of liquid quantities). Similarly, in the descripton of the second component, even though centered upon the coordination of the subject's action schemes, that is, essentially upon logical experience and abstraction, the three general schemata to be consciously grasped by the child may indifferently concern physical or logical properties, as can be seen from the examples used (e.g., collection of objects, liquid quantities); just as in the case of conservation of physical properties, that of classes of objects, of relations between objects, or of the number of objects likewise presupposes the child's recognition, first, of qualitative identity, of revertibility, and of the covariation of the logical properties introduced into the object. Finally, the differentiation of these schemata and the liberation from spatiotemporal constraints described by the third component of the model to explain the transition from empirical toward logical necessity apply as much in the case of conservation of logical (or infralogical) as that of physical properties.

After these preliminary considerations, we can now proceed to the examination of the first component: the dissociation of the physical properties of objects. In order to be able to assert that a particular physical property is conserved (e.g., length, weight, substance, space occupied) in spite of certain changes performed on the object (as change of color, shape, texture, temperature, position, etc.), the child obviously needs to be able to differentiate, first of all, within any given situation, the property that is conserved from those properties that change (are not conserved). For instance, as long as a child cannot dissociate the shape of an object from its weight, or the spatial arrangement of objects within a collection from the number of objects present in the collection, it is quite obvious that, for this child, any change in the shape of the object necessarily must appear as a change in weight, or any rearrangement of the elements in a collection as a change in the number of elements, so that this child cannot possibly effect any coordination between the properties in question (of which more will be said later) in order to affirm invariance for one while the other varies. This is all the more obvious as quantity is not perceptible in itself, as Piaget has shown a number of times (Piaget, Sinclair, & Vinh Bang 1968), and has to be inferred by additive or multiplicative composition of certain of its attributes, the relevance of which cannot even be recognized without prior differentiation of the properties in question. In fact, they need to be distinguished to a degree sufficient to prevent interference in a situation where they intervene simultaneously within a context of cognitive conflict. The necessity of this dissociation is in fact so obvious as to seem almost trivial, and one might be inclined to take it entirely for granted, to set aside the question whether this dissociation is the final result of a long development, and to content oneself with an explanation of conservation based uniquely upon the coordination of the activities performed by the subject upon the physical properties already structured and differentiated from the beginning. In this respect, it is quite striking to realize that the many studies Piaget did on the development of fundamental concepts (space, quantity, time, motion, etc.) in the child focus essentially upon the aspects involving the subject and his actions upon objects, without giving explicit attention to describing the development of the physical properties of objects.[1] Even his later studies of the development of causal concepts, which are by definition directly concerned with knowledge of objects and their various modes of interaction, still seem to be essentially dominated by the perspective of the subject. That this is so becomes particularly clear in the fairly direct developmental isomorphism Piaget establishes between the domains of operational and causal thought, where the former is constituted by operations *applied* to objects, and the latter by the same operations but this time *attributed* to the objects.[2]

There is no doubt that research was necessary to study more explicitly the manner in which the child develops an understanding of object properties as such, and that this necessity provided the impetus for some exploratory and still incomplete studies, which will be discussed in Chapter 5, to be undertaken in this domain in certain centers. For example, in Canada, Morf and his research group (e.g., Migneron 1969) have carried out work concerned with the development of object qualities in the child. Further, one might cite my research done with Pierre-Joly (Pierre-Joly 1974; Pinard & Pierre-Joly 1979) on the weight concept, where it was clearly shown that the younger children show very little dissociation between the weight of an object and its texture, its temperature, position, motion, etc.; see also Pinard and Chassé (1977), which showed a highly persistent lack of dissociation between volume and surface, giving rise to certain kinds of pseudoconservations. One might also note the studies directed or inspired by Murray, which have been cited above, illustrating

1. At the Symposium of Genetic Epistemology in Geneva, 1966, according to a remark made by Mounoud (1978), Piaget himself "declared never having really studied anything but the subject and somewhat jokingly exclaimed . . . that all his developmental studies will have to be redone from the point of view of the object" (p. 21 of Mounoud's French text).

2. This distinction, already sketched in Piaget's early epistemological writings (1950b, pp. 341 ff.), is later developed extensively ([1971] 1974) and integrated within his most recent model concerning the equilibration of cognitive structures ([1975] 1977).

at least indirectly the way children confuse, for quite a long time, the property of weight with other attributes of objects. In addition, the well-known studies carried out by Mounoud and his group (see, e.g., Mounoud 1970, 1977; Hauert 1980) in Geneva as well as those done in Bresson's laboratory in Paris (Bresson 1971) also concentrate on certain object properties and the processes leading to their identification and isolation. As a final illustration of this trend to study specifically the object and its evolution, note the research carried out by Piérault-Le Bonniec and his coworkers (Piérault-Le Bonniec 1977; Piéraut-Le Bonniec & Vurpillot 1976–1978; Piéraut-Le Bonniec & Jacob 1976–1978) on the construction of certain properties (e.g., concavity and convexity) of objects in the infant and on the variations observed in the properties of an object (e.g., shape, color) as a function of the capacity for abstraction in children from two to about seven years of age.

It was probably this same concern with the object and its properties that has motivated a number of other researchers to put the accent on the latter (e.g., Trabasso 1968; Trabasso & Bower 1968; Gelman 1969; Miller 1973). These authors see conservation acquisition as primarily depending upon the child's ability to dissociate the different attributes of an object and to attend only to the relevant attributes while ignoring the others (e.g., length vs. nonalignment, in a problem of conservation of length; number of elements in a collection of objects vs. the length or the density of the collection, in a problem of the conservation of number). Seductive as it seems in its simplicity, such an interpretation calls for certain reservations. Let us consider as an example Gelman's (1969) study, where five-year-old children were easily taught conservation (of number and of length) by a method consisting of a series of exercises in discriminating length or number, in which the child had to identify at each trial, among three stimuli (three initial lines of which two, obviously, had the same length, or three collections of tokens of which two were identical in number) which could also vary in color, shape, size, etc., the two stimuli that were identical to each other or the one differing from the others. In the face of rather spectacular successes (relatively young age of the subjects, ease of learning, generalization to two tasks of conservation of substance, and stability in acquisition for the group receiving verbal feedback about whether their choices were correct or incorrect), two interpretations of these results come to mind. It may be that Gelman's subjects already had the notions of quantity and invariance, as the author suggests herself (1969, pp. 184–185)[3] and as Miller (1978) also hypothesizes later, so that the learning exercises could easily bring the subjects to make good use of their preexisting knowledge, not letting themselves get distracted by perceptual delusions, as if it were sufficient to remind oneself, in order to accept invariance, that length but not alignment needs to be considered in a conservation of length problem, and the number of elements instead of the density or spread in spatial disposition in a conservation of number problem, etc. But then, given this interpretation, it remains to be explained how the children may have acquired this preexisting knowledge (if it is not innate), which only puts the problem back to a younger age level; it remains to explain how the children could have acquired this preexisting knowledge without also having learned the equally prerequisite dissociation between length and alignment, number and density, etc., since accepting invariance implies in itself such dissociations. This amounts to recognizing that the learning exercises did not really teach any new ability to differentiate between relevant and irrelevant attributes but only helped the subjects to utilize an ability they already possessed, whose manner of acquisition still needs to be explained. If one accepts a second interpretation, that is, that Gelman's subjects did not already possess the notions of quantity and invariance, questions remain to be asked concerning the authenticity of these acquisitions. Such questions are all the more relevant as it is a priori difficult to understand how an exercise based essentially upon *perceptual* discriminations in the case of the length problems, and upon mechanical *counting skills* or even discriminations of simple *perceptual numerosity* in the case of the number problems (since the collections to be evaluated included no more than five elements), could lead a child to understand that no deformation or displacement performed on one of

---

3. "Since there was very fast acquisition, it seems more appropriate to say the five year old can work with quantity if 'told' to do so" (Gelman 1969, p. 184). "The five year old child apparently does have to learn to respond consistently to quantity and not to be disturbed by irrelevant cues, but does not have to learn, de novo, to define quantity and invariance. . . . It could be that these responses are present in a child's repertoire, but are dominated by strategies under the control of irrelevant stimuli" (p. 185).

the two stimuli, which had been recognized as being identical beforehand, will in any way change its quantitative characteristics (length or number). It has been known for a long time that the perception of length or of numerosity appears at a much younger age than the concepts of length and of number. Based on the nature of the explanations given by her subjects, Gelman notes the possibility that her subjects had learned not only to ignore irrelevant cues of a specific nature but also had learned more general cues such as maintaining an initial judgment in spite of changes performed. This leaves open the possibility that the subjects' responses were not so much referring to quantitative identity as such but rather to qualitative identity (e.g., choosing the "same" two objects as before the transformation was made), or referring to perceptual equivalence especially in the case of lengths.[4] Given this interpretation, it is hardly surprising that Christie and Smothergill (1970) obtained completely negative results when using Gelman's discrimination exercises for lengths to teach conservation of length to four-year-old children. In a more recent study, Vadham and Smothergill (1977) have reapplied Gelman's technique introducing certain kinds of additional controls: subjects aged four instead of five years, to eliminate the possibility of preexisting spontaneous acquisitions; use of three groups, one receiving only the exercises of length discrimination, the second numerical discrimination, and the third both types of discrimination, in order to test for specificity of learning effects based on Halford's (1970a) criticism of Gelman; use of more stringent criteria in determining success on the learning tasks compared to those used by Gelman and by Christie and Smothergill. The results were rather disappointing on the whole: superior performance for the three experimental groups as compared to the control group, but gains no higher than 50% success rates on the posttests, considering only simple judgments of conservation, and falling to near zero when justifications were also considered; better performance of the group having undergone both types of exercises; absence of specificity of learning, each group giving no better performance on the conservation tests for which they were specifically trained than on three other tests; no relationship be-

4. *Mutatis mutandis,* the essentials of this criticism could also apply to Siegel's well-known research results (e.g., 1973; 1974; 1978) concerning the number concept by nonverbal methods.

tween success rate on the learning tasks as compared to that on the posttests; etc. Summarizing the main conclusions of Vadham and Smothergill, all the evidence obtained indicates that Gelman's interpretations receive little support and that if the children have learned the discriminations required in the learning tasks they have learned hardly any of the corresponding conservations. In fact, this may be a clear demonstration of the fact that, even though training exercises in perceptual discrimination or simple counting can easily be mastered by very young children, such exercises are hardly instrumental in bringing about acquisition of the corresponding conservation concepts.[5]

To conclude this discussion of the first of the three components implicated in the acquisition of conservation, suffice it to repeat that conservation of a physical property of an object (or a logicoarithmetical property of a collection of objects) presupposes prior dissociation between the properties defining an object. This dissociation then enables the child (1) to attend to the relevant attributes and to ignore the irrelevant ones in a conservation problem; (2) not to succumb to the dangers of contamination due to interference between certain properties that the child already knows how to recognize in an object, if they appear alone, but not if they intervene simultaneously in a conflict situation; and (3) to infer (to use a less simplistic and artificial interpretation) conservation of a particular property (e.g., quantity of liquid) by coordinating the perceptible attributes (e.g., height and width of containers) with which that physical property is associated. To arrive at such dissociation physical experience and abstraction are necessary, since the physical properties of an object are not given in advance in the child's knowledge but must be constructed and differentiated by the child. These physical experiences and abstracting activities are, however, not sufficient, as can easily be seen from the rather common observation that a child may very well be able to dissociate substance from weight, for example, in an object, without conserving either of the two properties (or conserving one without conserving the other), or be capable of differentiating height and width in two containers without conserving the quantity of liquid held by these. The rea-

5. In this general context, the reader is referred to the brief but incisive critical review by Larsen (1977) on what he calls the "strategy of simplification" proposed by Gelman or Miller.

son for this is, first, that conservation requires, in addition, the coordination of the already differentiated attributes; and, more important, as noted already in the preceding chapter, that in order to function physical experience necessarily requires logical experience, which serves as a framework for the processing and interpretation of empirical data. It should also be noted that physical experience, although dependent on logical experience in the spatiotemporal domain, proper to the conservation of physical attributes (such as quantity, space, etc.), still remains indispensable in the domain of logicoarithmetical conservations (e.g., number, classes, and relations), which are directly related to logical experience. This is true not only at the level of concrete thought, due to the constraints characteristic of pseudoempirical abstractions, but also at the level of formal thought when applied to problems of a physical nature.

Awareness of the Subject's Action Schemata

The second component necessary in the acquisition of conservation stresses directly the actions the subject performs upon objects, whereas the first focused on the objects as such and the learning of the dissociations between physical properties. The fact that this second component occupies a rather privileged position in Piaget's model, while the first has for a long time, and still does to a degree, remained relegated to a secondary plane and treated as self-evident, is to be seen as being due to Piaget's epistemological position; in his constructivist approach, according to which knowledge of reality does not consist simply of a progressive incorporation or internalization of objects already constituted in the outside world but requires, on the contrary, a long process of construction or of reconstruction of reality by means of the actions the subject performs upon the objects, it is obvious that the acquisition of conservations is considered primarily as the result of such a reconstruction. We consider it useful to distinguish between these two components mainly for reasons of emphasis; perhaps not to the same almost exclusive degree as some of the current interpretations discussed above, a more substantial part and a more explicit role than in Piaget's model are here given to the first component. It may even be assigned a privileged position in some cases, especially with respect to certain forms of conservation where deformations are not implicated (e.g., conservation of weight in spite of a change in color or in temperature). In fact, it is obvious that dissociation of the physical properties of an object and conscious awareness of internal action schemata are not processes that are independent with respect to each other; rather, they develop concurrently and in direct association, in the same way as the two kinds of experience (empirical and logical) which constitute the privileged basis for one or the other of the two processes, respectively.

The claim that becoming consciously aware of internal action schemata should be necessary for the acquisition of conservation is likely to raise certain objections at a time in the history of psychology which generally rejects allusions to any kind of introspection as completely unacceptable. Whatever the merits of this kind of interdiction, formulated in certain positivist circles—a rather questionable kind of interdiction, which is becoming increasingly challenged (see particularly the position of Hebb 1968; Paivio's neomentalism 1975; and Lieberman's recent appeal 1979)—it may be useful to reconsider in this connection the distinction drawn by Piaget (Beth & Piaget [1961] 1966, pp. 233–234) between psychological experience involved in the phenomenon of introspection, and logicomathematical experience involved in the actions the subject performs on objects. The former concerns the subjective aspects of an action in progress (e.g., the sentiments associated with it, the difficulties it presents), and the kind of awareness it entails concerns the subject as an individual in the process of carrying out some action. Logical experience, on the other hand, concerns the results, that is, objective and, therefore, in some way necessary aspects of certain kinds of activities, such as to separate, seriate, count, etc., which later turn into mental operations once they become internalized and grouped into integrated structures. The kind of awareness that accompanies this type of experience concerns any subject engaged in such activities, since it touches the most generalizable and objective aspects of these activities, that is, their structures or schemata. Thus, it is the role of logical experience, by which a subject can apply a particular activity to new contents, modify its contingencies, compare the results of these changes, etc., to enable the subject to become conscious of this action schema, not in direct fashion, since an action schema is not perceptible as such, but indirectly through the conscious discovery of the observable

constants resulting from the repeated and varied applications of
the action. This kind of awareness is therefore in no way related
to introspection in the usual sense, often smugly condemned in
the name of a certain scientific objectivity.

Returning to the difficult question concerning the acquisition of
conservations in the light of the preceding considerations, it is
now possible to show, using as an example the problem of the
conservation of quantities, what the observable constants and,
thus, the action schemata are which the subject needs to become
indirectly conscious of in the course of his discovering conservation, by means of the logicomathematical and abstracting experiences he undergoes in acting upon the objects. While admitting
that the quantity of matter constituting an object may not be
immediately dissociated from its shape or any of its properties (as
was seen in the preceding discussion), one can assume that, in
order to arrive at an affirmation of conservation, the subject
needs to consciously grasp three interdependent action schemata,
even though these do not necessarily all intervene in every situation of conservation, and even though knowledge of the empirical
laws and constants resulting from awareness of each of these
schemata is not sufficient to guarantee conservation.

The Qualitative Identity of Objects[6]

The first general schema the child needs to become aware of,
when he coordinates the result of his repeated actions on various
objects he encounters, implies simply the understanding that an
object can stay the same in spite of certain transformations it
undergoes, such as a change in color, temperature, form, spatial
location, etc. There is no need to repeat here what Piaget has
described at length (Piaget, Sinclair, & Vinh Bang 1968): how the
qualitative notion of identity develops in the child and its relationship to conservation, showing, in particular, that it is quite

6. The kind of identity discussed here has nothing to do with the "identity-
equivalence" dichotomy introduced by Elkind (1967) several years ago to indicate
two ways of asking the conservation problem. Whether or not there exists a
décalage separating the acquisition of the two kinds of conservation is still a
debated question. In any case, the identity and the equivalence defined by Elkind
are both quantitative (e.g., "there still is the same amount of water to drink") and
must be distinguished from the kind of qualitative identity considered here (e.g.,
"it's still the same water").

possible for a child to recognize the qualitative identity of an object having undergone certain transformations without conceding at the same time that its quantity is also conserved (e.g., "it's still the same water to drink, but now there is more of it"). The empirical law or constant corresponding to this chema in the child's consciousness, as derived from coordination of his actions performed upon objects (logical abstraction), may be something like, "You can change the color, the shape, etc., of a thing, but it is still the same object." This first general schema needs to be, in our view, completed by a complementary schema for achieving qualitative identity when associated with a particular form of transformation an object may be made to undergo. This complementary schema, of which the child needs to develop conscious understanding in the course of his experience with objects, is more directly related to conservation as such. It appears as a general empirical rule according to which one can add to or subtract from a particular object (material, substance, etc.) which is given beforehand. Adopting certain distinctions introduced recently by Piaget and his colleagues (e.g., Piaget [1975] 1977; Piaget et al. 1977b; Sinclair DeZwart 1977), these additions and subtractions may take on various forms and therefore become affected in a variety of ways: (a) either by successive actions carried out independently, directed from or to a point external to the object (e.g., add marbles to a collection by taking them from some other place; take away marbles from a collection and placing them elsewhere), where each addition may or may not be followed by equivalent or nonequivalent subtraction, and vice versa; (b) or by successive actions carried out on an object, but related to one another and taking place within the limits of the object considered (e.g., take away part of a collection of marbles and then put them back in the same place in the collection) so that the subtraction of matter first effected on the object is followed by the corresponding addition inside the same object without any contribution from outside; (c) or by one single action performed on the object, with no outside contribution, but incorporating both addition and subtraction simultaneously within the same object (e.g., add to the width of a collection of beads by simultaneously reducing its height with no transfer to or from the outside of the collection). Each of these three subschemata within the general schema of addition-subtraction corresponds to an empirical law or constant which the child comes to abstract and to become conscious of by means of the same process of coordinating his actions on objects, for example: "if you have something and then add to it from another place, you have then more of the same," or "if you have something and then take some of it away, you have less of the same than before" (subschema *a*); "if you have something and then take some of it away to put it back afterwards at the same place, you have at first less, then later more of the same" (subschema *b*); "if you move the parts around on something you have, it's still the same object, but there is a bit more in one place and a bit less in another place of the same object" (subschema *c*). Conscious grasping of these schemata seems to us a prerequisite to conservation without being a sufficient condition, however, since the different actions of adding and subtracting in no way preclude the possibility that something may be lost or gained in the transaction.

The Revertibility of Certain Actions

The second general schema to access a child's consciousness is both simpler and more general than the first and the third. It is simpler because it refers to a property characterizing certain kinds of actions the child may know from his daily experience (such as to go somewhere and return, move an object and put it back, etc.). Of course, the child does not necessarily notice this property of his actions on every occasion, nor does he have to be aware of how this property can influence the way he structures his environment. The greater generality of this schema of revertibility compared to the two others derives from the fact that the categories of actions to which it may be applied is almost unlimited; the additions and subtractions pertaining to the first schema are obviously also part of the second, and so are the manipulations inherent in the covariations of the third schema, to be discussed further on.

It is suggested that the awareness of this second schema may appear in three different modalities, distinct yet interrelated, even though it is not always easy to establish a developmental sequence among them a priori. The first of these modalities consists of the child becoming aware of the fundamental fact, however trivial, that there are some phenomena and some actions he performs himself which can be undone or inverted, while there are others that are not invertible. His daily experiences, from his first years on, have certainly confronted him with this fact many times (e.g., whereas it is possible to put a piece of fruit back from where it was taken, or to reheat something after it has cooled down, it is impossible to retrieve the fruit after it has been eaten, or to get back the object if it has burned down). But, as some of Piaget's recent research ([1974b] 1976, [1974c] 1978) has shown, there is often a very substantial décalage between consciously grasping an action and the successful execution of this action. Similarly, as seen in Piaget's research concerning identity (Piaget, Sinclair, & Vinh Bang 1968), children experience particular difficulties in recognizing the identity of an object or a person when these have undergone nonrevertible transformations (a person or an animal growing older, a burning candle, etc.). Thus, it takes the child many observations and experiences with external phenomena and the result of his actions before he comes to consciously realize that there is a distinction to be made between phenomena and actions that are revertible and those that are not. When applied to the conservation problem—to stay with the same example—the rule or empirical constant corresponding to this understanding consists in the child's assertion that, among the things that can be done with a material (either liquid or solid), some are revertible (e.g., change containers, warming up) while others are not (e.g., drink or eat it, burn it).

The second mode that the awareness of schema can take grows directly out of the first. That is, the schema of revertibility becomes an empirical rule for the child, which specifies that, when a phenomenon is revertible, if one performs some action upon an object, the result of this action is removed by the same action performed in the opposite direction. In this way, for example, the increase observed in the water level, when water gets poured into a narrow container from a wider one, is removed when the water is poured back into the first container. Other examples are the additions-subtractions and the covariations discussed in relation with the other two schemata, as it can be shown that the schema of revertibility can also apply to the two types of action included in those other schemata.

The third mode of the revertibility schema incorporates a further element in addition to the preceding ones: that of representation or mental imagery, which makes it possible for the schema to apply not only to (direct or inverted) actions performed in reality, as when the child engages in actions like transferring the contents of liquid containers, but also to the same actions when carried out in thought only, with the anticipated results only imagined. In other words, an imagined representation of an inverted action enables the child to anticipate the return of the initial situation preceding the direct action, for example, imagining that the increase in water level will be canceled if the water were retransferred from the narrow into the original wide container. This form of internalization of actions obviously has nothing in common with those hypothesizing or deductive behaviors characteristic of formal thought, because the notion of "possible" implicated in these anticipated image representations never goes beyond the level of material actions, which can be concretely realized (or have been realized in the past). It is also evident that the conscious realization of this revertibility schema, in one or the other of the modes just described, in no way assures the conservation of the properties implicated in the direct actions and their reversals. In fact, a child may perfectly well believe that some direct action performed on an object (e.g., pouring water into a narrower container) changes some of the object's properties (e.g., can augment its quantity by raising the water level) and that the reverse action performed subsequently (e.g., pouring the water back into the original container) can bring about the opposite change (e.g. reduce its quantity by lowering the water level). In sum, for all the internal consistency that the child's thinking shows, applying the reversion schema thus results not in conservation but in two successive nonconservations. Certain experiments performed by Murray and Johnson (1969, 1975) bear eloquent testimony to such confusion, as already indicated in Chapter 1.

The Covariation of Object Properties

The third general schema the child needs to consciously apprehend in situations where, for example, some material undergoes a deformation, is an explicitation of subschema c within the general qualitative identity schema. In its most general form, it simply expresses the fact that some object attributes (e.g., length, width, height) are interdependent in such a way that a variation in one will ipso facto produce a variation in the other as long as no outside contribution intervenes. The conscious grasp of this schema, resulting from the multiple experiences the child has with objects, does not come about all at once but in a series of sequential steps, each marked by a particular acquisition. Each of these acquisitions may be considered a different subschema, or rather a more or less evolved form of the same general schema in which the more evolved forms exceed the preceding ones in terms of greater extension of content and the definition of their objects.

The first of these subschemata does not bear on a covariation between two properties as such, even though this constitutes one of its prerequisites and is the earliest acquired. It involves the child becoming aware of certain empirical constants or certain functions (functional dependencies) inherent in the actions he performs upon objects. Thus, to stay with our earlier example, the child comes to realize, in the course of his manipulating liquid substances, that the level the liquid attains in a container depends necessarily on the form of the vessel and that this dependence effectively becomes a kind of constant or law that has no exceptions, for example, when water is poured into a thin glass it always rises higher than when the same water is poured into a wider glass, etc. It should be pointed out from the start that these empirical constants are necessary but not sufficient conditions for conservation in the compensatory form. They are necessary because compensation requires not an abstraction or detachment, as is frequently maintained in the literature, of the perceptual dimensions—misleading as they may be—of an object, but a conscious appreciation of these perceptual dimensions which constitute the material upon which the child's compensatory activity can be performed; they are not sufficient, however, as is eloquently shown by the large number of nonconservations found in children who nevertheless are quite capable of correctly predicting the variation in the levels, but inferring from this a similar variation in quantity due to a lack of dissociation between level and quantity.

The second form that the general schema of covariation can take, as it evolves into conscious awareness, is developmentally more advanced for two reasons. For one thing, it enriches the simple functional dependency relationship defined by the first subschema by transforming it into covariation proper. At first, this subschema appears in a very rudimentary form, devoid of any kind of quantification: everytime one dimension of an object is made to vary in one direction (with nothing being added from the outside), a second dimension simultaneously varies in the opposite direction. It is immediately apparent that this covariation reintroduces, in a different form, the empirical constant of the addition-subtraction subschema c described above, from which it is distinguished, however, in that this time the accent is placed on the additions and subtractions involved in a covariation in the dimensions of an object; for example, one cannot increase (or decrease) the height of a water column or a clay ball—if nothing is added or taken away outside of the object—without simultaneously reducing (or increasing) along the width dimension in the case of the water column, or the length dimension in the case of the clay. The second reason why this form of awareness goes beyond the first is the fact that it includes not only the positive effects or characteristics of an action (e.g., augment the height of the water column) but also the negative ones implicated in the action (e.g., reduce the width). Both characteristics are complementary and cannot be separated from each other, because the two constitute what may be termed the two opposite poles of an action. For Piaget, the conscious appreciation of the negative pole of an action plays a crucial role in development, to the extent that it constitutes one of the central components in his recent model of the equilibration of cognitive structures (Piaget et al. 1974b, pp. 52–53, 165–172; Piaget [1975] 1977). If it is true that every action aims at a positive result (e.g., move an object, go to another place), it is also true that it includes at the same time a negative aspect, not only because any particular action differs from all other possible actions and thus excludes everything it is not (e.g., the simple act of moving the elements of a collection excludes in and by itself the action of adding new elements), but also, and more important, achieving the positive result, that is, arriving at the situation aimed at (e.g., lengthening a ball of clay) implies necessarily a movement away from the initial situation, a correlative of the positive aspect of the same action (e.g., reducing the diameter of the clay ball). Now, Piaget has shown that the child's thinking remains for a long time dominated by the positive aspects of an action outweighing the negative aspects. The reason for this is that the positive aspects of an action at whatever level are always presupposed with respect to the negative ones, so that knowledge of the latter becomes the result of second-order observations or inferences: for example, perceptual activity can only attain the positive aspects of an object; sensorimotor action aims at positive goals only, even when it seeks destruction of an object or removing of an obstacle; internalized action (or thought) only arrives late at a systematic and logical use of negation, such as is shown in the difficulties experienced by the child to manipulate the inclusion of complementary classes in a subclass; this primacy of affirmation is even reflected in language, that is, in the linguistic distinction between "marked" and "unmarked" terms, etc. Piaget (Piaget et al. 1974a, 1974b) has also been able to show that the child, before being able to understand that each affirmation implies the negation of its opposite, that is, before achieving mental reversibility, gets himself trapped in multiple contradictions. Thus, if any particular action does not exclude what it is not, or if the positive aspect of an action does not always imply a corresponding negative one, then it becomes possible for an action to result in contradictory effects (e.g., the act of removing some elements of a collection can have the same effect as adding some; a quantity of water poured into a glass of different dimensions may be judged to be either greater because the water column is higher, or smaller because the column is less wide). In sum, to return to the second form of awareness of the general schema of covariation, it can be concluded that this form of consciousness is both necessary and insufficient; it is necessary because it is obviously a prerequisite for compensation, but it remains insufficient because it does not yet go beyond a mere registration of a factual covariation appearing, furthermore, only in a qualitative form (e.g., one cannot increase the height of a water column without reducing its width).

Only in its third form does the conscious experience of the general schema of covariation reach a level of precision sufficient to include a minimum of quantification. What characterizes this more advanced form of awareness is that the child no longer considers only the general dependency between two variations going in opposite directions, or between the positive and the negative aspects of an action performed on an object, but that he now becomes aware of the fact that there is a relationship between the values each of the covariates can take. Thus, instead of merely noticing that for each increase in height there is necessarily a corresponding decrease in the width of a water column, the child now begins to pay attention to the magnitude of these variations and to discover the law or empirical constant stating that, for a given water column, the higher the level, the narrower its diameter. The quantitative relation expressed by this law, to adopt a terminology often used by Piaget (e.g., 1950a, pp. 77 ff.; Piaget et al. [1968] 1977, pp. 186 ff.), is certainly not numerical or metric, that is, based upon estimates formulated in terms of cardinal numbers; but it attains at least a first level of extensional quantification, since it includes a comparison and even a seriation of differences (e.g., the greater the increase in height in a particular water column, the greater also the change in its width). In spite of the indisputable progress this more advanced form of the general schema of covariation represents, the child's conscious understanding of it is still not sufficient to ensure the logical necessity of conservation, precisely because it concerns still only covariation, that is, an empirical law or function, whose explanation remains to be discovered. Furthermore, it does not yet necessarily bring about an explicit form of quantified proportionality, a requirement—at least in extensional if not metric form—for the conversion of covariation to compensation (e.g., the initial height of the water column is to its terminal height as its terminal width is to its initial width).

To conclude the discussion of the second component necessary for the acquisition of conservations, let us simply recall that conscious understanding, as discussed, is mainly a result of reflective abstraction at work in logical experience, since the action schemata described above only become accessible to the child's consciousness when he takes note of the results that are produced through the coordination of his actions upon objects.

The Coordination of Physical Properties of Objects with the Subject's Action Schemata

So far it has been shown that the differentiation of the physical properties of objects involves mostly physical experience and abstraction, whereas the conscious understanding of the subject's action schemata primarily implicates logical experience and abstraction. It remains to show how the combined interplay of

these two kinds of complementary experiences can lead the child
to affirm the logical necessity of conservation so that he no longer
needs recourse to new experiences in order to prove conservation.
In other words, it needs to be demonstrated how, so to speak, experience becomes unnecessary when replaced by logical deduction.

The simplest and clearest way to illustrate this process is
perhaps to take up one after the other the three action schemata
just discussed and to show for each in what way the transition
from experience (or induction) to logical deduction may take
place. This method to proceed recommends itself especially,
since it calls up directly the three types of argument (identity,
reversibility, and compensation) upon which the child may base
his affirmation of conservation at one time or another.

From Qualitative to Quantitative Identity

Considering the first of the three general schemata, it may be
said that the transition of experience to deduction consists
essentially in a changeover from qualitative to quantitative identity, the former becoming integrated[7] within the latter, which assures the logical necessity proper to conservation. For this
changeover to take place, it is first of all required that the
schemata representing qualitative identity, which the child has
already become conscious of, and the physical properties of objects, which he has already been able to isolate, be explicitly
confronted and integrated with one another. Only if this condition
is met is it possible for these schemata or empirical rules to become directly applied—using our earlier example of the conservation of substance—to the quantity of matter contained in a
particular substance, and not applied to its texture, color, position, shape, etc. In other words, first of all it is necessary that the
child's reasoning, whatever its value, should be directed at the
relevant property of an object and, consequently, be capable of
posing the problem of invariance (or variance) with respect to the
quantity of matter contained in the object, one of whose prop-

7. Piaget is careful to point out that this qualitative identity does not disappear
in the process but "changes its nature by becoming integrated into a more complex structure, to which it becomes subordinated and which gives it certain new
characteristics. Thus, identity and conservation are not related in a filiative manner, rather they become integrated, so that the latter cannot be reduced to the
former" (Piaget, Sinclair, & Vinh Bang 1968, p. 73).

erties has been modified. What makes this process of conscious appropriation particularly difficult is the fact that quantity as such is not a perceptible property like other physical attributes of an object; the child needs to learn to infer it by means of an additive or multiplicative composition of certain perceptible attributes (or indices) of the object, which he first has to learn to dissociate from one another and from quantity itself, as designated by these indices. This complex process is what is meant when we speak of the child's action schemata becoming applied to those, and only those, object properties that are relevant to and permit inferences of a quantitative nature.

Second, in order for qualitative identity to complete its development into quantitative identity, it is necessary that the child establishes an explicit contrast between the general and the specific forms of qualitative identity—of which he has already become conscious—so that he is capable of drawing a clear distinction between two different kinds of change carried out on an object: one which includes observable additions and subtractions of matter, and another without such modifications (such as a change in color, temperature, position, etc.). This rather simple[8] first discrimination, however, is not always sufficient. In those cases where observable additions and subtractions of matter are involved, it is also particularly important that the child establish a contrast between the different subschemata (and their corresponding empirical rules) of which he has become conscious so that he can easily grasp the essential difference between a form of addition or subtraction of matter carried out on the same object by *successive actions*—either originating from a source outside of the object (subschema *a* of the general qualitative identity schema), or within the object (subschema *b*)—and another form of material addition or subtraction carried out on the same object by *one single action* originating within the object and producing two simultaneous and complementary effects (subschema *c*).

Applied to conservation of liquid quantity, for example, this distinction enables the child (1) to comprehend that when water is transferred from one container to another of a different shape, neither subschema *a* nor *b* become operative (nothing is taken away to be replaced thereafter, nothing is put elsewhere to be

8. This undoubtedly explains the relative ease with which children succeed in recognizing conservation in cases of modifications without deformation.

taken again, in two successive actions), but that subschema c is involved (e.g., one adds to the height and reduces the width of the water column in one single action, which produces two simultaneous effects: one of addition, the other of subtraction); and (2) to infer from this distinction that the transport of the liquid has done nothing but transfer the same water from one place to another and has not changed its quantity, since the part subtracted in one location has simultaneously been added in another on the same water column. But, however important this distinction introduced by Piaget into his recent model may be, it seems to us that it still does not suffice by itself to guarantee the logical necessity of conservation, basically because even a single action which produces the two effects of addition and subtraction simultaneously still remains an action physically accomplished. And a physical action is always particularized and as such inevitably subject to spatiotemporal limitations: two displacements can have different forms and magnitudes, two displacements are necessarily successive and may be independent of one another, one displacement necessarily takes time to be accomplished, even the simultaneous effects of addition and subtraction resulting from a single action occur in time, etc. Therefore, unless it is assumed a priori that the child possesses in advance that knowledge of conservation which he is just in the process of acquiring, there remains always the possibility that spatiotemporal limitations lead the child to assert conservation for a particular displacement while denying it in the case of another; it is even entirely possible that a child who is quite aware of the fact that the same displacement produces two complementary and equal effects of addition and subtraction still holds that the total quantity is not conserved. For all kinds of reasons—such as some precausal dynamism "magically" attributed to the very act of transferring the water from one container to the other, or to constrictions imposed by the containers themselves—there is no a priori condition preventing a child from recognizing the equivalence of the two effects produced simultaneously by a single action (e.g., that what is taken away at one point is equal to what is added at another at the same time), while remaining convinced that the absolute value of these two equal quantities is not conserved in the course of the transfer, which necessarily takes a certain amount of time to get accomplished (e.g., the amount taken away here is equal to that added there at any moment of the action, but still the quantity of matter transferred may increase or decrease during the exchange). In sum, due to the spatiotemporal restrictions inherent in any physical action, the child whose thinking remains tied to the use of empirical schemata and laws, as consciously internalized, still is unable to comprehend and deduce the logical necessity of conservation; the most it can do is to extend, by some sort of experiential induction or progressive generalization of these empirical rules, the range of known instances of conservation further and further, but with no provision for excluding exceptions to the rules, because their reason is not yet understood and consequently the transition from simple empirical to logical necessity has not yet been accomplished. Incidentally, this is the reason why we believe that what seem to be operational conservation responses in children classed at intermediate levels, in fact, do not surpass the preoperational level of thought (Pinard 1975).

Third, therefore, in order for the transition from qualitative to quantitative identity to be accomplished, it is necessary that the child free himself of the spatiotemporal restrictions inherent in any physical action and thus to escape, so to speak, the hazards of successivity. But the only way to carry out this transformation from successivity to simultaneity is to complete the process of confronting the schemata and empirical laws discussed in the preceding sections by another form of experience or mental reflection directed toward the physical actions performed by the subject or witnessed by him. To the extent that these mental experiences are not simply image representations of the physical actions but are concerned with analyzing the internal structure of these actions and their coordinations—a task properly assumed by logical, reflective abstraction—the child then comes to grasp the fundamental fact that physical displacements that can be performed successively on the parts of the same whole are all mutually equivalent, because the parts within a single set are both permutable and interchangeable (or vicariant) in the case of simple displacements without transformations involving addition or subtraction from a source outside of the set (to employ certain notions introduced by Piaget [1975] 1977; Piaget et al. 1974b, in his latest model). They are permutable in the sense that they can be placed in any position within the set without losing their proper identity: for example, the parts of a set A can be arranged equally well as $a_1 + a_2 + a_3 \ldots + a_n$, or as $a_3 + a_1 + a_2 \ldots + a_n$, etc., and thus can be substituted one for the other. They are vicariant in the sense that any set can always be considered as the union of any one of its parts (whatever its size) with its complementary parts: for example, in constructing the set A, one may equally well first choose part a_1 or another part a_2, etc., each time joining the part thus chosen to the remaining parts of the same set: $a_1 + (a_n - a_1) = a_2 + (a_n - a_2), \ldots = A$. As soon as the child has become aware of this mobility of parts within a set, he becomes capable of understanding that any displacement actually performed is only a particular instance of all cases possible. More important, he will be able to infer on the basis of this equivalence that the sum of the parts is conserved whatever the arrangement one might impose on them, since it is always possible to go from one to another by a simple internal transformation. A child who asserts conservation (e.g., "there is always the same amount to drink") by giving an argument of identity (e.g., "because no water has been added or taken away, but only the containers are changed") attempts to render explicit the difference between a transformation involving additions and subtractions outside of the set and one involving only displacements of permutable and vicariant parts within the same set. It is now easy to see how this awareness is equivalent to the transition from successiveness to simultaneity: each physical displacement of parts of a set—this being subject to the spatio-temporal constraints inherent in any physical action—implies simultaneously, by a simple mental transposition, all other displacements the parts may successively be subjected to within their set. In other words, this amounts to transforming a physical union of parts, which necessarily takes place in time, into a mental one, which per se is free of these temporal constraints: this difference is reflected in normal language use when we speak, for example, not of *constructing* a set A by uniting the parts $a_1, a_2,$ $a_3, \ldots a_n$, but of a set *composed* of the parts $a_1, a_2, a_3, \ldots a_n$.

In sum, it is through this awareness of the commutativity and vicariance of parts constituting a whole set that the successive physical transformations performed on one object come to restructure themselves in an integrated structure (*structure d'ensemble*) or closed network of atemporal mental transformations.

Since these are all interrelated, there can thus no longer be any gains or losses, as is always possible when the changes take place in time. This restructuring of successive physical actions into atemporal mental operations not only has the effect of enabling the child to assert conservation—which he can already do at an earlier, intermediate stage with respect to certain kind of particular physical transformations—but also of altering profoundly the nature, certainty, and generality of these assertions: (1) *experience is replaced by mental deduction*—whereas the former had given rise only to the empirical rules or constants the child had learned by himself (or could easily be taught), but which are devoid of any kind of explanatory value, mental deduction does explain the rules and, therefore, eliminates the necessity of reverting to experience[9]; (2) *a form of logical necessity* comes into being out of the fact that the operations grouped together in one closed network are mutually derivable; this form of necessity at once surpasses any empirical necessity, which depends entirely upon the nonexistence of exceptions to the empirical rules learned; (3) predominant use is made of a *"constructive"* or *"reflective" mode of mental generalization* (see the distinctions introduced in Chap. 2), which can include all possible cases, since it is based on deductive inference and logical necessity, as just discussed, whereas the "inductive" or "extensional" mode of mental generalization is limited in its application to recognize only that a given empirical rule abstracted from observation of a certain number of instances also can apply to an ever-increasing number of other instances, but without trying to find the reason or logical necessity for this extension.

From Revertibility to Reversibility

With respect to the second schema discussed above, it may be said that the transition from experience to deduction is essentially that of revertibility to reversibility. The process involved is also

9. This change brings to mind the difference made once by Piaget (Apostel, Mays, Morf, & Piaget 1957, pp. 67–69) for logicomathematical thinking, between analytical actions of type I ("any composite act such that the truth value of its component actions constitutes the necessary and sufficient condition for the truth of its outcome"), and analytical actions of type II ("any composite act such that the truth of its outcome is completely determined (= necessary and sufficient condition) by inference from the truth value of its component actions").

essentially the same as just described for the transition from qualitative to quantitative identity. To avoid unnecessary repetitions, therefore, the present discussion will take up the same three conditions treated above, showing how each of them applies to the change from revertibility to reversibility.

First, what is needed is a confrontation of the general schema of revertibility, of which the child has already become conscious, with the physical properties of objects that he has come to discriminate. It is quite obvious that a child could never arrive at the conservation of physical quantities as long as the schemata or empirical laws of revertibility he uses cannot unambiguously be applied to that particular property of which he attempts to determine whether it is or is not invariant. This presupposes necessarily the ability to distinguish between various pairs of invertible actions that can be performed on an object (addition-subtraction of substance, heating-and-cooling, displacement-and-replacement, extension-and-compression, etc.).

Second, it is necessary for the passage from revertibility to reversibility that the child can compare the various modes of the general schema of revertibility, which he has already internalized: distinguish between invertible actions (or phenomena) and those that are not, remove the effect of an action performed in one direction by another performed in the opposite direction, be able to predict this cancellation by representing to himself a mental image of the inverted action. In order to arrive eventually at conservation, the child needs to be sensitive to the fundamental distinction between an invertible and a noninvertible action so that he can take note, by a process of differentiation and comparative analysis, of the fact that this schema can be generalized to any invertible situation, even though certain kinds of action are less amenable than others to inversion, either actually carried out or simply imagined, or even though some actions can be inverted more easily in imagination than in reality: for example, in a problem of conservation of substance, it is evidently much more difficult to carry out or even to imagine a return to the initial state when the problem involves the dissolution of sugar than in the case of transferring liquid from one container to another; in a problem of conservation of distances in a mountain landscape, it is probably much easier to imagine than to actually accomplish the return to the point of departure after a direct descent from the top. However necessary this discrimination and generalization of the schema of revertibility are, they do not in themselves suffice to guarantee conservation, even in the simplest cases (e.g., empty out and reempty; displace and replace), since both the direct and the inverted actions remain physical and successive actions taking place in time. This allows for the possibility that something may be gained or lost in the process.

Third, for this reason, it is necessary that the child ultimately free himself of the spatiotemporal constraints inherent in any physical action. Again, the process is similar to the one described above with respect to the passage from qualitative to quantitative identity. By considering the internal structure of these successive actions and of their coordination, the child ultimately comes to realize that the parts of a set, to which nothing is added or taken away from the outside, are permutable and vicariant, and thus equivalent within the set of elements, independent of each element's spatial position therein. When applied to the particular case of reversibility, this awareness means essentially to understand that the couple addition-subtraction involved in a direct action, that is, change of spatial position of parts of an object (e.g., increase the height and decrease the width of a water column between two containers, increase the length while decreasing the density of a row of elements) is necessarily equivalent—by simple internal permutation of the two components or simultaneous effects of the direct action—to the couple subtraction-addition involved in the opposite or inverted action (e.g., decrease the height, while increasing the width of a water column). In this way it becomes possible to go from direct action to inverted action by simple internal transposition in such a way that the sum of parts cannot possibly vary because any change in position is seen as only one instance among all others possible and includes implicitly—and therefore simultaneously—all others, including return to the initial state. In sum, it is by forming an integrated structure (*structure d'ensemble*) that the successive physical actions become mental operations, interrelated by mutual implication and, therefore, capable of being transformed one into the other, which precludes the possibility of gains or losses in the course of the transformation. This difference between an invertible physical action and a reversible mental operation is implicitly expressed by a child when he asserts conservation, basing himself upon the possibility of removing an effect produced by an action, by performing the same action in the opposite direction (e.g., "there is always the same amount to drink; it does not matter if you pour the water into another glass, because you can always pour it back into the first, no matter what kind of glass it was"), instead of denying conservation twice in succession, in the belief that the inverse action should reverse the initial effects of increasing or decreasing the quantity, to decrease or increase the respective amounts (e.g., "now there is more water to drink; you have to pour it back again to have the same as before"). In sum, the systematic recourse to arguments of this nature to justify conservation indicates clearly that the child is able to make the distinction between a physical transformation, which modifies (by addition or subtraction) the sum of the parts of a set, and a simple displacement, that is, a physical transformation limited to repositioning the parts without affecting the sum. It further shows clearly that, for such a child, performing the inverse action is nothing but a way to explicate in time a possibility which the physically realized direct action already implied at the time of execution. But once the spatiotemporal constraints inherent in physical action are removed, both the direct action and its inverse imply each other, so that one can be transformed into the other without possibility of either gain or loss in the course of the transformation. As in the case of quantitative identity completing qualitative identity, it is the transition from physical revertibility to mental reversibility (from the successive to the simultaneous) which confers an explanatory value upon the empirical rule invoked by the child, as it shows why and how the possible return to the initial situation makes it possible to infer *deductively* the invariance of quantity with no recourse to experience, and especially without interpreting such recourse in terms of a simple way to follow up a first variance with a second. This substitution of experience by deduction brings about (*a*) a logical character in addition to the purely empirical necessity which can never be overcome by simple repetition of experiences; and (*b*) the possibility for deductive or constructive generalization, instead of the earlier simply inductive or extensional one, modifying the empirical rule already acquired by the child and making it applicable to all possible cases.

From Covariation to Compensation

Considering, finally, the third of the general schemata the child needs to become conscious of in his progression toward conservation, and taking as an example a situation involving the deformation of an object, it may be said that the transition from experience to deduction essentially means, in this case, a transition from the empirical schema of covariation to the operational one of compensation. Even though compensation is less frequently invoked as an argument for conservation than the others, and this for reasons that will be discussed below, the passage from covariation to compensation follows the same general processes as that from qualitative to quantitative identity and that from empirical revertibility to operational reversibility. It is thus subject to the same three conditions, of which it shall suffice here to repeat the essentials.

Once again the child needs first of all to come to adjust, so to speak, by progressively coordinating his actions upon the objects in his environment, his schema of covariation to the various physical properties he has learned to discriminate in objects. This will allow him to apply his general schema to those properties that matter in any particular situation. Such a confrontation thus implies both a differentiation and a generalization of the general covariation schema. There is differentiation of the schema to the extent that the child becomes aware of two aspects: first, that covariation does not necessarily occur with all transformations an object may be subjected to in a situation of conservation (e.g., change of color, of temperature); and, second, that in those cases where it does occur, it is necessary to clearly dissociate the properties to be considered as being in covariation from the other properties of the same object (e.g., height and width of the water column in the conservation of liquids, length and density of a row of elements in the conservation of number). In complementary fashion, there is generalization of the schema of covariation to the extent that the child comes to recognize the same basic structure in all kinds of different situations, without attempting to extend this generalization to situations where it does not apply.

The second condition is closely linked to the first and is also contemporary with it. It requires that the child become explicitly conscious of the relationship that exists between the covariation schema and the schema of addition-subtraction in its third form (''when you change the form of an object, it still remains the same object, but there is a bit more in one place and a bit less in the other''). This relationship consists in the possibility of considering the former of the two schemata as an application of the latter to the dimensions of an object. Furthermore, the child needs to become conscious of the differences between the various modes or modalities in which the general covariation scheme appears, as it becomes more differentiated and generalized. By this confrontation the child (1) comes to better understand what it is the second mode adds to the first, that is, the necessity of considering the negative as well as the positive aspects of a transformation, and also what it is the third mode adds to the second, that is, a kind of equivalence between the two simultaneous effects; and (2) becomes more aware of the contradictions resulting from exclusive reliance on the first mode and from the neglect of complementary observations, which become progressively more accurate, pertaining to the second and particularly the third mode. Yet, this differentiation and generalization of the child's scheme of covariation do not suffice—in spite of their essential contribution—to ensure conservation, since the laws and empirical rules this schema generates still lack any kind of explanatory power. More important, the spatiotemporal character of the actions and transformations to which this schema is applied fails to exclude, in principle, the possibility of nonconservation.

It is for this reason that the transition from covariation to compensation requires ultimately that the child be able to free himself of spatiotemporal limitations. This is true because, even though covariation is an expression of the product of two simultaneous effects within a single action, the covariation itself takes place in time, and the magnitude of the effects produced, even though completely equivalent with respect to each other, can vary from one time to the next as a function of the extent of the transformation effected. In this way the child can always believe that, even though there is complete equivalence between the portion added in one place (e.g, height increase in a water column) and that subtracted in another (e.g., decrease in width), this quantity may itself change in the course of the transformation. Therefore, once again, as in the two cases discussed previously (identity and reversibility), the child needs to understand that a whole is made up of mutually equivalent parts, that is, parts that are permutable and vicariant so that any of the parts may be placed in any position whatsoever (commutativity), no matter what its size (vicariance). Thus, to the extent that the union of parts of a whole is no longer seen as a physical union or construction (necessarily spatiotemporal) but as a mental union or composition (extra-temporal and extraspatial), and to the extent that nothing is added or taken away from the outside, it becomes then inevitable that the whole is conserved, as it is possible to proceed mentally from any state to any other, by simple internal transposition or re-arranging of parts. In other words—to go back to our example of the transfusion of liquid quantities from one container to another of different diameter—that a quantity contained in a water column of height $H_1 \times$ width W_1 can be judged as being invariant when it is transformed, by a physical transfusion, into a column of height $H_2 \times$ width W_2, or of height $H_3 \times$ width W_3, is due to the fact that this change can be understood as a different form of understanding the disposition of the parts within the whole of the initial object, which, in turn, is seen as only one of the ways in which it is possible to arrange the parts. In this way it is evident that any increase in height must necessarily be compensated by an equivalent decrease in width. This passage from empirical covariation to operational compensation manifests itself when a child invokes, more or less explicitly, an argument of "compen-sation," as it is called (e.g., "there is still the same amount to drink, because even though the water rises higher in this one, this glass is not as wide and it comes to the same thing"), when asserting the conservation of the initial quantity. The acquisition of the operational schema of compensation leads to the same three consequences, already noted in the case of operational identity and reversibility, in the child's reasoning: experience is replaced by deduction, which furnishes an explanation of the em-pirical rules acquired previously; empirical necessity based upon simple observable constants is surpassed by logical necessity, based upon the deductibility of mental operations; operational generalization of compensation is extended to all possible cases, replacing the simple progressive extension of that schema to new instances.

Conclusion

To sum up the preceding considerations concerning the origin of conservations, let us simply recall that the general process involved may be summed up as consisting essentially of three principal components; the first two, the dissociation of the physi-cal properties of objects and the conscious grasp of the subject's own action schemata, which he uses in interacting with objects, develop together in close association and interdependence; yet, the rules and empirical constants acquired by the child, in the course of the physical and logical experiences implicated in the first two components, are not sufficient to give an understanding of the necessity of conservation. This is so because they do not go beyond the level of mere legal investigation and are thus devoid of any explanatory power, and moreover remain subject to the spatiotemporal limitations inherent in the physical actions from which they have been abstracted. Thus, as we have tried to show in taking up systematically each of the three kinds of argument invoked in the justification of conservation, it is the role of the third component to complete the first two—considered necessary but not sufficient—by a form of mental experience or reflection upon the physical actions performed on objects whose goals are triple: first, an integration of the activities of dissociation of the physical properties of objects with the action schemata become conscious by the acquisition of empirical rules which give them expression; second, a comparison or confrontation of these schemata and empirical rules, which differentiates and general- izes them; third, and most important, a liberation from spatiotemporal limitations, which are invariably present in any physical transformation, and which always allow for the possibil- ity of gains or losses incurred during a transformation. The re- alization of this last goal depends essentially upon the child's becoming aware of the fact that all the parts making up a single object are equivalent with respect to one another in terms of commutativity and vicariance, so that any transformations one might successively perform upon an object, as long as they re- main within the limits of the same object, will be considered as just special cases of a whole class of transformations, which imply one another by simple internal transposition. It is this mutual implication—with its underlying transition from succes- siveness to simultaneity—which allows the child to substitute de- duction for experience and thus to go beyond purely empirical necessity and purely inductive generalization to which all empiri- cal rules or laws are limited by definition.

Finally, it must be made clear that even though the examples given to illustrate our model are almost all taken from the conser- vation-of-liquid quantities, it should not be concluded that it cannot be generalized to other forms of conservation. As can be briefly indicated, taking up in turn each of the three components of the model, the general structure will remain essentially unchanged when certain transpositions are introduced into the model by extension to other content areas.

To begin with the first component, it is clear that the dissociation of physical properties of objects is necessary for any form of conservation. If the confusion shape-quantity is the most frequent one observed in the conservation of substance, equivalent types of confusion can be found in all other forms of conservation: the weight concept presupposes among other things a distinction between perceived volume and resistance; length requires a distinction between interval occupied and extension beyond, or between extensibility and mobility; volume between weight and form; speed, between distance covered and duration of travel; etc. In certain forms of conservation, more than one dissociation may be required (e.g., in weight conservation one needs to dissociate resistance from form, from position, from color, etc.), and, other things being equal, a conservation gets more difficult as its dissociations become more difficult to make.

Similarly, the second component of the model, that is, the child's awakening consciousness of his action schemata, also is essential to all forms of conservation. In the simplest cases, where no deformation is involved (such as in conservation of substance or weight with concomitant changes in color, temperature, etc.), only the schema of qualitative identity is necessary, once the physical properties are dissociated. The schema of covariation evidently does not apply, and the schema of revertibility, when produced by the child, can only serve to justify judgments of nonconservation. In most cases, however, the three schemata may apply. Whether we are dealing, for example, with conservation of number, of space, of length, weight, etc., each time the child needs to become aware that the object in question remains the same in spite of the transformations or displacements to which one might subject it; that the additions and subtractions imposed may remain inside the object (by displacement of parts with simultaneous effects of increase in one location and decrease in another), or, on the other hand, may include contributions from outside (addition) or losses (subtractions) in independent actions. On the other hand, the schema of revertibility can also intervene in most cases, except that it should be stressed that the child also needs to take account of the fact that a return to the initial situation may be more or less difficult to realize or to imagine in certain situations (e.g., conservation of sugar dissolved in water). As for the schema of covariation in certain attributes of an object, even though it may not necessarily apply to all forms of conservation, it does intervene in a great many situations where a variation in one attribute of an object is always accompanied by a variation in another (e.g., length of a row vs. density, proximity of its elements, in number conservation; extending on the right vs. extending toward the left in the conservation of length of two staggered rods, etc.). In sum, it is clear that there are changes in content, when the empirical rules which express the child's awareness of his action schemata are used in different situations; but their functions remain always the same and are everywhere subject to the same limitations.

As for the coordination of the physical properties of objects with the subject's action schemata—the third component—it necessarily intervenes in any form of conservation, whatever its content, because it is only the processes involved in this last component—particularly the freedom from the spatiotemporal constraints of physical action—which can explain the transition from experience to deduction and from empirical to logical necessity. This may occur in any one of the three ways (from qualitative to quantitative identity, from revertibility to reversibility, or from covariation to compensation), one or the other of which may be privileged by the child, depending on the particular characteristics of the situation. In the simplest case (that of transformations without deformation), the freeing from spatiotemporal constraints necessarily takes the form of quantitative identity (e.g., "you can do anything you like, there will always be the same amount, if nothing is added or taken away"). In those situations where deformations are involved, the freeing from space and time can likewise be expressed in the form of identity, but may also proceed by way of reversibility through compensation or through inversion (e.g., "you can do what you want, there will always be the same, if you add here what you take away there," etc.). Finally, in those situations where conservation is implicated in a reasoning process without taking the traditional form of a conservation problem (as in the many situations cited in Chap. 1), the freeing from spatiotemporal constraints is still necessary, even where it does not proceed along the specific and explicit paths of identity, compensation, or reversibility. For example, in order to admit that a class of objects is conserved (e.g, wooden beads) in spite of its division into subclasses (e.g., red and green beads), the child needs to comprehend that the same bead may be simultaneously—mentally, if not physically—part of two different collections (e.g., part of a necklace of red beads and part of one made of wooden beads). What is common to those three types of situations and explains why the third of the components necessary to conservation is present in all three situations is the fact that, in each case, the different parts of an object are commutable and vicariant so that any possible organization they can successively take on are but internal transpositions, which imply one another and thus affect in no way the sum of these parts.

4   On Some Controversial Topics and Alternative Models

Before proceeding to present a set of empirical data illustrating certain aspects of the descriptive model of the child's acquisition of conservation, proposed in the preceding chapter, it may be useful to devote a chapter to a discussion of two somewhat related topics: a comparison of the most usual arguments for conservation, and the role played by cognitive conflict in the acquisition of conservation. This chapter will also compare the present model to certain alternative proposals.

A Comparison of the Usual Arguments for Conservation

The first point we wish to consider concerns the comparison between the three arguments usually invoked to justify conservation, that is, identity, reversibility, and compensation. Considering first a purely theoretical or logical analysis of the three types of justification, it may suffice to recall (Piaget 1950b) that each represents a particular form of mental reversibility. First, *identity* is a form of reversibility by cancellation of an additive direct action $(+ a)$ through an opposite subtractive action $(- a)$, but without those actions being carried out in reality, as is indicated by the term "null operation" to designate the general identity operation $(a \pm 0 = a,$ or $a - a = 0)$. The specific argument of *reversibility*, on the other hand, is an expression of the inversion of physical actions having been carried out and proceeding in a specified direction in one sense as well as in the opposite sense; this form of mental reversibility thus involves composition of the actions themselves, but without taking account of the quantitative relations inherent in these actions. Finally, the argument of *compensation* expresses in turn a form of mental reversibility by reciprocity of the relations appearing as a result of the actions performed. This involves, thus, the composition of the results of the actions rather than of the actions themselves, and, in this way, allows for a minimum of quantification of the changes brought about by these actions: the equivalence between two operations $(a_1 + b_1 = a_2 + b_2)$, as expressed by this form of reversibility, is therefore the result of the cancellation of one difference $(a_2 = a_1 - x)$ by the opposite $(b_2 = b_1 + x)$ rather than that of a direct action by the opposite in its totality. Even though a particular subject does not have to give explicitly all three kinds of argument in a given situation, it is quite obvious that these arguments belong together by virtue of their sharing that fundamental characteristic of mental operations, which is reversibility. This primacy of reversibility in its most comprehensive sense is what we have tried to emphasize when, in Chapter 2, we have attempted to show that it is mental reversibility which determines the transition from successiveness to simultaneity, necessary for conservation, under whatever form this transition appears. The main reason for this is that mental reversibility is, by definition, that property of mental operations which makes possible the internal transpositions inherent in the various operations constituting a single network, including those operations involved in the notions of commutativity and vicariance of parts pertaining to an object, and these notions provide the direct and equal basis for the usual three types of justification.

When one compares this theoretical interdependence among the three types of justification with the relative frequency with which each can in fact be observed, one might ask why it is that identity is more frequently invoked by the children than is reversibility and especially compensation. That compensation is the least frequently given as a reason for conservation is due not only to the fact that in some situations it cannot be applied (e.g., change of temperature, of color, etc.), but it is perhaps mainly because it is easier and less abstract to imagine and to explicate an inverse action which cancels the effect of its corresponding direct action (reversibility) and produces the null operation (identity) than it is to imagine or explicate an inverse action that cancels one difference by another, in which case the cancellation concerns only the relation between two terms, without canceling the terms as such. In trying to explain why identity is more often encountered as a justification than is reversibility, even though it is logically based upon the latter, one might refer to an argument given by Piaget (Berlyne & Piaget 1960, p. 112) to the effect that simply asserting conservation only activates a progressive, direct process, while subsequently justifying this assertion presupposes a regressive analysis which, by definition, inverts the order of events used in the mental construction of justifications. However, it seems to us that the observed prevalence of identity arguments (e.g., nothing has been taken away or added) over arguments involving reversibility (e.g., it is possible to undo what was done) can be explained more simply perhaps with reference to two reasons: that a direct transformation is not always reversible or easy to invert in reality (e.g., dissolution of sugar in water), and that, unlike the identity argument, reversibility can often be used in the form of simple empirical revertibility, in the justification of nonconservation (e.g., "when you flatten the ball, then you have less, and when you make it again as it was before, then there is more").

Before terminating the discussion of the first point, it may be interesting here to bring up the specious objection raised by Murray (1978) in a brief consideration concerning the value and relevance of the usual arguments invoked by children to justify conservation. Astutely taking as a hypothetical example the conservation of the weight of a clay ball subjected to X-rays, the essence of Murray's objection resides in asserting that none of the three usual arguments are capable of supplying the information crucial to the inference that no weight change has occurred. This is easily seen the fact that even nonconservers admit without hesitation—at least in the usual situation of form change, if not in the case of Murray's example where reversibility and reciprocity are rather difficult to envision—that nothing has been added or taken away, that it is possible to reestablish the original situation, that the clay ball is both longer and less tall, etc. According to Murray, who incidentally makes reference to certain texts written by the Geneva team in order to solve the difficulty he has raised, what makes these three arguments interesting from the point of view of genetic epistemology, even though they are in themselves irrelevant and even unacceptable, is not so much the fact that they are used by conservers but that "their integration is taken as a manifestation of the operational system the conservation test was designed to diagnose in the first place" (pp. 5–6). In this way, then, "the conservation task provides a projective test for operativity" (p. 6). And Murray concludes that here again one finds another example of Piaget's well-known idea that the errors children make are more instructive than their correct answers. Seductive as they may seem by their elegance and their subtlety, Murray's objection and the answer he provides himself seem to us to pursue a line of reasoning which raises more problems than it can solve. Suppose, first of all, that the usual arguments for conservation are indeed irrelevant and can be considered "instructive" child errors, then it is hard to imagine how it is—by what mysterious trick—that such irrelevant arguments when integrated by the child, or even by an adult, can constitute a valid test of operational thought and thus acquire epistemological relevance. The fact that Piaget and his co-workers speak of such integration of the three arguments, based on their interdependence, or again that nonconservers likewise acknowledge these facts without considering them as a reason to assert conservation, in no way implies that these arguments are in themselves irrelevant, nor does it imply that the conserving child necessarily always "cites" all three—as Murray falsely has Piaget claim. When Piaget speaks of "the only legitimate answer" ([1947] 1950, p. 141), which Murray refers to (1978, p. 5), he is not speaking about the answer the subject has to give to the conservation question but about the only legitimate answer, as Piaget conceives it, to the question Piaget poses himself in that particular context, that is, the question of how it happens that the three usual arguments come to have for the subject this absolute degree of confidence, even before he was well aware of the fact that nothing had been added or taken away, etc. The answer is for Piaget that "the various transformations invoked . . . in fact depend on each other and, because they amalgamate into an organized whole, each is really new despite its affinity with the corresponding intuitive relation that was already formed at the previous level" ([1947] 1950, p. 141). It seems to us entirely clear that this text as well as the remaining two cited by Murray, while emphasizing the interdependence between the usual three arguments, carry no implication whatsoever as to a requirement that the child give overt expression to each of the three arguments in a given conservation task. It further seems to us that simply likening them to what Piaget calls children's instructive errors is going somewhat too far. In fact, as easy as it is to agree that the errors committed by the children at earlier stages can tell us about the intuitive or purely functional nature of preoperational thinking, or that the errors observed even in problems at the concrete level in children who begin to use the tools characteristic of emerging formal thought can provide information about the kinds of processes involved in the transition between concrete to formal thinking, as unclear does it seem to us how errors committed with supposedly irrelevant and unacceptable arguments can possibly provide us with any kind of information concerning the nature of operational thinking and even make a conservation task a suitable and valid test of operational functioning, unless one can find some other way of showing its validity. Thus, in accordance with the model proposed in Chapter 3, it seems to us more correct to assume that the usual reasons are in fact relevant to the extent that the child who makes use of them in asserting conservation has reached the point where he is free of the spatiotemporal constraints inherent in each physical transformation. As long as the child has not yet arrived at this crucial stage, one is always justified in asserting not so much that the arguments are incorrect or irrelevant but that they are insufficient and thoroughly fragile. This is so because, before achievement of the decisive level, the arguments given only refer to simple empirical schemata or rules, which, as we know, are insufficient to guarantee the logical necessity of conservation, since they still lack any kind of explanatory value and always allow for the possibility of gains or losses (real or imagined) in the course of the transformation. Thus, in going from the physical to a mental mode, a process which we have tried to describe, the empirical schemata or rules get transformed into operational schemata or rules, and the arguments invoked by the child to assert conservation thus acquire their full logical force or, if you wish, their relevance. For example, when a child uses the classical identity argument he expresses a logical necessity going beyond the spatiotemporal constraints: if nothing is added to or taken away from what there was to begin with, there will always be the same amount, this being quite unrelated to the fact that the physical changes performed upon the object, such as a change in temperature, irradiation, transfer into another container, deformation, etc., cannot always be done without the danger of something getting added or lost. Looked at it this way, it seems hardly astonishing that children can recognize the facts without considering them arguments in favor of conservation; what would certainly be very surprising is that such denial should be due to an understanding of the irrelevance of these facts qua arguments rather than to lack of appreciation of their relevance. Nor is it surprising to find these arguments used more or less consistently by children of intermediate levels or by children undergoing training exercises based on systematic teaching of these arguments. However, the use they make of them never goes beyond the level of empirical rules or schemata, lacking in explanatory value and thus in logical necessity, as shown by frequent inconsistencies, incomprehension, instability, lack of resistance to countersuggestions, and lack of generalization to all possible cases. It is not even excluded that some children invoke these same arguments not so much to assert conservation but to explain their judgments of nonconservation. For instance, it can easily be observed that a child, when asked what could be done to establish equality ("to make it the same"), will answer that one should go back to the initial situation (which implies a second nonconservation). Paradoxical as it may seem, in principle at least there is no reason why one should not expect to hear a child justify judgments of nonconservation with arguments that appear to have all the characteristics of identity or compensation; for example, a child who denies conservation of liquid quantities following an exchange of vessels, explaining that "we just poured the water out, but we did not take away any (or add any)," may very well just mean to say that water should be taken out of (or added to) one of the containers to make the water levels equal again. Similarly, a child who explains his nonconservation by the fact that the liquid was transferred into a "thinner and taller" vessel may simply be voicing his (precausal) idea by giving an accurate description of these containers, that the action of pouring liquid from a wider and lower container into one that is narrower and taller has effected a change in the liquid's quantity. In sum, with reference to the model described above, it appears that this use of the traditional arguments in justifications of nonconservation is a direct consequence of the fact that these children have not yet surpassed the level of the most elementary empirical rules or schemata, and in order to transform these rules into operational ones these children must first liberate themselves of spatiotemporal limitations. That they are still subject to these shows itself, as Murray himself notes (Murray & Johnson 1969,

1975), when they use these rules (qualitative identity, re-vertibility, and covariation) in justifying nonconservation responses (e.g., "now, we have to take something out of the taller one"; "we should pour the water again into the wider, lower vessel"; etc.).

It hardly seems possible to discuss the relative validity and interdependence of the traditional justifications without taking up, at least briefly, the controversy raised by Brainerd (e.g., 1973a, 1974, 1977a) concerning the possible erroneous interpretations brought about by the common practice of asking children, in conservation tasks, for example, to justify verbally their conservation or nonconservation judgments. Strictly speaking, this controversy does not really seem relevant in the present context, since it raises the much more general question concerning the relations between thought and language, whereas the model proposed in the preceding chapter directly and primarily seeks to indicate the development the child's thinking must undergo in order to be capable of a conservation judgment, whether or not he is able to or cares to give verbal expression to the reasons upon which his judgments are based. The reader interested in knowing how the nature of the success criterion (i.e., simple judgment or motivated judgment) influences performance on certain specific problems (e.g., the age of acquisition of particular conservations, acquisition sequence, etc.) may consult not only the publications by Brainerd already cited but also those studies or comments occasioned by these publications (e.g., Reese & Schack 1974; McCarthy-Gallagher & Kim-Reid 1978; and especially Larsen 1977), which advocate the use of both criteria. This latter solution seems to us more commendable if one is interested in understanding the nature and significance of the solutions offered by the children rather than drawing up a psychometric catalog or Markov chains of the child's "yes" and "no" answers.

The Role of Cognitive Conflict in the Acquisition of Conservations

The second point to be mentioned concerns the role of cognitive conflict in the acquisition of conservations. One criticism frequently addressed at Piaget's theory is that it fails to explain how the process of reequilibration, to which Piaget assigns a primary role in the development of cognitive structures, gets initiated. In his latest model (Piaget [1975] 1977, pp. 12 ff., 65 ff., and passim; Piaget et al. 1977b, pp. 313 ff.), Piaget assigns an increasingly important role to the notion of cognitive conflict, that is, that of initiating and driving the mechanism of reequilibration, a factor he still considers to be the one really responsible for development. According to Piaget, congitive conflict or dis-equilibrium arises when a child encounters obstacles in his inter-actions with his environment. Such obstacles or perturbations may take the form of a resistance against the child's efforts at assimilation (with corrective or negative feedback following) or of gaps to be filled with reference to the conditions necessary to the maintenance and generalization of assimilatory schemata (with reinforcements or positive feedbacks following). It is precisely the necessity or the need felt by the child to resolve the con-tradictions and perturbations of the environment which is said to initiate the mechanisms of compensation or reequilibration. In the course of development these become increasingly efficient and qualitatively different, since the first regulations are always in-sufficient and thus lead to new perturbations. The different forms of reequilibration are: (*a*) conflict resolution by simply ignoring the obstacle or by giving up the ongoing action with no effort to accommodate the schema in question (e.g., abandon a classifica-tion activity as soon as an unpredicted object comes up, or treat it like the other objects without accounting for the differences), (*b*) conflict resolution by means of an attempt at accommodation of the schema in question to permit assimilation of the obstacle (e.g., enlarge a classification by introduction of a new type of class, which can account for the unforeseen object), (*c*) conflict resolution by anticipating possible perturbations so that these can be deduced and resolved in advance by inserting them into a more general system (e.g., predict a classificatory structure that is sufficiently open and flexible to ensure that different and unex-pected objects can be inserted).

While it must be acknowedged that the model for explaining the acquisition of conservations, as described in Chapter 3, does not explicitly invoke this notion of cognitive conflict, it is easy to see, with respect to each of the three components of the model, how contradictions and perturbations arising in the child's interaction with his environment function to initiate and to catalyze the pro-cesses implicated in each of the components. First, with respect to the dissociation of the physical properties of objects, it is evident that the experiences and abstractions necessary for the construction and the coordination of the physical properties of objects simply could not come about without obstacles arising from the resistance of objects and without all kinds of contradictions due to the confusions that follow from the child's ineptitude to recognize the relevant properties of the objects. Second, regarding the empirical rules corresponding to the child's schemata that he needs to become consciously aware of in order to acquire conservation, it is equally clear that these cannot come to be established without undergoing a series of revisions and modifications demanded by problems and contradictions the child encounters when meeting new contents or interference from the multiplication of variables involved, or when having to compare the results of his experiences, etc. Finally, the third component, the coordination of the physical properties of objects with the subject's action schemata also cannot be realized without the reequilibrations and transcendence necessitated by the following kinds of perturbations: (a) those inherent in the application of the empirical rules established by the child to the relevant physical properties of objects; (b) those inherent in the differentiation and generalization of the empirical rules or schemata of which the child has become conscious; and (c) those inherent in the liberation from spatiotemporal constraints, which acts precisely to remove the obstacles implicated in the successive physical transformations, integrating them into a system of possible transformations derivable one from the other by purely internal transpositions.

Even if it may be relatively easy to see the role the notion of cognitive conflict may have theoretically in the acquisition of conservations, it is much less simple to show that this is not a mere theoretical fiction but that cognitive conflict really intervenes in actual acquisitions. True, one can see it at work in giving children a conservation task, and not only with tasks including countersuggestions of a verbal or factual nature, such as those used in a great many of Piaget's experiments using a method of critical exploration. Cognitive conflict also can be observed when simpler and more standardized methods are used such as in most studies derived from Piagetian theory. Especially if one takes the care to ask children to justify their conservation or nonconservation responses, the results clearly show that the experimental situations constitute a source of conflict to the children. This can be seen in the numerous hesitations and oscillations evident in their behaviors and verbalizations. However, all this shows is that a conflict situation can produce internal conflict in children. This in itself seems a rather trivial statement, but it raises the more important question of why such conflictual situations do not induce conflict in the younger age groups. The role of cognitive conflict also can be studied by introducing it systematically in experiments teaching conservation to nonconservers, as determined in pretests. There is an extensive literature concerning this type of research, of which one can find three different varieties: (a) studies using training methods based on conflict of physical origin (e.g., Lefebvre & Pinard 1972, 1974), that is, conflict resulting from counterdemonstrations invalidating the child's anticipations and accepted rules; (b) studies using methods based on conflict of a social origin (e.g., Murray 1972; Botvin & Murray 1975; Fortin-Thériault 1977), that is, conflict resulting from the confrontation of two subjects of different age or different operational levels disagreeing on a particular problem; and, finally, (c) studies employing modeling techniques (see the critical review by Rosenthal & Zimmerman 1978, chap. 3), where the child does not participate in the experiment in the sense of actively performing the training exercises but rather observes passively—that is, without making any kind of intervention—the series of exercises administered to a model; the model may be of varying age, operational level, etc. Incidentally, it is not excluded that the child, who is thought to be "passive" in this method, also does not experience internal conflict (see Charbonneau, Robert, Bourassa, & Gladu-Bissonnette 1976; Charbonneau & Robert 1977; Botvin & Murray 1975). Still, all one can show with any of these methods, granted that the training produces results satisfying strict criteria of authenticity and stability of learning, is that a conflict situation of physical or social origin may be sufficient to induce or accelerate the learning of conservation. Even here one has to be careful to assure that the so-called conflict situation does in fact produce a conflict in the child. Since it is known how impermeable young children can be to contradiction, and also that there are rather considerable individual differences as to the degree of sensitivity to cognitive conflict (see, e.g., Lefebvre & Pinard 1974), the negative results observed in certain learning experiments claimed to be based on cognitive conflict must be said to be entirely nonconclusive with respect to the eventual efficiency of such methods. This problem was raised in the critical review by Lefebvre-Pinard (1976a, 1976b) of the Geneva experiments (Inhelder, Sinclair, & Bovet 1974).

In sum, it remains an open question to what extent cognitive conflict plays a role in the acquisition of conservations. In fact, there is a difference between saying that a conflict situation can often produce a cognitive conflict in the child or that it may be sufficient to induce learning, if it is systematically introduced, and showing that cognitive conflict actually does play a role in spontaneous acquisitions of conservation and that it constitutes a necessary factor in the learning of conservation. In our view, while research concerning experimentally induced learning of conservation should not be discontinued but should be pursued mainly toward the systematic comparison of divergent models of mental development and toward the relative efficiency of the various factors that are likely to influence this development, it is absolutely necessary to extend the research to include the systematic observation of children in natural environments, as was already done for certain types of Piagetian tasks (e.g., Kuhn & Brannock 1977; Capun & Kuhn 1979). Given the current state of knowledge with respect to the problem considered, it appears that the ethological approach used by Strayer (1980), for example, to study social interactions among children, an approach recently adopted by Charlesworth (1978) to study cognitive development, offers perhaps the best promise of success, even though, to some, it may seem somewhat risky and even backward to give up the sheltered security of laboratory methods in favor of the troublesome complexities of observational methods. However, provided that one can find the time and the ingenuity to detect those situations in which the child in his everyday experience encounters real conservation problems, and further provided that objective and reliable codification schemes can be worked out with which to code and assess behaviors in such situations, it seems to us that the ethological methods are without substitute, if one wants to validate a model of the development of conservations and determine the influence of cognitive conflict upon mental development. In any case, it would be extremely instructive to compare directly data obtained, from the same children, by both laboratory (descriptive and experimental) and observational methods from "natural" settings.

Discussion of Some Alternative Models

At the end of this chapter, dealing with some questions related to the model of the origin of conservation proposed in the previous chapter, it may be of interest to compare this model to certain alternative formulations existing in the literature. Since the models to be considered are already well known, no detailed or systematic analysis seems required; rather, it suffices to examine their essential scope, thereby indicating their limits.

Brainerd's Model

The first model considered, that put forward by Brainerd (1978a, 1979), proposes a Markovian analysis of the process implicated in the acquisition of conservations. This model essentially applies within the context of learning studies. Basically, what Brainerd's theory stipulates is that the process operating in the acquisition of conservation consists in a sequential selection of rules or strategies upon which children depend in making a conservation judgment. For Brainerd, these rules have a very neutral sense and are defined by three subclasses of simple judgments (N = rules of nonconservation, which always lead to erroneous judgments; C = rules of conservation, which always lead to correct judgments; P = rules of partial conservation, yielding alternately erroneous or correct judgments); nothing is postulated about the content of these rules, and it is left to other methods (e.g., asking for a justification of conservation judgments) to specify their nature (verbal, perceptual, or motorical). A Markov-type analysis can identify the parameters operating in the progressive acquisition of the probability of correct choices made by a child in the course of a learning experiment. Brainerd then demonstrates that the three states corresponding to the three subclasses of rules adopted by the children are necessary and sufficient to account for the data gathered in three experiments showing provoked learning of certain kinds of conservations (number, length, and quantity) performed by him using a simple method of verbal feedbacks already used in some of his earlier studies. According to Brainerd, this theory also can account for three other facts which he says are generally recognized and considered important by researchers working in this area: (*a*) older children learn faster than younger ones because of the fact that the efficiency in making choices and the degree to which rules of type *C* are available to the child increase naturally with age, as is predicted by his theory; (*b*) the amount of learning achieved does not seem to be related to the children's initial level of cognitive development, when learning is evaluated by the increase in performance from pre- to posttest, and this is also predicted by the theory, which distinguishes the parameters influencing initial level from those affecting learning itself; (*c*) transfer of learning is generally limited to tasks rather similar to the learning task because, as predicted by the theory, the relative specificity of *C*-type rules with respect to the task learned makes it more likely that these will be objectively and effectively applied to rather closely related tasks.

A theory of this kind seems to us of little interest, in spite of the statistical fireworks that illuminate it and the Markovian cloak that shelters it. That a certain obsession with the problems inherent in the demands for justification of responses, as they are usually addressed to children in traditional conservation tasks, should lead a theoretician to restrict himself merely to enumerate the child's simple judgments (correct or incorrect), and to define the rules used by the child only in terms of the effect they produce upon the choice of his answer without any concern for the content or form of these rules, may very well facilitate the scoring of the protocols and the statistical treatment of the data; but if one is interested in finding out about the mental processes involved when a child acquires conservation, one may ask what psychological interest the simple statistical fact represents that the probability of a correct response develops as a Markov sequence, if this does not tell us anything about the origin, the nature, the significance, etc., of the content of the rules determining these responses. It is not without interest that the results observed in learning experiments show that the probability of a correct choice increases in accordance with the predictions of the model; but this in itself is hardly surprising, since the method involves only simple judgments and, more important, is based upon a simple routine of verbal feedback, which corrects directly every error and provides the child with the true outcomes (laboratory rats trained to change their responses would undoubtedly exhibit the same type of development). The prediction made by the theory concerning specificity of transfer is in itself quite trivial (most models make the same prediction), and the explanation offered in terms of the specificity of C rules during acquisition remains rather undemonstrable as long as the definition of these rules by the theory avoids systematically any reference to content. On the other hand, the predicted relationship between chronological age and learning rate, which is to be explained in terms of a progression in the efficiency of choices and in terms of the degree of availability of C rules, is in itself also quite trivial; the only way to rid such an explanation of its tautological flavor would to be to include explicit references to the content of the rules and an analysis of the factors responsible for the differences in availability as a function of age. Finally, the apparent absence of a relationship between learning rate and initial level of the subjects as shown by a preliminary analysis, made by Brainerd (1977b) of a series of learning studies, and as predicted by his theory, rightly points to the methodological necessity to use difference scores between pre- and posttest in evaluating the amount of progress made during learning, when the experimental subjects are not all at the same level initially. Before one can accept this absence of relationship as demonstrated, however, and before one can give it a clear and unambiguous interpretation, it is necessary to be able to analyze and to isolate a host of factors, among which one might mention the following as examples: (*a*) the method used in assigning subjects to an initial level: depending on the homogeneity of the pretests employed, the criterion for success adopted (e.g, justified or unjustified responses), the numerical score used to assign subjects to initial levels, when point scores are used, etc., the resulting classifications of subjects are more or less reliable and graded—any error of classification can obviously fog all further comparisons; (*b*) the training methods used, which may have quite different effects depending on the subjects' developmental level (e.g., a crude method of simple verbal feedback may be as efficient, if not more so, with subjects of a lower level as compared with more advanced levels); (*c*) the relative efficiency of the method used, which may introduce floor or ceiling effects, which Brainerd himself (1977b) rightly calls attention to in his reanalysis of certain experiments as having possibly influenced the results but which he considers without influence in two other experiments (Brainerd 1972; Murray 1972), without giving attention to some of the other factors just mentioned (e.g., scoring method without justification). In any case, what seems of critical importance to us when evaluating the progress made by subjects in any kind of learning experiment, and whatever the initial level of the subjects, is not so much the progression on a scale of points, more or less arbitrarily converted into stages, but rather a progression on a scale of well-defined stages, which may or may not subsequently be transformed into numerical scores if it is useful for statistical treatment.

Before proceeding to examine the following model, it may be pertinent at this point to consider the attempt, made by Brainerd (1978b), to represent the logic implicated in a conservation task in terms of the INRC group used by Piaget to describe the logic implied in the solution of problems at the formal level. Brainerd begins by identifying the INRC group with a Klein group but without observing the distinction made by Piaget (see Piaget et al. 1977a, chap. 7) between the concrete and the advanced forms of a Klein group. Thus, Brainerd reduces all forms of the Klein group—including the group INRC used by Piaget—to a single general model, in which there are two mutually exclusive variables (e.g., A and B) intervening within one system, and where the following relations can be envisioned in succession: leave the system unchanged ($AB = I$), change variable A only ($\bar{A}B = N$); change variable B only ($A\bar{B} = R$); change both variables ($\overline{AB} = C$). Then, he applies this general model to a conservation-of-number problem, in which the two variables are said to be the two rows of items to be compared, and he adds that the same model can be applied easily to other conservation tasks and also to tasks involving multiplication of classes or relations. According to Brainerd, whose aim it is to show that the INRC group is not a characteristic of formal thought, this application of the Klein group to conservation tasks of the concrete level is closely analogous to that made by Piaget (Piaget [1946b] 1970, chap. 5; Inhelder & Piaget [1955] 1958, p. 318) to the well-known problem of the snail moving upon a board which is itself movable: I = advance of the snail; N = backward motion of the snail; R = backward motion of the board; C = advance of the board. What

Brainerd does not seem to notice, however—even though it is true that both of these forms of the Klein group permit the total set of internal transformations typical of this group (RN = C, RC = N, CN = R, and NRC = I)—is the essential difference between this elementary and concrete form of the Klein group and the higher level forms it takes when it becomes an INRC group, as described by Piaget in his study of the development from one to the other form of this group. In the INRC group, the two operations N and R are radically different from each other. Operation N (backward motion of the snail) is the complete negation of the initial operation I (advance of the snail), with no change in the term to which the operation is applied (N is the inverse operation applied to the same object), and it expresses simultaneously the reciprocal of the operation C (advance of the board) which it can thus compensate. Operation R (backward motion of the board), on the other hand, expresses the negation or change in the term to which operation I is applied (advance of the snail), without negation of this operation I of which it is the reciprocal and which it can thus compensate by a simple permutation of the terms (the action of the snail's forward motion is not directly cancelled, but its effect is simply compensated for by the backward motion of the board). It is essentially this distinction and the coordination of the two forms of reversibility (NI = RC, as RI = NC) which defines the more advanced form of the Klein group, the group INRC. On the other hand, in the elementary and concrete form of the Klein group, *as applied by Brainerd to conservation* (or to problems of the multiplication of classes or relations), the operations N and R do not differ at all in the same manner as they do in the group INRC, in that both operations are only partial negations of the initial operation (AB), of which $\overline{AB}$ is the complete negation and not the correlative. The operation $\bar{A}B$ is only a partial negation of the operation AB without being the reciprocal of $\overline{AB}$ and without compensating it; similarly, the operation $A\bar{B}$ is itself only a partial negation of AB without being its reciprocal and without compensating it; finally, the operation $\overline{AB}$, which combines the two partial negations, is obviously not reciprocal to $\bar{A}B$ either. In sum, this elementary form of the Klein group can be reduced, not to the INRC group but to the well-known multiplication matrices typical of concrete thought with no integration of the two forms of reversibility, since the differences between the four operations can always be reduced to simple negatives (null negation, partial, or total negation). Incidentally, if Brainerd had chosen, in his example taken from the conservation of number, two of the dimensions that covary inversely (e.g., length and density of a row) instead of arbitrarily using two equal rows as variables,[1] he would have at least noticed the essential difference between a conservation problem and a problem involving the coordination of two reference systems. In a conservation problem, the dimensions affected by a transformation (length vs. density, in the case of number; height and width, in the case of quantity of matter; etc.) are not independent from each other (e.g., it is not possible to make the row longer without lessening its density, or increase the height without decreasing the width of a water column). For this reason, the compensation involved in this kind of conservation reduces necessarily to the concrete grouping of the multiplication of relations (increasing length × decreasing density = decreasing length × increasing density), with no possibility to concretely dissociate the inverse of an operation (e.g., lengthening a row) from the reciprocal (decreasing its density). At least the necessity of having two independent systems to make possible the integration of the two forms of reversibility did not escape Murray (1977), who likewise attempted to translate the logic of the nonconservation of weight into that of the INRC group, taking care that the two variables introduced be independently variable, at least in principle (I = add plasticine, N = take it away, R = heat the plasticine, C = have it cool down again); but, as was already stated above (p. 31), this INRC group reduces quite simply to a mere inversion of two successive physical actions, if one assumes, as indeed we do and Murray does too when he attributes nonconservation to the child's failure to distinguish the denotative and the connotative sense of the weight concept, that the child cannot yet distinguish clearly between a change in quantity and one in temperature (or shape, etc.), so that a temperature change can be seen as

1. It will be remembered, in fact, that a conservation test does not necessarily involve two rows to start with, as is the case when a method of conservation by equivalence is used. It may just contain one row, as in the case of conservation by identity. The two variables may then be length of row and density of elements (two variables that cannot be transformed independently of each other).

equivalent—but without real reciprocity or compensation—to a change in quantity (I = add-heat, N = subtract–cool down). On the other hand, if we assume that there is no such lack of dissociation or semantic confusion in the child, or that the child is capable of hypothetically considering the addition-subtraction of matter and the change of temperature as two independent ways to modify weight, then one is perfectly entitled to engage in the exercise of translating the subject's logic into an INRC language, as Murray has taken pleasure in doing. However, before one can accept the conclusion that this logic really plays a role in the solution of a problem by a child (or even an adult), where the problem in no way requires it in order to be solved, the least one can ask for is that the subject give evidence of being able to manipulate the two variables independently and to understand, for example, that it is possible to leave invariant the weight of an object while simultaneously adding (or subtracting) matter and decreasing (or increasing) its temperature and that the weight of an object can be doubled (or halved) by an addition of matter and an increase in temperature (or a subtraction of matter and a decrease in temperature). It seems to us that trying to give a formal interpretation to a problem at the level of concrete logic is to expose oneself unnecessarily to a dangerous cut from Occam's razor.

Gagné's Model

Another interesting model is the one proposed by Gagné (1968) as an alternative to the one described by Piaget. Gagné's model is one of development essentially centered around factors of learning, to which, according to Gagné, Piaget has only attributed a secondary role. For Gagné, the development of the child consists in the cumulative learning of a hierarchically organized set of abilities, which are constructed on one another by a process of differentiation, recall, and generalization by transfer of learning. This sequence begins with elementary associations, which become organized into more complex chains permitting multiple discriminations; which in turn serve in the learning of concepts leading to learning of rules—first simple rules and then increasingly complex ones governing behavior. Gagné then applies this general schema to the classical conservation-of-liquids task, using as an example the transfer of liquid from a rectangular container to other rectangular containers of different dimensions.[2] In this kind of situation, the operational definition of liquid conservation is given by the judgments concerning equality or inequality of the amount of liquid contained in each of the rectangular vessels, and the complex rule regulating this behavior may be expressed as follows: the volume of a liquid is determined by its height, its width, and its length within the vessel. The learning of this complex rule is seen as the highest point in an ordered series of learning experiences: first the learning of concepts, then learning of rules of increasing complexity (e.g., the concept of the length of a straight line; the concepts of rectangle, of length, and width; the rule defining the surface of a rectangle by its length and its width; a rule for the comparison of rectangular surfaces; a rule saying that volume equals cumulative "slices" of area; a rule stating that volume increases when the values on one dimension are changed with the other dimensions held constant; a rule stipulating that, when one dimension is held constant, the remaining two may compensate when volume changes). Once conservation is acquired with respect to rectangular containers, it can be generalized and transferred to cylindrical containers by means of the additional learning of the concepts of cylinder, volume of cylinders, and surface of circles. Combining the principles applicable to the volume of rectangular with those applicable to cylindrical containers should then make it "easy" to learn to estimate the volume of irregularly shaped containers. Gagné specifically points out that this type of generalization by transfer of learning exists in the subject and constitutes a measurable aspect of his mental capacities; but, according to him, it would be quite false to think that a "principle" of conservation as such, designating the whole set of specific rules the child learns about conservation, as well as other "principles" mentioned by Piaget such as reversibility, seriation, operational groupings, etc., have any existence in the child's thought. These represent only certain abstractions in terms of which an outside observer may choose to

2. The reference given by Gagné to Piaget and Inhelder (1964) is curious in two respects: first, the two authors are not cited in the correct order; and second, the cited publication (Inhelder and Piaget ([1959] 1964) has nothing to do with the conservation of liquids.

describe the child's mental processes, abstractions existing undoubtedly in the mind of the observer but not in that of the child.

Gagné's model is certainly not without ingenuity or elegance. It would be ungracious to discredit the merits of a model which demonstrates the essential role of learning in mental development. One is immediately struck by the effort at objectivity which characterizes it, and especially by the merits of a systematic analysis of a complex task and the ordering of the components which progressively lead to the learning of this task. When Gagné insists on the cumulative character of such learning, with the notions of differentiation, generalization, and memorization implied by this characterization, one is reminded of the properties in terms of which Piaget has repeatedly described the development of schemata in the child (repetition, generalization, and recognition). The notion of cognitive rules regulating the child's behavior is in itself quite compatible with the notions of strategy, law, function, or principle, in terms of which Piaget attempts to describe the progressive evolution of the child's conducts in the acquisition of conservation. But this is where the analogy ends. When Gagné criticizes Piaget, for example, for not giving sufficient weight to learning, one can agree with him insofar as this criticism concerns the possibility of induced learning of logical structures or that of a marked acceleration in the acquisition of these structures by the child, the kinds of learning and acceleration of which the Geneva group believes, right or wrong, that they are neither easy to accomplish in reality nor even desirable. But the criticism is not justified when consideration is given to the four volumes produced by Geneva in a single year (Apostel, Jonckeree, & Matalon 1959; Goustard, Gréco, Matalon, & Piaget 1959; Gréco & Piaget 1959; Morf, Smedslund, Vinh-Bang, & Wohlwill 1959) on the learning of logical structures, and to the important distinction made by Piaget (Gréco & Piaget 1959, pp. 35 ff.) between learning in the strict sense, where the resulting acquisition is a function of physical or logicoarithmetical experience, and learning in a wider sense which includes, in addition, a separate process of preoperational coherence or equilibration. It is mainly the first type of learning to which the Geneva group attributes relatively little importance and efficiency, even in a more recent publication (Inhelder, Sinclair, & Bovet 1974) which deals exclusively with the experimentally induced learning of certain logical structures. Learning in the wider sense, however, implies spontaneous processes of equilibration, which lie at the heart of cognitive development. It is this second form of learning to which Piaget essentially refers when he considers development as primary with respect to learning, since the latter necessarily depends upon the former in the elaboration and possible efficiency of any learning method. With respect to Gagné's affirmation that conservation of liquids may be subject to cumulative learning, and with respect to the possible sequence of concepts and rules to be acquired by the child he offers, it is far easier to agree with the principle of hierarchical learning than with the sequence he proposes. In any authentically developmental perspective, new acquisitions obviously depend upon certain prerequisites. It is also quite clear that the child's progression toward conservation is marked by an ordered sequence of steps which can be described, as in Chapter 3, in terms of a series of levels through which the child passes in dissociating the physical properties of objects and in coordinating his own action schemes. A sequence such as proposed by Gagné (1968), however, raises a number of problems. The concept he chooses to illustrate his model is the "conservation of liquid, as studied by Piaget," using a task in which the child has to compare "volumes of liquids" contained "in rectangular containers" (p. 183). But the description he gives of this task in the same article refers explicitly to a traditional test of the conservation of *substance* or *quantity* of matter and, thus, has nothing to do with the volume occupied by an object in its environment (external physical volume), nor with metric volume (measurement of volume as studied by Piaget as part of his research on the development of spatial notions (Piaget, Inhelder, & Szeminska [1948] 1960). The sequence proposed, however, concerns explicitly the acquisition of metric volume, and so one is led to the somewhat odd conclusion, in terms of the logic used by the author, that in order to come to recognize the invariance of a quantity of matter (or of the "volume" of a liquid) the child needs to proceed via the acquisition of metric volume and needs, for example, to have comprehension of the following: (1) the *concept of a straight line* (first level of the sequence), which is a rather late acquisition (Piaget, Inhelder, & Szeminska [1948] 1960; Laurendeau & Pinard [1968] 1970); (2) the *concept of length* (second level of the sequence), which is conserved later than that of substance; (3) the *notion of the surface of rectangles* (third and fourth levels of the sequence), a concept which is acquired later than length; (4) the *notion of continuity,* necessary for a comprehension of the rule stating that volume consists of a cumulation of slices of area or of a projection of an area in any direction (fifth level of the sequence), a notion not accessible before the stage of formal thought; (5) the *dissociation of various factors,* required for the comprehension of the last levels of the sequence, a dissociation which cannot be performed fully before the level of formal thought. From this point of view, it is not surprising that the child has to begin the same long sequence of steps almost from the beginning—by transfer of learning from the invariance of liquid volume contained in rectangular to that contained in cylindrical, and then irregular-shaped vessels—by learning the new concepts specific to the new shapes of vessels. To use the conservation-of-liquid *quantity* as an example, it has been known for a long time that, once the child admits conservation of liquid in cylindrical containers, there is ipso facto generalization to other types of containers of other shapes, regular or irregular, without any new kind of learning, since the reason the child gives go beyond these empirical contingencies. Further, when Gagné declares (1968, pp. 188–190) that there is serious danger of going wrong in thinking there is a "principle of conservation" or other "principles," such as "reversibility," "seriation," "grouping of logical operations," in the child's thinking, and not merely in that of the external observer as pure "abstractions" representing "collection of specific capabilities," it is again easy to agree with him, if what he means to reject is a form of mentalism according to which these so-called principles constitute substantial entities of a mental character that are amenable to direct observation and completely accessible to the child's conscious understanding. Piaget himself ([1968] 1970) readily recognizes that a cognitive structure—like a social or even a physical structure—"is a theoretical construct, not an empirical given" (p. 98) and that cognitive structures "do not belong to the subjects' consciousness, but to his operational behavior, which is something quite different. . . . Not until he becomes old enough to reflect on his own habits and patterns of thought and action does the subject become aware of structures as such" (p. 68). More recently again, in an article in which are examined the relations between structures and procedures adopted by the child, Inhelder and Piaget (1979) attempt to answer the same criticism:

> If it is true that the structures consist of systems which are or, at least, appear non-temporal, the reason might be that they do not exist in the child's mind, which never employs anything but procedures; rather they might be only the mental products of the psychologist observer or logician interpreting the subjects' behavior in his own way. But in fact, this would be a bit like saying that if children are conscious of eating or even breathing, their stomach and lungs exist only in the mind of the physiologist. In actual fact, the structures concern what the child "can do" in his cognitive behaviors, independently of whether or not he is conscious of them; if he is conscious of his procedures but not of his structures, it is because it is far easier to mentally follow a temporal sequence of actions than to bring together in a single act of knowing all the various connections of a single simultaneous set. (P. 169)

However that may be, Gagné's statements are even more equivocal when one considers the following: (a) conservation is for Piaget not a "principle" but the consequence of a property of mental operations, that is, of reversibility, which in turn is, therefore, not a "principle"; (b) operational groupings are not "principles"—nor is seriation, which is simply one grouping among others—but they are the subsets of mental operations interrelated by certain properties (one of which is reversibility) which organize them into whole structures; (c) there are several possible levels of structuring and of generalization of mental operations, so that the conservation acquired by a child in one domain does not necessarily imply conservation in another, as is evident from the décalages observed; (d) there is nothing any more unpleasant to infer the existence in the mind of a subject (epistemic), on the basis of behaviors, of a set of mental operations organized into whole structures (direct operation, inverse, identity, etc,) than to infer the existence in the thought of a subject, again on the basis of behavior, of "increasingly complex and interacting structures of learned capabilities" (Gagné 1968, p. 190).

Halford's Model

One last model conceptualized by Halford (1970a, 1975), in a cognitivist perspective much more closely related to Piaget's theory, thus leads to the present model. It is not easy to sum up the theory, presented by Halford (1970a) in a rather dense article, whose internal structure is perhaps not always transparent. To limit ourselves to what appear to be the essential aspects, it seems that the perspective adopted by Halford seeks to bridge the gap separating the models that are based on traditional types of learning from those that are based on equilibration, by showing how equilibration can be translated into learning terms if it is accepted that the learning of a logical structure, such as conservation, implicates tasks that are relatively different from those usually demanded in other forms of learning. In the case of conservation-of-liquid quantities, for example—later to be extended to other types of conservation—Halford believes that the indices the child might be able to use to infer conservation, indices which frequently constitute the focus of learning methods, are not really relevant, since children can recognize them without necessarily using them to infer conservation. For example, identity, by which Halford means simply what Piaget calls qualitative identity, is recognized even by the nonconserving child. Similarly, reversibility—that is, the fact that a liquid poured into a container of a different shape regains its original dimensions when poured back into the initial container—as well as covariation of dimensions—that is, that such a transfer may bring about an increase in width and a decrease in height of the water column or vice versa—may be recognized by a child without necessarily leading to conservation. Even what Halford calls the "more primitive quantity cues" (addition, subtraction, or neither)—in which we recognize Piaget's quantitative identity—are phenomena which may be noticed and admitted by nonconserving children. For this reason, while recognizing that conservation training might have been successful with methods using one or the other of these indices, Halford admits that a theoretician of the equilibration model can always contest the logical authenticity of such learning results. Halford's own model asserts, in effect, that in order to acquire conservation a child needs to learn to integrate, in a single system, the quantitative indices (addition, subtraction, and neither addition nor subtraction) with the conjunct variation in the two dimensions (length and width) of the containers: the notion of quantity is said to imply the recognition by the child of this interdependence between the two kinds of indices. This recognition then causes each of these indices to become relevant by making the child aware of the fact that the two lead to the same result. The path leading to the integration of these indices in a single system—which becomes the goal of a kind of generalized learning or learning set—includes a series of partial acquisitions on the basis of the repeated observation of particular cases leading to generalizations (if not to rules in the strict sense). These become more and more stable and structured (e.g., if there is transfer of liquids, without addition or subtraction, then variation on one dimension necessarily implies variation on the other; if there is variation on one dimension only, there has to be either addition or subtraction; if there is neither addition nor subtraction, returning the liquid into its original container restores the original dimensions; if in a transfer there is only one dimension that varies, then simply pouring the liquid back to the initial container, will not restore the original dimensions), Once the child has learned this interdependence, he can justify conservation by citing indifferently either one of the two indices, in themselves not relevant but acquiring relevance through their integration within a single unified system. To illustrate his theory, Halford (1969, 1970b, 1971)[3] makes reference to various experiments showing that (a) conservers are capable of performing tasks which require judgments of this kind (the child has to distinguish among a number of containers, each of which is filled and differs from another container B on one dimension only, containers that fill either partially, exactly, or overfill a container A, which he had previously seen being filled and then emptied into a container B, equal in size to A but differing in its dimensions); (b) even children that are not conservers, if they are five years old or older, are already capable of utilizing "logical" criteria of this kind with some success; (c) methods based on such "classifications" are efficient in bringing about learning of conservation.

Compared to the two models discussed earlier, Halford's theory is immediately more appealing and promising. It is remarkable, in the first place, by its attempt to give an operational connotation to certain aspects of the Piagetian notion of equilibration, emphasizing the functional interdependence between certain indices of conservation, and particularly on the reciprocity implied in the covariation of the dimensions of an object in a

3. The 1971 article was in press at the time Halford (1970a) referred to it.

single physical transformation. But, the most interesting aspect of the theory seems to us Halford's fundamental intuition that the acquisition of conservation depends on experiences, both empirical and logical in nature, which essentially consist in the child's progressive coordination of actions and judgments that can lead him to a "logical" affirmation of conservation. In spite of these indisputable merits, it seems to us that the proposed theory calls for certain comments and reservations. One might first note the ambiguity that surrounds Halford's treatment of what he calls "quantity cues," which refer globally to observable actions like adding and subtracting, without differentiating explicitly between additions-subtractions originating outside of the object and those remaining interior to the object. As shown in Chapter 3, this distinction implicitly contains—because of its focus upon the *simultaneity* of the effects of addition in one place and subtraction in another on the same object undergoing some transformation—the essential range of facts to which the covariation scheme makes reference by explicitly applying to the dimensions (length, width, etc.) of an object the additions and subtractions simultaneously performed upon the object, with or without a minimum of quantification. However, there is no reason to think that such explicit application is necessary, as Halford may be led to believe perhaps because the notions of simple addition-subtraction—by means of which he defines what he calls the "quantity cues" that are "more primitive," according to him, than identity and reversibility—are too narrowly defined in his system.

To this first is related a second, more important reservation. Halford underscores the irrelevance of the usual criteria for conservation, as Murray (1978) has done later—whose interpretations have already been disputed above (see pp. 76 ff.)—by noting that even nonconservers recognize that the object is still the same ("qualitative identity"), that nothing has been added or taken away ("quantity cues"), that the initial situation can be restored ("reversibility"), that the height decreases as width increases ("compensation"). He then finds in the integration of the "quantity cues" with the "compensation" cues the one best method for making these indices relevant. But it seems to us essential, for the sake of dispelling all ambiguity, to specify precisely the significance of the facts recognized by the nonconservers. Since these children deny conservation in spite of these facts—and sometimes even use them to justify their nonconservation judgments—one is led to the conclusion that what they recognize is not quantitative identity but the absence of addition or subtraction from a source outside of the object, not reversibility but simply the possibility to retrieve the initial situation, not compensation but a simple observation of how a transformation makes two dimensions covary. One is led to conclude, as we have tried to show, that the rules which result from the conscious understanding of these facts (and of the corresponding schemes) are still only empirical laws or observations without any explanatory value or logical necessity. In our view, it is these limitations that explain the irrelevance of the facts recognized by nonconservers. But it is surely not through the simple combination of irrelevant cues, which can lead only to purely empirical and factual laws, that these cues will become relevant; rather, it is through the radical change of these empirical rules into operational rules. This change presupposes, as we have tried to show, (*a*) a confrontation of the subject's action schemes with the physical object's properties, which he must have learned to dissociate; (*b*) a differentiation and generalization of these action schemes; and particularly (*c*) a liberation of the spatiotemporal constraints inherent in any physical action. Through this transformation, *each* of the usual criteria becomes relevant, and there is no need to assign a more privileged role to one or the other or to explicitly integrate one with the other. This conceptualization in no way precludes recognition of the functional interdependence of the various criteria. They are all interrelated by the fundamental notions of vicariance and commutativity, which we have shown play an essential role in the transition from qualitative to quantitative identity, from physical revertibility to mental reversibility, or from functional covariation to operational compensation.

Finally, a last reservation deserves to be briefly mentioned. This concerns the empirical data collected by Halford in his very elegant experiments and used by him to substantiate his theory. The fact that conservers are capable of combining quantitative cues with the indices of covariation cannot be taken as showing that this combination of cues is a necessary component in the process leading from nonconservation to conservation. Let us add that the fact, as observed by Halford, that nonconserving children (provided they were at least five years old) are also capable of such combinations would even seem to indicate that this ability is not a sufficient condition for conservation. Even granting that it might be a prerequisite, it seems to us unjustified to conclude, as Halford does (1970a, p. 309), that these children are capable of using "logical criteria of quantity" as the conservers do. Of course, one might call this a kind of logic; but this logic is—as much in the conservers as in the nonconservers—nothing but a functional logic of essentially preoperational nature, since the form of classification implied in Halford's task does not go beyond the kind of functional relations (unidirectional or univocal) which Piaget (Piaget et al. [1968] 1977) calls equivalence classes (e.g., all containers of the form X, X', etc., give the same results when they are applied to the same Y), and thus do not imply reversibility by co-univocal correspondence essential for operational logic proper. For this reason, it was possible to use a task of this kind (see Lefebvre & Pinard 1974) to estimate initial levels of sensitivity to cognitive conflict in children who then underwent conservation training. That a training method using classification exercises of this kind may be quite effective is in itself not surprising, considering that the logic of functions in whatever form it may operate is a normal step in the child's development toward operational logic. But it remains necessary to assure oneself whether and to what extent the observed advances go beyond the level of this functional logic and attain that of authentically operational logic. In the case of Halford's experiments, one is well advised to take into account, even though his pretest may have been sufficiently difficult, first, that the method he used was fairly strongly directive (with verbal corrections and demonstration of errors), and, second, that the learning achieved did not resist the countersuggestion devised by Halford.

Before concluding this analysis of the model proposed by Halford, it may be interesting to mention two later articles by the same author (Halford 1975; Johnson & Halford 1975). They fall within the same conceptual framework, except that Halford does not particularly insist on the combination of quantitative indices with the indices of covariation, as was done in the preceding publications. Essentially, the novelty of these later contributions can be summed up by saying that what is necessary for conservation to be understood is the ability to interpret an ambiguous action (a transformation). This capacity, in turn, requires that the child be in possession of a system of quantification, which enables him to interpret a combination of successive actions (adding, subtracting, transferring to another container) that are performed on a given quantity. For example, if three successive actions performed upon a quantity A (*transfer* it to a container of different dimensions, i.e., $A \rightarrow A^1$; *add* to it another quantity x, i.e., $A^1 + x$; then *transfer* $A^1 + x$ into another container C, i.e., $A^1 + x \rightarrow C$) produce the same result as two actions performed upon a quantity B first recognized as being equal to A (add the same quantity x, i.e., $B + x$; transfer it to another container C^1, equal to C), then it can be inferred that the first transformation performed on A has no effect upon its quantity: if $A \rightarrow A^1 + x = C$, as $B + x = C^1$, then $A^1 = B$ just as $A = B$, since $C = C^1$. Thus, combining in different ways the three actions of transferring, adding, and subtracting, one arrives at a system of quantification (a 3×3 matrix), which makes possible stable and consistent predictions concerning the effects produced upon a quantity by several successive actions. For Halford, such a system constitutes a groupoid, that is, "a set with a single binary operation, defined on a set of three actions" (1975, p. 126). A system of this kind is said to be a minumum requirement for conservation, and a subject capable of using the rules governing the combination of actions implied in the system should be capable of operational thought.

This model is not without ingenuity and seems to insist, quite correctly, on the necessity to introduce the coordination and integration of action schemes as factors in the acquisition of conservation. However, it raises so many problems that it is difficult to endorse it. First, one might question the validity of the criteria used to judge the quantities resulting from the actions performed upon the initial quantities. The conservation problem, it should be pointed out, arises essentially from the fact that the quantity as such—and thus quantitative identity in the strict sense—is not directly perceptible, as are color, position, shape, and dimensions of objects. And as shown by the diversity of reasons offered by children for denying conservation, it is clear that quantity as such remains for a long time indissociated from the perceptible attributes of the object and dependent upon the actions performed upon these attributes, so that for the child there is no way of being sure that the successive actions have not had some impact upon quantity itself. Therefore, unless one assumes that the child already has acquired conservation, one may ask how he could have constructed the system of quantification which he needs to possess in order to affirm conservation. Even if quantities C and C^1 are judged to be equal after the transformations performed upon A and B, there is nothing that prevents a child from thinking that the quantity $B + x$ has changed in becoming C^1, as has $A + x$ in becoming A^1, or even x by getting added to A^1 or to B. In sum, strictly speaking, the fact that the child perceives equality in the end does not rule out possible gains or losses in the course of transformations. In other words, it may be that Halford himself is somewhat guilty of question begging, as he accuses Wallach (1969) of being, in spite of the action $+ x$ which his system adds to that of Wallach, particularly when he takes care to specify that this quantity $+ x$ is the same for A^1 and for B. Basically, what to us seems to constitute an essential reservation is that Halford's groupoid only structures a set of empirical rules, which cannot have operational meaning leading to logical necessity, as long as the successive actions upon which they are based are not transformed into mental operations through the liberation from spatiotemporal constraints inherent in any physical action, and in this way liberation from possible gains or losses incurred in the course of the action.

It is possibly this latent question begging that accounts for the uneasiness apparently felt by Halford (1975) in deciding whether the quantificative system he proposes is of operational level or not. He states variously (pp. 127–128) that a subject who could use this groupoid "would be employing operational thought," that this groupoid is "a system of operational quantification" and that it is a "pre-requisite for conservation." The essential problem is to decide whether the manipulation of this groupoid presupposes comprehension at the level of operational thought. If the answer is yes, then it is hardly surprising that Halford's conserver subjects, serving in his experiments designed to illustrate his model, showed themselves capable of understanding the rules of combination for this grouping structure and also capable of interpreting a greater number of transformations than did the children at the preoperational or intermediate levels. But if the use of these rules requires comprehension at the operational level, one may then legitimately ask, first, what else some of the older nonconservers need to have in order to understand conservation, since these children knew the rules, as Halford observed, an observation which led him to consider this system of quantification as simply a "pre-requisite for conservation." More important, if it is assumed that this condition is of an operational nature, one may ask also (*a*) how the child could come to learn this system of quantification, which puts the problem one step back; and (*b*) how an older nonconserving child can be, within a single circumscribed domain, both at the operational and the preoperational level. It seems to us far simpler to suppose that the rules implied in Halford's groupoid do not require operational-level comprehension but may simply represent a set of observational statements which, in order to be transformed into operational rules, require an additional process, the liberation from spatiotemporal constraints inherent in all successive physical actions—as such irreversible and not necessarily conserving—which lie at the basis of these empirical rules. This would explain both the facility with which conservers manipulate the rules (whether or not in an operational manner) and the relatively good ability of nonconserving children, depending upon their level of preoperational development, to manipulate a certain number of them (in nonoperational fashion). In sum, the idea of a combination of actions leading to a "system of quantification," as proposed by Halford, appears to us quite valid to the extent that it represents, in simple form, a way to conceptualize certain aspects of the coordination and of the confrontation of action schemes or empirical rules used by the child, as described in our own model. In our view, however, what is missing in Halford's model is a necessary emphasis on the process of dissociation of the physical attributes of objects (to remove the confusion between nonperceptible quantity and perceptible indices), and on the process of liberation from the spatiotemporal constraints characteristic of successive physical actions (to transform successiveness into simultaneity, i.e., action into operation, and in this way preclude the possibility of losses or gains in the course of action).

5   Of Some Empirical Data

Given the largely speculative character of the considerations constituting the subject matter of the preceding chapters, it certainly does not seem superfluous to devote this chapter to the presentation of certain empirical data that may help to clarify some aspects of our theoretical model. Let us emphasize from the start that some of the studies to be presented—a number of them not so recent—were in no way intended to provide any kind of confirmation for our model, even though they may have, to a certain extent, provided the inspiration for it. Obviously, in order to demonstrate the validity of the model, one would have to systematically test specific predictions derived from parts of the model—which would first have to be given operational definitions; in addition, it would be necessary to devise experiments confronting our model with models based on different principles or ideologies. Only in this way would it be possible to determine, with some degree of certainty, whether or not the components of the model represent both necessary and sufficient conditions for the acquisition of conservations. In the meantime, by citing a few experimental studies of variable scope and quality, it would seem to be of some interest to indicate in what way at least one or the other of the components of the model can manifest itself in actual child behavior.

Dissociation of the Physical Properties of Objects

To begin with the dissociation of the physical properties of objects, it will be recalled that in Chapter 3, according to one interpretation, conservation acquisition depends essentially on the child's ability to focus his attention upon the elements relevant to the situation and to ignore the irrelevant ones. For Gelman, for example (see her 1978 critical review), given the situation of conservation of number, even very young children already know something of the rules involved in quantitative invariance, are able to distinguish transformations that change from those that do not change (irrelevant transformations) numerical quantity, and are able to reason about quantity under certain conditions. While acknowledging the fact that this kind of competence may be much less complex in the child compared to the adult, Gelman nevertheless estimates that many learning experiments may be interpreted as methods for discovering an already existing ability rather than as a way to create this ability "from scratch" (p. 300).

There is no difficulty in accepting the principle that the child must be able to distinguish the relevant from the irrelevant aspects of the situation, or that the degree of success achieved in a learning situation depends normally upon the amount of knowledge already present in the child. However, the question soon arises as to the nature, the origin, and the limits of this preexisting knowledge and of the child's abilities to distinguish the relevant from the irrelevant aspects of the situation in a conservation task. To answer some of these basic questions, what is needed first is an analysis of the progressive formation of object structures in the child so as to be able to establish at what time in his development the child becomes capable of identifying and of discriminating the different properties of an object. One also has to ask at what time and under what conditions the child's representation of the object, initially of a global and syncretistic nature, becomes sufficiently differentiated to forestall the interferences and deformations that are likely to be brought on by the simultaneous presence, in the same object, of the various properties which are, however, already constructed and thus identifiable by the child. The discriminations are even more important in a conservation task, since quantity is not a perceptible property of objects, such as color, shape, position, etc., and must be inferred on the basis of certain perceptible properties, which the child first needs to isolate from one another and often also to combine with each other to recognize their relevance or irrelevance in a given situation. To these and similar questions the few experiments that follow have attempted to furnish certain answers.

First, we might mention an experiment (Migneron 1969) performed under the direction of Albert Morf, a former member of the Geneva research group now in Montreal. This not very recent, yet highly interesting study deals with the origins of the child's awareness of various properties of objects. It attempts to show the role of physical experience or abstraction in the child's construction of reality—the kind of experience and abstraction the author blames Piaget for not having given sufficient attention to. Further, the study has investigated the role played by the identification of object attributes in this structuring of reality, following a perspective inspired by Henri Wallon rather than by Piaget. In this experiment—still of a rather exploratory nature—Migneron has studied the process of the differentiation of object properties in three groups of children of mean ages 4-7, 5-5, and 6-7 years. Two levels are subjected to analysis. First, on a level of verbal expression, the child has to identify and label verbally the characteristics of different objects presented by pairs. Second, on an action level, the child has to recognize and correctly apply a particular relevant property of an object in order to reach a concrete goal. In the *verbal situation,* the child is presented with 14 pairs of blocks successively, where the two members of each pair always differ from each other by various attributes, all of them perceptible: color, form, dimensions (height, length, width), overall volume, material, and weight. The child holds each pair in his hands and simply has to say how the two are similar or different. Statistical analysis of these verbal comparisons reveals a highly significant difference between the three age groups, compared by pairs, with respect to the naming of the various object attributes. In general, the number of attributes mentioned increases with age (e.g., at four years, 91% of the attributes mentioned concern color); further, the order of increase is: color, form, size, material, and weight (even at six years, only 3% of the attributes mentioned concern weight). It is also interesting to note that the naming of an attribute does not immediately generalize from its first appearance to all items but, at first, only to those that differ in terms of that attribute before being extended to the items that share the property in question. In the *nonverbal, active situation,* the child is presented with three consecutive problems where, first, the relevant dimension (length, weight, or form) has to be isolated before the problem can be solved; the child is also asked to explain why a particular choice of object is efficient and to predict from sight whether one of the objects not selected may be efficient too. The first problem concerns the differentiation of length, where the child has to make a candy come out of a box (three times in a row) by pushing on a rod, which is about 6 inches too short but which can be made longer by inserting a block to be selected from a set of nine (where five measure 6 inches, three 4 inches, and one 2 inches in length or diameter). The blocks differ from each other by shape (rectangular, circular, or irregular), by size, or by thickness. The analysis of the selections and predictions made by the children—a rather crude analysis—indicates that even at four years of age errors do not exceed 25%. This suggests that length is an attribute relatively easy to differentiate from the other attributes, particularly in a situation where length is made perceptually prominent, offering the subject a fair choice of objects of sufficient length. But what needs to be particularly noted are the following two phenomena observed by Migneron: first, that the correct choice, least frequently made, is the one object differing in color and form from the original stimulus object (which is used as an example); and second, that the most frequent inadequate choice is one having the same color and form as the original stimulus. Migneron quite rightly interprets these two observations as indicating a kind of lack of differentiation of the objects' qualities and insufficient generalization of these qualities (e.g., that the diameter of a spherical object is not perceived as having length in the same manner as the others). The second problem is one of *weight* differentiation, where the child has to hang, from an elastic, a box sufficiently heavy to go down lower than a comparison band, which is either red (in the case of a 3-ounce weight), white (for a 6-ounce weight), or black (for a 9-ounce weight). The experimenter begins, for example, by placing a 3-ounce box, and the subject has to choose one which would give the same result from a set of six boxes (two of each weight), which differ from each other by color, by length, by width or thickness; each time the child has to justify his choice. The same procedure is followed in the case of a 6-ounce box, and then of a 9-ounce box, again with the child being asked to explain his choice and the effect produced. Then the child is asked to predict visually the effects produced by each of three boxes pointed out successively, where each box has one of the three weights used in the task (3, 6, or 9 ounces). The results show that success on this task is much less frequent than in the length problem for both choice and predictions—at four years the success rate is less than 50%. Further, it appears that the errors, as revealed in the children's explanation, which are based upon color, size, general appearance, and do not mention weight—weight is not even checked by these children—can be explained as failure to dissociate the different attributes of the objects. The third problem requires differentiation of *form*. The child has to identify (by choice and by prediction) from among 13 blocks all differing in color and size the four which fit exactly into four molds (rectangular, cruciform, cylindrical, and triangular) carved into a form board. This problem is fairly easy to solve even for the youngest children, but the nature of the errors observed (the most common one being adequate shape but too short) shows that the child has some difficulty in taking into account the other aspects of an object when he has to estimate the form. In spite of the obvious methodological shortcomings (e.g., not enough systematic control in the use of experimental materials, insufficiency of statistical analyses)—which the author readily acknowledges—this study suggests at least that there are chronological décalages with respect to the recognition and utilization of the various qualities of objects and that this décalage is at least partly due to the fact that this recognition and utilization are differentially affected by the perceptual context (the set of qualities possessed by a particular object), within which the relevant quality to be used and recognized is necessarily embedded.

Two ingenious studies by Osiek (1977) carried out within the theoretical framework of the developmental model proposed by Mounoud (see, e.g., 1970, 1977)[1]—who criticizes Piaget's model for not giving sufficient attention to the steps the child has to follow in order to isolate, extract, and identify the various properties of a given object—have directly examined the interferences

---

1. In Mounoud's model (see, e.g., 1970, 1977), the object concept develops in a sequence of steps as follows: (*a*) global organization; (*b*) analysis into partial structures corresponding to the specific qualities of the object; (*c*) reconstitution of the object through a nondecomposable fusion of its partial structures; (*d*) development of interrelations between these structures; and, finally, (*e*) a new organization of the whole, which may then serve as a starting point for a second cycle of developmental steps later on. It would be interesting to compare systematically some aspects of this model with Piaget's notion of décalage (both vertical and horizontal).

that may operate when the child attempts to dissociate some of these properties. The first of these studies deals with the rather special case of indissociation between form and center of gravity. Concretely, children aged from 4 to 11 years (10 subjects per age level) are presented with two objects of identical form and identical weight (800 grams), but in one of these objects the center of gravity coincides with the geometrical center, whereas in the other the center of gravity is located midway between the object's geometrical center and one of its edges. The child has to explore the objects by touching them (but he cannot see them), one after the other, and then describing the objects verbally and drawing their form. Analysis of these verbal descriptions and drawings—there was a very substantial correlation between these two forms of expression—reveals interference errors between form and weight. These appear mainly in the form of rectangular representations—both verbal and graphical—when the weight is off-center, and in the form of squares when the weight is centered. As predicted by Mounoud's model, which space does not permit discussion of here, such interference errors appear only at the age of five (i.e., at that stage of the model where the child analyzes a global undifferentiated object into partial structures based on the various properties of the object) and at eight years (i.e., at a stage where the child becomes capable of establishing relations between the partial structures following an intermediate level devoted to the recomposition of the global object but without any clear definition of the relations existing between the partial structures). Aside from the theoretical implications of such a model, what is of interest in the context of the present discussion is the indissociation form-weight revealed in children's representations of form as a function of the place of the gravitational center (for children at certain age levels). The parallel analysis of children's descriptions of the weight of the two objects—these are only spontaneous descriptions, since the method did not include systematic questioning with respect to weight—incidentally confirms the difference in the types of analysis of the object as used before and after the age of eight, where interference was observed; at either age, form is considered similar, but the off-center object is judged "heavier" by seven-year-olds, "heavier on one side" by nine-year-olds. The second study reported in the same article by the same author examines dissociation of form and texture of objects. In this experiment, 70 children between 7 and 12 years of age are presented with two sticks of identical weight (120 grams) and dimensions (25 cm. in length with a square section 2.5 cm on each side). Both are covered with sandpaper of either uniform texture (180 grains all along the length of the stick) or variable texture (320, 180, 100, 180, and 320 grains arranged on five sections in the order mentioned). The child explores each stick by touch (without seeing it), and then has to describe it verbally and choose among four drawings showing identical lengths but different forms (a regular rectangle, a trapezium, a rectangle with convex long sides, a rectangle with concave long sides) the one that corresponds to the object explored. The results show that the stick of uniform texture is identified correctly in 92% of the cases but that systematic deformations were observed for the stick of variable texture as revealed in frequent choices of the trapezoidal or the rectangular form with convex long sides. These deformations, however, are not statistically significant except in the case of the eight-year-olds, that is, the same age group that had shown interference effects between form and weight in the previous study. For 11-year-olds, the deformations are also frequently observed, again without reaching statistical significance. Osiek suggests that this might be due to a second stage of a further development, just as the interference effects observed at five years in the previous study were a reflection of a second stage in a more primitive developmental cycle.

Following these experiments by Osiek, we asked one of our students (see Doré 1979) to replicate this experiment in more systematic fashion by setting himself two main objectives. The first was to determine the degree to which tactilo-kinesthetic form perception of objects is influenced by the symmetric or asymmetric position of the object's center of gravity. The second, still more important goal was to examine directly if weight conservation is affected by visibly displacing the object's center of gravity. The results obtained with these two tasks for five groups of children with mean ages 4-3, 6-3, 8-3, 10-3, and 12-3 show that (a) position of center of gravity interfered systematically with form perception, a confirmation of Osiek's results, but there is a continuous decrease of this interference with age (the tactilo-kinesthetic impression of a change in the form of an object is from 80% in 4-year-olds to 50% in 6-8-year-olds, reaching between

30% and 20% only with the 10–12-year-old group), contrary to the cyclic kind of development observed by Osiek; (*b*) there is a strong correlation between the absence of such interference and the conservation of weight in objects that have their centers of gravity displaced. This leads us to think that the dissociation of the physical properties of objects as considered here is a necessary condition for weight conservation (no child conserves without dissociating), but not sufficient to guarantee its existence (there were several children able to dissociate without conserving).

The study to be considered next is one carried out by the author with the collaboration of Pierre-Joly (1974; Pinard & Pierre-Joly 1979). It deals with the same general problem, the specific aim of assessing the influence this dissociation failure can have upon children's judgments in a conservation-of-weight problem. It was partially derived from the work done by Migneron (1969), which was briefly summarized above. It also owed something to the large number of studies conducted by Murray's group (Murray & Johnson 1969, 1975; Murray & Tyler 1978; Nummedal & Murray 1969; Johnson & Murray 1970), which showed among other things that for quite a long period of time children tend to confuse the connotative and the denotative sense of the weight concept—an observation which seems rather important and much less simplistic than the interpretations given by Gelman (1969, 1978) noted above. In addition, our study exploits ideas expressed in some of Piaget's rather recent work ([1971] 1974) on physical causality, where he stresses the difficulty children have in dissociating weight seen in absolute terms as a quantity of matter (or mass), and weight as seen in the effects it produces in certain situations, and particularly in its ways of interacting with other spatial properties (such as surface, volume, etc.). Within this general perspective, one can ask to what extent children at different age levels (from kindergarten to grade 8) are capable of conserving weight not only in the presence of changes in form or when the object is divided into sections, as in most traditional conservation of weight problems, but also (*a*) when other properties of the object are subjected to transformations which do not entail any changes in form, (*b*) in the presence of variations in the concrete conditions under which the weight of an object may be observed to have an impact, and (*c*) when other physical properties are allowed to interact with weight. In order to create such conditions, one might construct four types of conservation problems, where the child has to verify first that two objects are equal in weight, and later decide whether they are still equal after a change is carried out on the object in front of him. In order to solve the first type of problem, a dissociation is required between the weight of an object and other properties of the same object. Such a problem involves the following types of transformations which affect one or another of the properties of the object without any change in form or deformation, as (a) *heating* a block of lead in a gas stove, (b) *cooling* a lead block in a refrigerator, (c) *change of color* by dipping the two initially similar blocks in two different color paints, (d) *punching holes* into a ball of plasticene with a fork, (e) *changing the perceptual volume* of a clay ball by grating it so that it appears "bigger" when the pieces are joined back together again. The second type of problem, which requires for its solution the dissociation of weight from the concrete situation in which it can be observed to have an impact, involves the following changes without any deformation: (a) *rotation* of a rubber ball attached to a string; (b) *displacement* of the surface upon which a lead ball rests, first on a stiff band, then on an elastic band; (c) *suspending* a ball first from a string and then from an elastic; (d) *raising* a polystyrene cone initially placed upon a table; (e) *lowering* a cone from the table to the floor; (f) *reorientation* of a pyramid suspended at its peak, then at the base. The third type of problem includes three traditional conservation items involving deformations as such: (a) deformation of a clay ball into a sausage, (b) deformation of a clay ball into a ring, (c) division of a ball into six pieces. Finally, a fourth type of problem, which involves a dissociation as well as a coordination between weight and other spatial properties, includes the following dimensions: (a) *coordination of weight with volume,* or the concept of density (comparison of two identical balls, one of which sinks while the other floats following transformation into a crucible); (b) *coordination weight-slope,* or the concept of force (comparison of two blocks which are counterbalanced on two identical slopes, one of which is subsequently changed into a horizontal); (c) *coordination weight-surface,* or the concept of pressure (comparison of two blocks of lead which were first placed on two springboxes of equal dimensions, then transferring one block to another box of larger surface area); (*d*) *coordination of weight with length,* or the concept of momentum (comparison of two clay balls, both of which were first placed at the ends of two rods of equal length, after which one of the balls was placed in the middle of its rod).

The set of problems was administered to five groups of 10 children each, aged 5-6, 7-7, 9-6, 11-5, and 13-7 years. The problems were given in two sessions (lasting about 20–30 minutes each) separated by an interval of two to four days. Each session included problems of all four types arranged in random order (the same for all subjects).

To begin with the first three types of problems, analysis of variance shows that the problems involving nondeforming transformations are not significantly more difficult than those involving situational transformations. In general, both types of problems diminish in difficulty with increasing age (the success rate at 5-6 years is 24% only, while it is 57% at 7-7 years, 93% at 9-6 years, and 90% at 11-5 years). Despite the fact that the problems involving nondeforming transformations are markedly less difficult than those involving situational transformations for the youngest age groups (5-6 and 7-7 years), the interaction age problem type is not significant. Comparing the problems involving deforming transformations to those involving nondeforming or situational transformations, it can be observed that the two latter problems are significantly easier than the former at all ages (24% success vs. 0% at 5-6, 57% vs. 33% at 7-7, 93% vs. 77% at 9-6, and 90% vs. 67% at 11-5 years). These differences become even more marked when the problem of *heating* is counted among the problems involving deformation rather than with the problems concerning nondeforming transformations. This can be justified by the fact that the reasons children give for denying conservation in this problem usually make reference to the possible change in form brought about by the rise in temperature (a deformation not noted in the case of the cooling transformation). Finally, a comparison of the items included in each of the categories cited indicates that (*a*) the deformation items have the same level of difficulty at each age level; (*b*) the items involving nondeforming transformations are likewise identical in difficulty at all ages, with the exception of the item *heating,* which is systematically missed in the youngest groups (5-6 and 7-7 years) by getting assimilated to the deformation items; and, finally, (*c*) within the category of items of the situational type, the items *rotation, suspension,* and *reorientation* are markedly more difficult than the items *displacement, raising,* and *lowering* for subjects aged both 5-6 and 7-7.

From the point of view of the difficulties of dissociating the physical properties of objects, the overall results seem very consistent and suggest two main conclusions: (1) up until the age of seven to eight years at least, weight is not clearly differentiated from other properties of an object, with form being the most difficult to dissociate, followed closely by temperature, texture, perceptual volume, and even color; (2) the changes introduced into the situation in which the weight of an object produces an impact lead to judgments on nonconservation just as often as do nondeforming transformations, especially when these changes create in the child the impression that the object has gained in force or that he has to expend more energy in certain situations as compared to others (e.g., *rotation, suspension, reorientation*).

Next, let us consider the results obtained with those problems where the child has to dissociate weight from certain other spatial properties (volume, slope, surface area, and length) which he has to coordinate with weight. Our data lead us to establish the following facts. At all age levels and for all the concepts studied, children have much less difficulty in asserting the conservation of weight (simple judgments with no justification required)[2] than in explaining the phenomena observed, once the transformation is carried out (at 7-7 years, e.g., for all problems taken together, conservation is asserted in 53% of all cases, but in no case is a valid explanation observed; even at 11-5 years, where conservation is asserted in 85% of all cases, only 40% of explanations were found valid). Second, of the four problems studied, the most difficult was that where weight had to be coordinated with volume (the percentage of correct solution being no higher than 30% at 9-6 and 60% at 11-5 years). The astonishing ease with which even the very young subjects assert conservation of weight in the remaining three problems (at 7-7 years conservation is admitted by at least 60% of subjects) must probably be seen as resulting from an artifact perhaps deriving from the fact that, in the three problems in question (interaction weight-surface, weight-length,

2. Unfortunately, it is impossible, given our questioning technique, to distinguish between the justification of conservation responses and explanations of the coordination of weight with the other spatial properties.

weight-slope), the object does not undergo any deformation as in the case of the problem interaction weight-volume. In sum, as can be seen also from the scarcity of valid explanations given by the children of the coordination of weight with the other spatial properties (no more than 8% of all explanations given in all four problems were found valid even at the age of 9-5 years), these problems are taken by the children as analogous to the other types of problem: the problem weight-volume is one of deformation like the others; the problems weight-surface, weight-length, and weight-slope are comparable to those involving situational transformations or changes in location, orientation, etc. Thus, it is hardly surprising to note that the level of difficulty of these problems is very similar to that of the problems involving nondeforming or situational transformations, which is just another indication of the lack of dissociation between weight and the other properties of an object or of weight and the particular situation in which it functions. With respect to the rather early age at which conservation-of-weight judgments were observed in this study—conservation of weight is generally considered not to be acquired before the age of nine—one may ask whether these conservation judgments really refer to the quantitative identity of the objects compared or if, at least for the youngest subjects, they refer to a form of qualitative identity, a prerequisite to conservation: when a child asserts that such an object "still weighs the same," perhaps what he means is simply that the object "is still heavy," "still has weight." One might also ask whether these early judgments of conservation do not perhaps refer to the quantity of substance rather than weight, which it would have been interesting to be able to verify; but this would not alter in any way the sense of the décalages observed with respect to the progressive dissociations becoming available to the child.

In spite of the obvious shortcomings, the main interest of this study of the dissociation of certain properties of objects lies in the fact that it seems to have some important theoretical implications: (a) on the limitations of a model of conservation acquisition based entirely upon compensation of dimensions, since nonconservation also can result from transformations that are nondeforming or even purely situational, and since the only way conservation can be justified in those cases is by identity arguments (in fact, in the experiment reported here, almost all of the justifications observed were of this type); (*b*) on the nature of certain factors responsible for décalage between different kinds of conservation; and (*c*) on the elaboration of methods of training conservation of weight by means of exercises involving the dissociation of weight from other object properties.

A final example may be given to illustrate the role of the process of dissociation in the acquisition of conservation. Following an earlier study by Lunzer (1965), which showed that children even at the concrete operational level tend to think that the surface of a rectangle does not change with a transformation of the perimeter when its length remains constant and, inversely, that the length of the perimeter of a rectangle does not change with a transformation of the surface when its area remains constant, Pinard and Chassé (1977) have been able to show that analogous forms of pseudoconservations occur with three-dimensional objects: when one deforms an object without changing its outer surface, children and even many adults are apt to think that this leaves also invariant the external volume (the space occupied by the object in its surroundings) as well as the internal volume (the quantity of material contained by the object). Inversely, if one deforms an object without changing its internal or external volume, subjects tend to think for a long time that the external surface also remains the same. The results of this experiment, the details of which can be ascertained in the article cited, are interpreted to show that these stubborn forms of pseudoconservation can be explained by the great difficulty subjects have in dissociating and then coordinating surface and volume in objects. It is perhaps for this reason that a notion such as external volume, which involves exactly the same concrete operational groupings as does weight and substance in order to be conserved, is in fact acquired only at the formal level of thinking. It is because the external volume of an object has to be first dissociated from the internal volume, and thus from the object itself, with which it remains confused for quite a long time.

In conclusion, the few examples given above in this chapter may, in spite of the purely descriptive or normative nature of the data reported, help to clear up the nature of certain dissociation failures, their gradual reduction with age, and their influence upon judgments of conservation. In our view, the main interest of studies of this nature is to show that the dissociation of physical properties of objects cannot be reduced to a simple prerequisite condition to which it is sufficient to alert the child in order for him to attain conservation. It seems to us rather that this ability to dissociate is itself the terminal point of a long development and that it represents an essential and contemporary component of the same rank as the other two in the complex process leading to the acquisition of conservation. In sum, the dissociation of physical properties of objects is just as important as the child's becoming aware of his action schemes. It would seem to be of interest to derive from such normative, descriptive studies training methods based upon the systematic exercise of dissociation (e.g., learning conservation of volume by dissociation of surface and internal volume; learning conservation of length by dissociation of form, elasticity, position, etc., of certain objects), and to compare the efficiency of such methods with that of methods based on exercises to make the child aware of his schemes or rules of action (falling under the second component of our model).

The Child's Conscious Awareness of His Action Schemes

Even a rapid survey of the extremely abundant and rich literature on the learning of conservation (see the extensive reviews by Beilin 1971, 1978) will reveal that the great majority of the methods used in these experiments somehow involve the child coming to a conscious awareness of certain schemes or rules regulating his behavior in a conservation situation (schemes of addition-subtraction, schemes of compensation or covariation, schemes of reversibility or inversion, etc.). Whether the methods are essentially didactic in nature (i.e., formal teaching of rules, explicit correction of errors, verbal explanations, etc.), whether they are of a less directive nature, engaging a more active participation of the child by means of varied exercises (see the various methods based on cognitive conflict of either physical or social origin), or whether they involve systematic observation of conserving models (see the training methods based on modeling), they all have in common that they seek to have the child reach an awareness of certain action schemes involved in the acquisition of conservation.

There is thus no doubt that of the three components mentioned in our model, it is this second one that is generally the most exploited in the literature. We have already discussed a number of outstanding examples of this, such as Murray's experiments involving the schemes of "reversibility," and those of Halford whose theory of the origin of conservations is based essentially upon the acquisition of the schemes of addition-subtraction and covariation. Therefore, for the sake of illustrating the importance of the child becoming conscious of his action schemes, we shall limit ourselves here to mentioning some experiments that are more closely related to our model and which employ methods that are only slightly directive, and for this reason may be thought to be more directly comparable to the processes involved in the spontaneous acquisition of conservation.

A few years back, a member of our laboratory, Fournier-Chouinard (1967) obtained rather spectacular results in an experiment concerning the conservation-of-liquid quantities by a method which aimed at making the child aware of the schemes of compensation necessary to conservation. During an initial phase made up of *anticipation exercises,* the experimenter presented five problems in which five containers with different diameters were successively hidden behind a screen. The child had to predict the level reached in each of these containers after the contents of a standard container had been poured into it. Each time the child was allowed to note the actual level attained, and the only intervention made by the experimenter was to have the child verify by sight and by touch the diameters of the two containers used in each comparison. Following this, there was a second phase consisting of *compensation exercises.* (*a*) First, the traditional conservation problem was given in which the child does not accept equality. Then, the experimenter made the two levels equal by subtracting liquid from one of the containers, and the same conservation question was asked again. Success at this exercise thus presupposes a distinction between equal height and equal quantity. (*b*) Next, two containers of widely differing diameters were presented, where the level attained in the narrower one only slightly exceeded that attained in the large container. The quantity question was asked again. To succeed with this exercise, the child would thus have to come to distinguish the difference in height from that of quantity ("taller = more to drink"). (*c*) In the third exercise, the two containers were identical to start with but contained visibly different amounts of liquid quantities. Then the contents of each were poured into two other containers so that the levels attained differed again, but in the opposite sense, and the quantity question was asked again. In order to conserve the inequality of the initial situation, the child once again had to dissociate level from quantity. In the course of these exercises, no verbal explanation was ever given to the child, nor was there any correction of errors. The only intervention from the experimenter consisted in drawing the child's attention to the obvious differences in level and diameter (by visual and tactile comparisons), so that the child was in a position to come to consciously grasp certain schemes of covariation or compensation. The *pretest* used to start with—administered again as *posttest*, once between two and four days after the exercises, a second time two months later—consisted of eight tests of conservation of quantities: (*a*) three traditional conservation tasks of three problems each—the first dealing with liquid quantity, the second with modeling clay, and the third with beads; (*b*) one conservation-of-liquids task (two problems), where the liquid was poured into containers of noncylindrical form (a U-shaped tube and a bowl), which obviously complicates the compensations to be made; (*c*) a task of liquid displacement, where a transparent container shaped like a cone containing a colored liquid was simply turned over in front of the child; (*d*) a test of arithmetic partition concerning the equality of two quantities, one of which was subsequently divided into parts two times in a row, and the sum of these parts was then compared to the standard; (*e*) a test of liquid quantification, where the child had to pour a standard quantity of liquid successively into two cylindrical containers of different diameters; (*f*) a test of comparison of quantities, where the subject had to seriate five cylindrical containers of varying dimensions already filled with different quantities of liquid; (*g*) a test of pattern displacement (two problems), in which a set of elements (16 red diamond shapes and 16 yellow triangles), which were first arranged in one configuration and then moved around to make a new configuration. The extent and variety of this pretest not only aimed at ensuring a certain degree of generality in the eventual learning performance, but also at eliminating from the start those subjects who already had reached a certain level of conservation, since the experiment had shown that some subjects start out by denying conservation at the beginning of the pretest but end up asserting conservation. There is a danger in giving too short pretests, as is often observed in this kind of research.

The experiment comprised three groups of 15 subjects each, of identical level at the pretest (with a few rare exceptions, none of the subjects surpassed stage 1 of nonconservation at any of the subtests) and equivalent in chronological age (mean = 6-2): (*a*) an *experimental* group who received the training exercises just described; (*b*) a *control* group trained with analogous situations involving various transformations of the material, but where the subjects simply had to emit an opinion as to the quantities before and after the transformations, with a candy for a reward after each response; (*c*) a *comparison* group not receiving any training. The results showed significantly greater advances for the experimental group as compared to the two remaining groups (and this was highly significant, with at least 12 out of 15 subjects having reached the operational stage on every subtest given as pretest and readministered as posttest on two occasions). The generality and stability of these learning effects allow us to conjecture, at least, that they are of operational character. The massive failures at the pretest show that these subjects were truly of preoperational level, even though their relatively advanced age may have accelerated their learning. Furthermore, it does not seem very likely that their initial failure should have been due to simple semantic confusion between the concepts of level and quantity for two reasons: the very realistic formulation of the instructions (e.g., "the same amount to drink"), and the fact that the majority of subjects made a very explicit distinction between "taller" and "amount to drink" in the course of the second training exercise of compensation, without this having an immediate positive effect upon their performance with the following exercises. In addition, the possibility that we are dealing with a mere transfer of a stereotyped equality response seems excluded by the fact that the subjects were never informed of the correctness of their answer and, second, that two of the three compensation exercises present situations of inequality. Similarly, the suggestion that the children learned nothing more than a simple empirical rule of the type "equal before–equal after" can be discounted, since this rule does not apply in the case of subtests *d, e,* and *f,* which were nevertheless solved successfully, and further because of the fact that these exercises were essentially of the compensation type, whereas the justifications given at the posttest were chiefly of the identity type.

Confirmation of the importance to be attributed to the child becoming conscious of the schemes of compensation and co-variation, as shown in Fournier-Chouinard's study, also comes from a second study carried out several years later using essentially the same method, but this time applied within the context of an intercultural comparison. The results of this study are reported in Pinard, Morin, and Lefebvre (1973), but it may be interesting to briefly describe them here. Two main groups were studied: (a) 64 children from Ruanda (Central Africa) from a rural environment, divided into two subgroups, one of which did not attend school (mean age = 6-8) while the other had completed between five to six months of schooling (mean age = 7-3 years); (b) 32 French Canadian children (mean age = 7-3 years) from Montreal at the beginning of their second year of schooling.[3] The pretest and the training exercises, given in the children's mother tongue, were a perfect replication of the pretest and exercises designed by Fournier-Chouinard (1967) as just described. The principal results follow: (1) all three experimental groups when compared to their respective controls of identical and clearly pre-operational level at pretest (highest score = 8.50 out of 24) showed highly significant learning effects, with 80% or more of subjects in all three groups obtaining at least a score of 21 out of 24 on the first posttest; (2) there was no significant difference between groups as to amount of learning achieved; and (3) there was no significant difference between the first and second posttest for any of the groups. In sum, it seems clear that a training method based on exercises of coordination and equilibration of compensation schemes implicated in the conservation of liquid quantities may be efficient enough to reduce or equalize the chronological lags which separate the spontaneous acquisition of this type of conservation in children of the two cultures.

Lefebvre and Pinard (1972) likewise have approached the same problem of experimentally provoked learning of the conservation-of-liquid quantities, retaining the same demanding pretest (and posttest) as in the other experiments just described but using a somewhat different training method which also avoids all forms

3. A few normative studies had previously revealed that 72% of the children aged 6-8 in Ruanda and 57% of those aged 7-3 were at the preoperational level in a test of the conservation-of-liquid quantities. In addition, almost the entire group was at stage 1 only. In Montreal, the corresponding proportion of subjects of the age level and milieu chosen was about 50%.

of direct teaching; its main purpose is to demonstrate the role of cognitive conflict in this kind of learning. The method is to create a contrast between two incompatible schemes or rules, which are due to a purely unidimensional mode of quantification, in such a way as to get the child to come to a conscious grasp of these rules and especially of their inadequacy. During a first phase of *preparatory exercises (exercises A),* aimed at the creation later on in the experiment of a true state of conflict, the child is led to (*a*) become aware of the inadequacy of his predominant conceptual rule ("when it's taller, there is more to drink"), and (*b*) resort to another rule different from his usual inventory, which may enter into opposition to his first rule ("when it's wider, then there is more to drink"). Following this preparatory phase, the subjects are given *conflict exercises,* which call upon either compensation schemes (*exercises B*) or schemes of addition-subtraction (*exercises C*), and which bring into play the same conflict dynamics: development of an opposition between two incompatible conceptual rules, bringing the subject to give contradictory responses, empirical confrontation with the facts, and registration of the final inequality of the quantities after the change of vessels. In this way, the child is constantly reminded of the inadequacy of all unidimensional quantification, and this facilitates the solution of the conflict. In the compensation exercises, the initial quantities in the two identical containers are clearly different; but when the contents of one of the vessels is poured into another container of smaller (or wider) diameter, this effects an equality of levels (opposition of the rules "equal level = equal quantity" and "taller = more quantity"). In the exercises of addition-subtraction, the initial quantities in the two containers are visibly equal; but the conflict dynamics remain the same: pouring the contents of one of the vessels into a larger one already partially filled (addition), or pouring a part only of the contents of one of the containers (subtraction) into a container of smaller diameter brings about a state where the two levels become equal or change inversely with respect to the quantities. In order to determine the relative efficiency of each of these varieties of exercises, five groups of subjects are formed, equivalent as to age (mean = 6-5) and sex, five subjects per group, each group being given a different set of exercises: exercises *ABC* (group 1); exercises *AB* (group 2); exercises *AC* (group 3); exercises *AX* (group 4), where

X designates certain tasks unrelated to the conservation tasks; exercises X only (group 5). The overall results show that, compared to the two control groups (groups 4 and 5), the three experimental groups (groups 1, 2, and 3) perform significantly better on the pretest tasks given as two successive posttests (with an interval of two months), but that the three experimental groups do not differ significantly from each other, neither in terms of number of training sessions needed for learning nor in terms of their global posttest score. The operational character of these acquisitions can be justified, first, in terms of the same arguments we have used for the results of Fournier-Chouinard and Pinard, Morin, and Lefebvre just cited. But the best demonstration is perhaps to be found in the results obtained by Lefebvre and Pinard's subjects on the generalization test proposed by Watson (1968), which was designed to produce different responses in subjects depending on whether their learning has resulted in an acquisition of a logical structure, or of a purely empirical rule resulting from simple instrumental conditioning. Since the three situations of conservation learning invented by Watson happen to correspond respectively to the present exercises of compensation (different initial quantities, with subsequent deformation of one quantity, but no addition or subtraction), those of addition-subtraction (equal initial quantities followed by deformation of one with addition and subtraction), and the traditional conservation tasks described previously, the subjects of groups 1, 2, and 3 were also given, after the second posttest, the generalization test of Watson (different initial quantities, then deformation of the lesser one with addition of an unspecified amount of liquid). If the children were applying a simple empirical rule, then, according to Watson, they should have given nonconservation responses because of the joint presence of two situations usually associated with responses of inequality (different initial quantities and addition of liquid). But all subjects having undergone training maintained the *probable* equality of the quantities, with 14 out of 15 making an explicit distinction as compared to a necessary kind of equality requiring the equalization of the differences (e.g., "about the same, but you can't be sure because you might have put a bit too much or not enough").

Following the preceding experiment, Lefebvre and Pinard (1974) have taken up the same method of training conservation of quantities in a complementary study, which was mainly directed at examining the influence the initial level of sensitivity to conflict may have on the learning accomplished by children between 4-6 and 6-8 years. From the point of view of the model presented here, the interest of this study resides precisely in the fact that each of the three tests used to evaluate this sensitivity to conflict is directly related to the second component of our model, the child becoming conscious of his action schemes, insofar as they permit an evaluation of (a) the presence of functional pre-operational schemes of sufficient elaboration, (b) the consistency with which the child uses his concepts, and (c) his ability to take account of the confrontation with the empirical facts. The details of these tasks can be found in Lefebvre (1973) and Lefebvre and Pinard (1974). Recall that the first, whose rationale was inspired by Piaget (Piaget et al. [1968] 1977) and the method by Halford (1969), seeks to determine the level of the logic of functions implicated in the formation of preoperational equivalence classes. It includes the two tasks designed to study the kinds of equivalence classes the child is able to construct from the dimensions height and width in a series of containers. The second test, adapted from Van den Bogaert-Rombouts (1966), concerns the child's logic of functions in the domain of relations. It evaluates the extent to which the child is able to recognize the relationship existing between two series of phenomena (a temporal sequence of events and a series of visible indices constructed as a function of the first) and to subsequently utilize this relationship to reconstitute the temporal order in which the events have taken place. Finally, the logic of functions studied in the third test, adapted from Szeminska and Piaget (1968), concerns the number concept and seeks to determine to what extent the child is able to estimate numerical inequalities and to understand that a difference y to be estimated depends on a transfer x which brought it about. The general hypothesis to be tested in this experiment predicted that, in children who are plainly preoperational (stage 1) at the pretest, the efficiency of training for conservation of quantities depends directly upon their initial level in functional logic, even though this preoperational logic is by definition unidirectional and thus irreversible. The method of learning used was the same as in the study previously described (Lefebvre & Pinard 1972), from which were also taken the seven pretest tasks and the test inspired by Watson (1968). Three groups of subjects, each having obtained the minimal score on the seven pretest tasks and equivalent as to age (mean = 5-6 years), sex, and grade level were employed: an experimental group, which received the pretest, the predictor tasks, the training exercises, and the two post-tests of conservation (with an interval of two months); a first control group, receiving only the pre- and the two posttests; and a second control group, receiving only the pretest, the predictor tests, and the two posttests, but no training exercises. The experimental and the second control group were to have obtained equivalent scores on the predictor tests, distributed over the range from minimal to maximal scores. Just to mention the essential results, the experiment has shown: (1) the conflict exercises have produced very considerable advances in the subjects of the experimental group (12 of the 21 subjects progressing to the operational stage and 5 to the intermediate level), and these advances remained at least on the same level on the second posttest; (2) the subjects of the two control groups maintained, with one exception, the same minimal score on the two posttests, showing that simply administering the predictor tasks does not produce any effect; (3) for the subjects of the experimental group, performance on each of the predictor tasks significantly influenced performance on the posttests, independent of chronological age. This last result, which is the most relevant in the present context, appears to show very clearly that the child's conscious grasp of his action schemes or empirical rules, as indexed by his level of functional logic, his consistency in manipulating his albeit pre-operational concepts, and his permeability to confrontation with empirical facts causes the child to be more sensitive to the contradictions provoked by the conflict exercises and to be more apt to engage in such activities as comparing and coordinating his action schemes, leading him to the threshold of reversible operations.

In a study done in the context of Pascual-Leone's (1970) neo-Piagetian theory, attempting to show the influence of subjective uncertainty, size of M-space, and of cognitive style upon the induced learning of conservation, Case (1977) adopted the training method developed by Lefebvre and Pinard (1972) in order to test the efficiency of the method and to specify precisely the role played effectively by the prior induction of uncertainty in the child (by means of the preparatory exercises specified by the method). To limit our consideration to this aspect, the results observed by Case did confirm the efficiency of the method, even though his results were not as spectacular as the original ones, this difference being partly due to the fact that his subjects came from below-average socioeconomic backgrounds. In addition, the study by Case has shown, by introducing the appropriate controls, that the efficiency of the method is not related, as was thought by Lefebvre and Pinard, to the uncertainty created by the preparatory exercises; rather, it seems that it may be related to the conflict situation itself as created by the compensation and addition-subtraction exercises, which have the effect of making the child come to realize that his judgments are inconsistent. In sum, the results of this study suggest that Lefebvre and Pinard are right in thinking that children tend to be quite sure of their judgments and that it is very difficult to make them aware of a conflict; but, according to Case, their subjective certainty is a result of their insensitivity to conflict, and not the reverse. Even to admit that the preparatory phase of the method does not play the role predicted by its authors, and is thus in fact unnecessary, it remains true that Case's interpretation (a) confirms the necessity for the child to come to a conscious grasp of his contradictory action schemes in a conflict situation—the second component of our model—and (b) is in turn confirmed by the results of the second experiment performed by Lefebvre and Pinard (1974), which showed that the initial level of sensitivity to conflict is related to the amount of progress produced by the conflict exercises of their method.

One last experiment, also carried out in our laboratories, merits mentioning, as it serves to illustrate indirectly the role in conservation as the child becomes conscious of certain of his action schemes or rules. Inspired by the experiments of Lefebvre and Pinard (1972, 1974), Fortin-Thériault and Laurendeau-Bendavid (1979) emphasize the necessity to re-think the notion of intermediate stage, which is usually described in such a way, even by Piaget, as to give the impression that the intermediate stage can be defined as a heterogeneous mixture of operational and nonoperational thought. It has already been attempted (see Chap. 1 of this volume; and Pinard 1975) to give a more positive definition to the intermediate stage by pointing out that Piaget's work on the logic of functions permits us to conclude that the thought of intermediate-level children remains essentially of a pre-operational nature in spite of some apparently operational arguments and behaviors. Within this frame of reference, Fortin-Thériault and Laurendeau-Bendavid, in their purely normative study, attempted to show that there exists a form of conservation which is preoperational in nature and limited to the logic of functions—designated as "simple" conservation in contrast to classical conservation; children at the intermediate level can become capable of this type of conservation before reaching operational stage conservation. To sum up the essential aspects of this experiment simply, there were six groups (from 4-6 to 9-6 years) who, before being given the classical conservation tasks (five of the tests used by Lefebvre & Pinard 1974), had to solve eight problems called "simple" conservation tasks, where the subject has to pour equal amounts into two opaque containers of identical dimensions by choosing the two he considers appropriate from among a set of three empty (and transparent) ones of various heights and diameters. In spite of the systematic bias that may have resulted from the invariant order of administration of these two groups of tests, and in spite of the rather rudimentary level of statistical treatment, the results of this normative study seem to indicate that the preoperational child can come to understand that, in order to equalize the levels of liquid in the two containers, he has to choose not only containers of identical height but also of identical diameter. In other words, before arriving at an explicit understanding of the operational scheme of compensation, the child can already understand at least that, with height remaining constant, a larger diameter necessarily leads to an increase in liquid quantity. The authors conclude from this that there exists a form of conservation which is simpler and acquired earlier than classical conservation: at this intermediate stage, even though the child is not capable of conservation when the experimental situation requires that the two dimensions be varied simultaneously and coordinated with each other, he is at least able to recognize the bidimensional character of the quantities and to understand that height alone may be sufficient to guarantee the correctness of his evaluations, but only if the diameters are also the same.

Without wishing to yield to some kind of superficial agreement, it seems quite obvious that the child's awakening awareness implied in this simple form of conservation, as demonstrated clearly by these authors, evokes directly the conscious grasp of the scheme of covariation of physical attributes, described by the model used in Chapter 3, in its most rudimentary and least explicit form: the empirical observation many times repeated that, if one pours some amount of water into a narrow glass, it always rises higher than if one pours the same amount into a larger, wider glass, leads naturally to the conclusion that one needs equal diameters if one wants to use height to make correct comparisons between containers. It is interesting to note, too, that these authors, in conclusion, consider it possible to suggest that this simple form of conservation may be based on the observation of the covariation of dimensions, and they refer to the early studies of Piaget and Inhelder ([1966] 1971) on the anticipation of water levels and to the more recent ones by Halford (1969, 1970a) on the combination of the dimensions involved in a deformation. However, referring to my previous comments concerning the range and diversity of these covariation schemas (see Chap. 3) and the limitations of Halford's theory (see Chap. 4), it remains true that this form of emerging "conservation" does not yet entail a capacity on the part of the child to dissociate explicitly the physical properties of the object (the first essential component of conservation): liquid quantity, itself not perceptible, is still defined in terms of the height attained in the vessel. For this reason, it seems more correct to speak of conservation of water level, which the child comprehends as being conditioned by the perceptible equality of the diameters, rather than to speak of conservation of quantity. It should be remarked further that even the most advanced and the most explicit forms of the preoperational schema of the covariation of dimensions, which was discussed in Chapter 3 (e.g., one cannot increase the height without decreasing the diameter of a given water column: the greater the increase in height, the smaller the diameter becomes)—even though this covariation entails, by definition, a conscious grasp on the part of the child of the *simultaneous* modification of the perceptible dimensions—are still not sufficient to ensure correct judgments, as can be seen in those children's responses which may deny conservation and give covariation as a justification. To recall once again the conditions necessary for the transition from preoperational covariation to operational compensation—the main reason for this is that the empirical rules expressing this covariation still lack any kind of explanatory value if, in addition, there is not coordination of the covarying dimensions. More important still, the spatiotemporal and thus successive character of the complementary and simultaneous variations, to which this schema is applied, does not, in principle, exclude the possibility of nonconservation. Finally, note that this form of preoperational "conservation" remains of limited scope; obviously it cannot generalize to those conservation tasks in which there is no deformation of material (e.g., weight conservation with concomitant changes in position, temperature). Of necessity it would have to change in content and express itself differently each time the child becomes aware of not the covariation of dimensions but rather explicitly of the qualitative identity of the objects or of the revertibility of certain transformations—and these latter are the most frequent cases.

In a follow-up study on the learning of conservation of liquid quantities, Fortin-Thériault (1977) wanted to compare the relative efficiency of a method involving conflict of physical origin with one using conflict of social origin in the acquisition of simple preoperational conservation, just discussed, and also of classical conservation of the operational type. The control measures used included the simple conservation tasks, described above, and the classical conservation tasks used by Lefebvre and Pinard (1974). The method of factual conflict was directly inspired by Lefebvre and Pinard (1972), from whom Fortin-Thériault borrowed the preparatory exercises (but required correct responses before proceeding further) and the conflict exercises of compensation and addition-subtraction (but added countersuggestions for the sake of attracting the child's attention even more to the dimensions to be compared or the addition-subtractions carried out). The method with conflict of social origin consisted of a type of conflict produced by the contradiction coming from a peer partner, who unlike the experimental subject was able to solve the problems presented. The results on the whole were very disappointing, with both methods proving equally inefficient for the acquisition of conservation as measured by the control tests. It may be, as was suggested by the author, that the changes introduced into the conflict method of Lefebvre and Pinard modified its nature to some extent so as to greatly reduce its influence. Yet, Groulx

(1974) had already used the same method without modifications and had not obtained positive results either. It is not easy to separate out the relative influence of the many factors (such as the effects of expectation,[4] of changes in the method, socioeconomic level and age of the subjects, degree of competence of the experimenters, the evaluation of initial levels, etc.), which might explain why the same method proves efficient in more than one case (Lefebvre & Pinard 1972, 1974; Case 1977) and inefficient in more cases than one as well. However that may be, faced with the analogous inefficiency of the method using social conflict, which she is inclined to attribute to the fact that the method did not permit control of the partner's assertions, Fortin-Thériault comes to the overall conclusion that the methods working with induced learning are undoubtedly not the best to study the acquisition of logical structures in children and, as already suggested by Wohlwill (1973) and Kuhn (1974), cannot replace longitudinal studies and observations of children's everyday activities. In Chapter 4 I have commented on the necessity to resort to systematic observation of children, by making reference to the ethological perspective recently adopted by Charlesworth (1978), in order to try and verify, in vivo so to speak, the processes responsible for the child's coming to a conscious grasp of his action schemata.

The Coordination of Physical Properties of Objects with Subjective Action Schemata

It will be remembered that the third component of our model—that is, the integration of the subject's action schemata with his activities dissociating the physical properties of objects—includes three requirements considered essential for the transition from qualitative to quantitive identity, from covariation to operational compensation, and from empirical revertibility to mental reversibility. The first one requires that the child be capable of applying his action schemata and empirical rules to the particular properties relevant in a given situation to which he is exposed, so that he can proceed to make the necessary inferences without falling back into those errors of indissociation that are typical of the period where these properties are still badly differentiated and thus liable to interfere with one another. The second

---

4. See, e.g., Kamii and Derman (1971).

requirement embodies the assumption that the child can compare, differentiate, and generalize the different schemata (or sub-schemata) of which he has become conscious, so that he is in a position to choose and to apply the ones most appropriate to the situation at hand. These first two requirements, which are both different from but related to each other, are basically prerequisites for the third and most decisive one, by virtue of which the child can go on to the kind of mental reflection necessary in liberating physical actions from their spatiotemporal constraints so as to transform them into mental operations.

The Adaptation of Action Schemata
to the Relevant Physical Properites

With respect to the first of the above-named requirements, the number of empirical data directly demonstrating the way they apply are rather limited. One might, of course, cite again the experiments performed by Gelman (1969) and Trabasso (1968), who see success at conservation tasks as being dependent on the child's ability to attend to those attributes of the stimuli that are relevant in any given situation. But it has already been pointed out repeatedly that this view is quite ambiguous, since the dissociation of physical properties is only the result of a long development and thus stands itself in need of explanation. What is of interest here, at this point in the discussion, is to show in what way certain schemata the child has already become conscious of come to be used appropriately in a conservation task and applied to the physical properties, already sufficiently differentiated to prevent the inferences to be made on the basis of certain properties (e.g., height and width) from being contaminated by other interfering properties (texture, position, etc.), so that even where confusions are difficult to avoid these do not result automatically in nonconservations or even pseudoconservations. In the absence of data bearing directly upon this particular requirement, perhaps the simplest thing to do is to cite some examples, taken from some of the studies already discussed, showing how certain empirical schemata are sometimes applied to irrelevant properties. One such example can be found in the experiment performed by Pinard and Pierre-Joly (1979)—for details see Pierre-Joly (1974)—on weight conservation, where the children do not seem to experience a greater degree of difficulty in asserting conservation of weight in situations where weight interacts with other spatial properties (weight-surface, weight-length, weight-slope: 60%–70% success at 7-7 years already) than they do in much simpler situations in which the modifications applied to the object leave its form and outer appearance unaltered, with only position, orientation, etc., being varied (67% success at the same age). As is shown by these children's total incapacity to explain why, for example, an object of the same weight is harder to transport when some other spatial dimension is varied, it is quite clear that this type of situation is unhesitatingly assimilated to other, more simple situations: the child indifferently applies the same schema of identity (quantitative, or simply qualitative) to the two types of situation without even entertaining the possibility that the application of a schema to a physical property must necessarily vary depending on whether the particular property comes to interact with other properties. This is a form of contamination analogous to that observed by Pinard and Chassé (1977) in their study of pseudoconservation for surface or volume, when the external surface of the object is transformed without modification in volume, or when volume is transformed without modification of the outer surface. These forms of pseudoconservation, which turn out to be extremely stubborn because of the notion of continuity entering into it, result precisely from a mistaken application of albeit operational schemata (identity and compensation) appropriate for the conservation of surfaces or of quantity of matter (internal volume) to a physical property (volume or surface), which in fact is not conserved in this particular situation. It would be very interesting, incidentally, to check (perhaps by means of learning experiments for the conservation of volume, using exercises based on the dissociation outer surface–internal volume) if the indissociations exhibited in these forms of pseudoconservation are not at least partly responsible for the generally late spontaneous appearance of the classical conservation of volume as compared to that of weight and substance. Finally, the experiment carried out by Osiek (1977), reported above, on the interference of form and the center of gravity of an object with the weight concept, has shown, by means of an analysis of children's verbalizations, that this interference for a long time renders the child incapable of a differential application of his weight conservation schema, which is in the process of being developed. This incapacity leads to massive denials of conservation among the younger children, who do not realize that changing the position of the gravitational center of an object fails to have any effect upon its weight other than simply redistributing it within the object. We have also reported Doré's (1979) experiment seeking to determine, in more systematic fashion, what role is played by this interference in weight conservation, using a method in which the child himself has to change the position of the center of gravity in an object before estimating the form of the object and making a statement about the conservation of weight.

The Confrontation of the Subject's Action Schemata

The second requirement necessary to the acquisition of conservation highlights the child confronting the schemata or empirical rules, which he already might have become conscious of in the course of his daily experiences. The amount of data available to illustrate this comparison process is a great deal more plentiful than in the case of the preceding requirement. Very clear examples are provided, for instance, by the many experiments which utilize cognitive conflict in order to attempt to provoke learning of conservation. The rationale of these methods consists precisely in getting the child to become aware of the contradictions into which he can become cornered by applying certain kinds of empirical rules that are of themselves inadequate, as long as he does not compare them one against the other so as to be able to reformulate them in a more differentiated fashion and, most important, integrate them with each other. Such is, for example, the goal— meeting with varying degrees of success—of the method used by Lefebvre and Pinard (1972, 1974), frequently (perhaps a bit too frequently) referred to above. Translated into the language of our model, these exercises of compensation by conflict are aimed directly at bringing about a progressive differentiation of the general schema of covariation, which is a prerequisite to compensation proper. Starting out from a first, very rudimentary form, which is really still quite alien to covariation as such (e.g., when water gets poured into a very thin glass, it always rises higher than in a very wide glass), the child gradually comes to be aware of the covariation itself, first in a purely qualitative form (e.g., you cannot increase the height of a water column unless you lessen its diameter), then in a more precise form which already contains a minimum of quantification (e.g., for any water column it is true that the greater the increase in height, the greater the decrease in width). Similarly, the complementary exercises of addition-subtraction are aimed at leading the child (1) to differentiate the additions and subtractions carried out on the same object by means of successive and independent actions coming from a source outside of the object (what we have called subschema a in Chap. 3) from the additions and subtractions brought about by a single action, without a cause external to the object, incorporating the simultaneous effects of addition and subtraction within the confines of a single object (what we called subschema c); and (2) to come to the recognition that the covariation schema appearing in the compensation exercises is basically only a more explicit version of the addition-subtraction schema (form c).

Another example illustrating the process of confrontation and integration of the child's action schemata can be found in the data collected by Halford (1969, 1970b, 1971, 1975) for the sake of providing support for his theory of conservation acquisition. It will be recalled that in the first version of Halford's model (1970a), concerning the acquisition of conservation-of-liquid quantities, the child has to learn to integrate in a single system quantitative indices (addition, subtraction, or neither) with the covariations of the dimensions of the containers. Learning about the interdependence and how to integrate these two kinds of indices, neither of which is meaningful in isolation, the child begins to understand their relevance and so to acquire the concept of quantity. In spite of my reservations with regard to the validity of the model and the efficiency of the learning method used by Halford on the basis of his model, as discussed in Chapter 4, it is easy to see how the integration of separate indices learned by the child in a series of partial acquisitions necessarily involves the same differentiation of the subschemata of addition-subtraction of our own model (i.e., addition-subtraction coming from a source external to the object vs. addition-subtraction taking place within the object), and likewise involves recognition of the fact that covariation itself is only an explicit form of the additon-subtraction subschema c (addition-subtraction of matter in a single action with two simultaneous effects). Similarly, considering the second model of Halford (1975), according to which the child, in order to understand conservation, needs to have at his disposal a quantification system that enables him to interpret a combination of successive actions (additions, subtractions, liquid transfers), one can at least recognize that the coordination of actions necessary for the construction of this quantitative system presupposes the kind of differentiation and integration of the addition-subtraction subschemata, as treated in the model discussed here.

Two more examples are to be mentioned briefly. The first concerns the normative study by Fortin-Thériault and Laurendeau-Bendavid (1979), already discussed, on the existence of a preoperational form of conservation found in children belonging to an intermediate stage before the acquisition of operational conservation. Assuming that it can be corroborated, which seems quite likely, one might think that this form of conservation of liquid level (if not of quantity) in a container presupposes a first discrimination between the two most elementary forms which, according to our model, the general schema of the covariation of object attributes can take: the simple functional dependence obtaining between the diameter of a vessel and the level reached by a liquid poured into that vessel (elementary form constituting a prerequisite to covariation as such), and the interdependence of the variations wrought upon the dimensions of an object subjected to some deformation (the first form of covariation as such, even in the absence of any kind of quantification of this interdependence). The second example refers to an experiment done in Geneva on the conservation of quantities from the dialectic perspective recently advocated by Piaget. This experiment, which Sinclair De-Zwart (1977) and Piaget (1979) allude to without specifying either the ages of the subjects, the method, nor the details of the results, is based on the idea that the actions which transform the objects in the traditional conservation-of-substance studies are not really productive actions but limited to displacements of small parts of the material. If it can be assumed that children tend to be interested mainly in productive actions, then it should be possible to get them to assert conservation more easily by a method based on a sequence of pairs of actions, partial productions (additions, then subtractions), which cancel out each time. In this way, one can gradually lead up to the last deformation to be performed all at once as in the usual tasks. For example, the experimenter might take off a part of a clay ball and ask the child whether there is still the same amount as before (which the child will deny), then he might add the same piece to another part of the clay ball and ask the same question again (this time the child will agree, explaining that the part that was taken away before is now added back on). The experimenter would continue in the same manner with the other parts, until the initial clay ball was transformed into a sausage. This method is reminiscent of Bruner (1966) in an experiment on the conservation of water contained in a vessel, with a duck floating on top, who gradually emptied "his water" out into another vessel of a different shape. It appears that children subjected to this method tend to admit conservation easily all the while during the series of partial transformations. They also maintain this advance during the classical conservation task administered afterward. Assuming that these results can be replicated and that they do not reflect simply the child's recognition of the qualitative identity of the substance, as Piaget himself doubts (Piaget, Sinclair, & Vinh Bang 1968) in his critique of Bruner's experiment, the method described by Sinclair DeZwart brings the child naturally (1) to differentiate the subschemata of addition-subtraction treated in our model (additions-subtractions coming from a source external to the object vs. additions-subtractions remaining within the object), and (2) to see in these additions-subtractions an application of the various modalities of the complementary schema of revertibility regulating successive and independent actions.

Liberation from Spatiotemporal Constraints

The third and last requirement involved in the coordination of physical properties of objects with the subject's action schemata is that the child has to free his representation of physical actions from their spatiotemporal constraints in order to transform his empirical schemata or rules into operational schemata or mental operations. This requirement, already described (see Chap. 3) as to its nature and modalities, is undoubtedly the most critical and also the most difficult to operationalize. The most critical, since it raises the essential problem of the transition from empirical to logical necessity: whether we are dealing with spontaneous acquisition or experimentally induced learning by whatever method (direct or vicarious experiences of conflict, rule teaching, etc.), essentially this transition demands of the child a mental reflection (reflective abstraction) on his own action schemata, which transforms successivity into simultaneity or, to put it differently, inductive and extensional generalizations of these schemata (source of empirical necessity) into deductive generalizations, which are the source of logical necessity. This requirement is also the most difficult to operationalize and, consequently, to illustrate with empirical data, for two main reasons. The first derives from the fact that the child's actions are necessarily physical and successive so that the subjective sense of necessity inherent in the coordination of his actions is always the result of an inference. As noted by Piaget (1977), "Necessity is not an observable datum that can be read directly from objects, but always the result of a construction internal to the subject" (p. 235). The second reason why it is difficult to illustrate the transition from inductive to deductive generalization has to do with the fact that this understanding of logical necessity itself undergoes a very long development, consisting of several levels, as Piaget tried to show in his recent papers on the logical modalities of possibility, impossibility, and necessity (1976, 1977). The notion of necessity appears in its fully developed form only with the implications inherent in the use of formal operations; but there are earlier manifestations of necessity, such as (a) a subjective sense of necessity, already detectable in the implications required for the coordination of sensorimotor schemata (e.g., in order to be able to take possession of an object, which is out of reach, by means of an instrument or tool, the tool must be placed right on the object rather than beside it); or (b) the empirical necessity, which can be detected in the schemata of functions typical of the pre-operational level (e.g., when the water level is higher in one glass than in another, it must follow that there is more to drink).[5] These earlier forms of necessity are thus apparent well before that which is characteristic of operations, even at the concrete level (the implicational relations existing between an observer's changes of position and the various perspectives of spatial representations, those between direct and inverse operations in conservation, etc.).

5. The subjective sense of necessity observed by Murray and Armstrong (1976) in nonconserving children is typical of this level.

It is precisely the passage from the form of necessity involved in sensorimotor actions and in the preoperational schemata of functional logic toward the forms of necessity characteristic of concrete and formal operations in which we are interested here. On the empirical level, the challenge to be met consists, then, in drawing the distinction between what Piaget has called "pseudonecessity" and authentic necessity, depending on the level and kind of inference supporting the child's explanation of a phenomenon. Authentic necessity, at the operational level, proceeds by deduction, which takes into account the phenomena observed but by transcending them. On the contrary, pseudonecessity, at the preoperational level, proceeds by simple induction, remains limited to observables (actual or possible), and is essentially due, still according to Piaget, to two kinds of indifferentiation: (a) lack of differentiation between the factual and the regular, which leads the children to believe that things cannot be other than what they are (many examples of this are provided by the analysis of precausal belief systems); (b) lack of differentiation between the general and the necessary, the former being nothing but simple empirical constants limited to entities already observed in the past or generalizable only by extension through addition of other observables, whereas only the use of a deductive mode of generalization enables a subject to know the reason—and therefore the necessity—of these empirical constants. It appears to us that these distinctions may be directly pertinent to the problems discussed here. If it is true, as we have tried to show, that the empirical rules of qualitative identity, or revertibility, and of covariation can eventually lead to conservation, it is because these rules, through a process of liberation from spatiotemporal constraints which inevitably govern all observable phenomena, become transformed and integrated into a deductive system of operational rules (quantitative identity, reversibility, and compensation). This system explains the purely inductive generality of the earlier rules to that conservation becomes a necessary result of a process of internal transposition of the operations constituting the system.

Looked at in this way, seeking to illustrate the passage from induction to deduction means to try to illustrate the degree of logical necessity that a statement of conservation carried for a subject. There are two ways in which such illustration may be provided. First, one might focus on the stringency of the tests used to determine the child's level of conservation and of the criteria used to evaluate the degree of logicality in the child's reasoning. Illustrations of this first type are abundant in the experimental literature; so copious, in fact, that it would be quite tedious to cite specific examples. Regarding the kinds of tests used most commonly, it is often quite easy to see that they are not sufficiently rigorous so as to permit establishing with certainty the level of conservation achieved by a child, not to speak of the degree of necessity underlying a child's conservation responses. This is particularly true in the case of the tests used in many of the learning experiments to establish the subjects' initial level before the beginning of training: such as tests that are too short, consisting of a very limited number of items to which the child may simply give "yes" or "no" answers; tests which even though long enough are not sufficiently diversified or even purely repetitive, including, for example, only situations with initial equality, which lend themselves naturally to the use of a simple, more or less mechanical rule (e.g., "if it's the same before, it must be the same after"); it also happens frequently that the subjects are classified as conservers or nonconservers in terms of a rather arbitrarily set minimal number of conservation responses; control measures that are so very similar to the learning exercises that it is hard not to believe the children did not simply make a transfer by reversing their initial responses; etc. Concerning the other, related problem of the degree of stringency of the criteria used to evaluate the logicity and the authenticity of the observed acquisitions, it is equally easy to note inadequacies or even useless applications: for example, no generalization to different tasks of identical structure to keep the subject from adopting a simple rule derived by means of a purely extensional generalization mode rather than a deductive one, difficult as it may be to establish this distinction (see Piaget et al. 1978); use of different yet inappropriate generalization tasks, where neither a theoretical analysis nor previously known facts demand such a generalization and may even suggest the opposite (generalization from the conservation of substance to that of weight, of length, etc.); failure to analyze systematically the justifications adduced by the children (such an analysis might lead to an apparent increase in the number of false nonconservations, but the result is less undesirable than the opposite increase of false conservations, especially when one wants to know precisely the kind and level of necessity underlying the child's affirmations); failure to test for resistance to countersuggestions designed to probe the subjects' degree of certainty, even though the child's spontaneous tendency to accept the countersuggestion of the adult may just as well reflect a real uncertainty as a mere attitude of compliance, which in no way shakes his true certainty (false nonconservation); instability of the learning achievements observed, sometimes evident in additional posttests, where these are given, at variable intervals, which however is not always done; etc.

This first avenue to illustrate the passage from pseudonecessity to real necessity certainly has its merits in the sense that it suggests a certain number of minimum requirements, well documented in the existing literature in terms of positive instances but more often, as we see it, by negative examples. In spite of these merits, it seems that this first way would lead us nowhere, since the data actually available are inadequate to demonstrate the difference between a sense of necessity based on the child's simply applying certain empirical rules and a sense of logical necessity based rather upon the use of authentically operational rules. The main reason for this is undoubtedly that the inferences to be drawn, which should establish this distinction on this basis of stringent techniques and criteria, still allow too much leeway in the interpretation of the data, even in the more rigorous studies. This can be seen first from the essential fact that these experiments never explore directly, that is, without relying on the child's conservation responses as such, the degree of generalization and necessity of which the child is capable, when he affirms and justifies conservation. It can be seen also from the correlated fact that all the techniques used to determine the level of conservation in the child, whether it is in spontaneous acquisition or in induced learning situations of whatever variety (rule teaching, equilibration exercises, modeling, etc.), can give results that satisfy the usual criteria (generalization to different tests, resistance to countersuggestions, stability of acquisition, etc.). Finally, it can be seen from the fact that, depending on their theoretical affiliation, the same methods or techniques of evaluation and the same

criteria of logicality are considered either sufficiently or in-
sufficiently rigorous by different authors, as is shown, for example, in the frequent use of the term "pseudoconservation" to
describe certain positive results of training, the authenticity of
which is being questioned, or in the rather byzantine dispute initiated by Brainerd concerning the legitimacy of having or not
having the child justify his conservation judgments (see, e.g.,
Brainerd 1973a, 1974, 1977a; Larsen 1977; McCarthy-Gallagher &
Kim-Reid 1978).

A second way one might choose to illustrate the passage from
the level of pseudo- or purely empirical- to logical-necessity
seems to us at once more promising and less ambiguous, even
though this way is still relatively unexplored and has as yet not
given rise to a great many empirical researches. It is more promising and less ambiguous, because the experiments done (or to
be done) in order to determine the type of necessity underlying
the child's assertions and justifications of conservation can be
more or less independent of conservation experiments as such,
and, more important, the experiments pertaining to this second
way are aimed directly at an exploration of the processes implicated in the emergence of logical necessity. Within this perspective, two main lines of research are worth mentioning. The
first concerns the development of the notions of commutability
and vicariance of parts within a whole set, while the second, even
more directly, concerns the development of the concept of necessity itself in the child.

To begin with the notions of commutability and vicariance,
which, as was shown above (Chap. 3), are essential for the transition from empirical- to logical-necessity—these still need to be
studied systematically as they develop in the child. That is,
studies need to be designed to specify the successive levels in the
child's growing awareness of the fact that the different parts of a
whole set may be rearranged in any way whatever within this set
without losing their identity (commutability) and are complementary and equivalent with respect to each other within the
set (vicariance). In the absence of such direct analysis, a good
number of examples illustrating the child's growing capacity to
comprehend commutability and vicariance may be found in
Piaget's recent researches concerning contradiction (Piaget et al.
1974b) as well as in Piaget's even more recent studies concerning

the relations between the notions of transformation and correspondence (Piaget 1979). These studies concerning the relations and correspondences between the positive and the negative aspects of an action show how the primacy of the positive over the negative aspects of an action gives way to a compensatory correspondence between the two, and how this process presupposes a capacity in the child to distinguish between a form of addition-subtraction having its source outside of the object (a noncommutable change) and one taking place within the object (commutable change in position). The experiment quoted by Sinclair DeZwart (1977)—briefly summarized above—and also recalled by Piaget (1979) provides a nice example of a method that might be useful in bringing about an understanding of this distinction, a prerequisite to conservation. The same capacity to understand the necessary correspondence between the positive and negative effects of an action is required not only for conservation but also in a host of other domains, as shown in examples to be found in the two publications of Piaget's cited above (e.g., the correspondence between what the subject gains and the experimenter loses in an exchange of tokens). In this way, it becomes possible to evaluate the child's ability to handle the relations between affirmation and negation independently and outside of the context of a classical conservation problem.

Considering next the development of the concept of necessity itself, it seems that this may be a still more direct way and one which, at least theoretically, is still more independent of the specific domain of conservations as such, for establishing the distinction between empirical-necessity or pseudonecessity characterizing the preoperational level and logical-necessity characteristic of operational thought. The empirical data apt to illustrate this distinction, which we consider to be the essential criterion for authentic conservation, are extremely few and far between. There is at least one ingenious study by Piéraut-Le Bonniec (1979), which attempted specifically to evaluate the sense of impossibility or of necessity accessible to the child. This was done with a simple problem employing a box with two kinds of openings, one of which would let through either balls or small rulers, while the other would let through only balls. The child had to decide if and how one could be absolutely sure (without seeing) through which opening either a ball or a ruler could have passed.

One might refer also to some articles by Piaget (1976, 1977), already cited, where he discusses the related notions of possibility and necessity in reviewing a number of Genevan studies dealing with the development of these notions and reinterpreting, within this new framework, earlier studies carried out in several areas. Let us simply recall that preoperational necessity (or impossibility) is based on inferences limited to observables. The only form of generalization to which it can give rise, therefore, is one of a purely inductive or empirical nature by extension to other observables, which can of course lead the child to rid himself of some purely subjective pseudoimpossibilities, but which still do not enable him to go beyond the level of empirical or purely legal constants without any real explanatory value in themselves. Let us take as an example, often used by Piaget from the domain of logicoarithmetical thinking, a problem of exchange of tokens between two partners: the child, having for a long time believed it necessary that an exchange of n tokens will produce a difference of only n tokens between the partners, will finally come to notice that this difference can never be one of only n tokens, without being able to understand why. Similarly, to take a second example from Piaget from the domain of causal thought—a problem where the child has to keep the balance of a ruler, part of which extends beyond its resting point—the child quickly realizes and can even predict that the task is impossible if more than half of the length extends beyond the resting point, whatever the length of the ruler. In order to be able to explain a law or empirical constant and thus understand its necessity, what is required is, first, an extension of the domain of possibilities, rendered accessible through, among other things, the development of the representational function and, more specifically, that of anticipatory imagery; but, most important, what is needed is that the child's actions and operations (either real or only possible), which he applies or attributes to objects, become constituted in a closed system of reciprocal implications so as to confer a constructive and deductive mode—and thus a character of real necessity—upon the child's generalizations. Thus, to take our two examples just cited, if the child becomes capable of understanding why an exchange of n tokens always produces a difference of $2n$ and of asserting that this will necessarily always be so, without having to try out other exchanges and without having to suspect possible exceptions, then this is due to his ability to compose additions and subtractions that result simultaneously from a single action so that they become integrated into a single system of reciprocal relations. This system, then, depends in no way upon the particular magnitude of such and such an exchange and thus is generalizable to all actual or possible exchanges. Similarly, if the child can explain the constant observed in the problem with the ruler to be kept in balance, as well as recognize its necessity, then this is due to his ability to coordinate with each other the direct and inverse actions attributed by him to the weight exerted by the physical object.

In sum, the empirical studies apt to illustrate the transition from an inductive to a deductive mode in the acquisition of conservation are still to be done. With all the rigor the methods of evaluation and the criteria commonly used for estimating logicity of reasoning—desirable though this may be—in the studies concerning spontaneous acquisition or provoked learning of conservation, it does not seem likely that the data resulting from even the best controlled of this type of study could furnish a decisive answer to the problem of the authenticity of the conservation acquisitions. The responses given by a child, even if care is taken to require a justification, a certain stability and resistance to countersuggestions, can almost never suffice to establish the distinction between a sense of necessity based on generalizations that are merely inductively derived from certain empirical constants or laws and a sense of necessity that is based upon deductive generalization resulting from a system of certain operational rules. For this reason, it seems to us more promising to proceed to a more direct kind of analysis, one that is independent of conservation judgments as such: one might either analyze the child's comprehension of the notions of commutativity and of the vicariant relation between parts and a whole, notions that are essential to conservation, or else one might make a systematic analysis of the development of the notion of necessity itself in the child, in different contexts that are more or less independent of the domain of conservations as such. By comparing the development of these notions to that of conservations, one might hope to be able not only to establish the relative efficiency of the various learning methods currently in use or of new methods which are based on these notions but, more important, to shed some light on the difficult and almost insoluble question concerning the authenticity of the conservations acquired by the child. This is by no means an easy undertaking. It will undoubtedly meet with a great many difficulties, not the least of which is the problem posed by what Piaget (1976, pp. 293, 295) calls the purely "local" necessities characteristic of the concrete operational level, since they are still limited to a particular content, which seems again to raise the thorny issue of horizontal décalages. Still, it seems that, in spite of these ambushes, it is well worth trying to do such studies for the sake of escaping from the almost inextricable maze into which have become enmeshed the researches both past and present concerning the acquisition of conservation.

6   Conclusions:
      Perspectives and Prospects

In this concluding chapter, instead of trying to sum up the essentials of the preceding chapters and to risk unnecessary repetition, it seems preferable to dedicate the remaining pages to a discussion of a few more general questions. This discussion may help situate the present volume within its proper perspective. It can also, to some extent, suggest the directions for the orientation of future research in this area. Three questions will be taken up for discussion: the importance of conservation for the study of cognitive development; the scope and limits of experimental studies of conservation learning; and, finally, one problem that is still more general and that will retain our attention somewhat longer—a comparative consideration of the cognitivist and the behaviorist approaches in developmental psychology.

The Importance of Conservation
for the Study of Cognitive Development

If the importance of a developmental problem were to be evaluated only in terms of the quantity of research done on it, one would have to admit that the acquisition of conservation constitutes one of the most important problems in the study of cognitive development. In spite of a certain decline during the last few years, the study of conservation has long been and still is being given a special privileged position within the literature specializing in the development of cognitive functions, up to a point where it is now practically impossible to make an even approximately exhaustive review of the literature. The chapters in books and journal articles treating different aspects of this general problem are countless: normative and transcultural studies, studies of conservation learning by various methods, synchronous or asynchronous development of various kinds of conservation, models

147

or theories designed to explain these acquisitions, etc. This pro-
fusion of researches and studies—a flow that necessarily carries
much repetition, inconsistency and even some drift, studies
which quite often represent nothing more than a diversion rather
costly in terms of material and human resources—still can be seen
as an index or symptomatic of the importance of conservation for
the study of cognitive development. There are three main reasons
for this.

The first is that, even though the great majority of studies is
oriented toward certain privileged forms of conservation (substance, weight, volume, number, space, etc.), the sense of the
term "conservation" is not as narrow as one might suppose if one
looks only at the most obvious examples, those with which the
literature is oversaturated. As indicated at the beginning of this
text, where I insisted upon the polymorphic character of conservation, conservation is not really a notion to be acquired in the
same sense as other notions or concepts such as space, number,
time, quantity, etc. It is neither a principle nor a specific cognitive
operation but is situated at the center of each of the logical and
spatiotemporal concepts the child has to acquire; it is a consequence of the reversibility of the cognitive operations constituting
each of these notions and makes possible, because of its invariant
character, the coordination of these operations. Thus, the importance of conservation derives mainly from its implication in
each and every one of the concepts that the child has to learn. For
this reason, one would be ill-advised to confine one's research to
only the most obvious forms of conservation, no matter how
diversified and sophisticated the techniques may be that are deployed in such studies. One should be particularly wary not to fall
prey to the illusory goal of trying to establish—as one might think
it to be required by the stage concept (e.g., Brainerd 1973b,
1978b)—whether the various forms of conservation implicating
different concepts are in fact acquired simultaneously and may be
part of a single integrated structure. But this is in no way required
by Piaget's stage theory nor is it possible to be empirically observed. This idea springs from a misconception of the notions of
integrated structure and horizontal décalage, which fails to distinguish the different levels at which these notions may manifest
themselves (see Pinard & Laurendeau 1969). It seems both
legitimate and necessary, however, to continue to do research on

the problem of conservations, but under the condition of increasing considerably the theoretical scope of this type of research by orienting it, for example, in one or the other of the following directions: (a) trying to specify the particular form that conservation takes in the acquisition of different concepts, given the fact that conservation is necessarily implicated in the coordination of the cognitive operations required for the construction of each concept (e.g., the conservation of a class of objects in a logical inclusion task, the conservation of neighborhoods implicated in the construction of topological space relations); (b) studying the development of particular forms of conservation without separating it from the particular concept to which it refers naturally, by specifying the place and the role it has in the development of that particular notion; this will make it possible to put into proper perspective and in the appropriate scale the problems related to the notions of integrated structure and horizontal décalages; (c) to attack directly the study of the development of logical necessity in the child, which is decisive for the authenticity of conservation and which depends precisely upon the fact that the actions and operations imply each other by reciprocal deducibility, as they become constituted within a unified system (or integrated structure). And this presupposes once again an integration of conservation within the development of the operations involved in a particular concept.

The second reason that explains the importance of conservation has to do with the fact that even the forms of conservation most frequently studied are not to be considered as more or less artificial or artifactual phenomena that are only observable in laboratory situations, completely removed from children's everyday life. Since, as we have tried to show, conservation is at the center of every concept the child has to acquire in the course of his development, it obviously follows that the more or less standardized tasks to which children are submitted—despite the dangers of fragmentation and unreality brought on by the otherwise quite legitimate concerns to identify clearly and to control the variables involved in children's acquisition of certain conservations—evoke in principle, at least, analogous problems from the child's everyday experience. In his everyday life, the child is confronted, as he adapts to his physical and social environment, with problems of classification, of relationships, number, space, time, speed, causality, etc. In the formation of each of these notions, conservation becomes a concrete problem. Unfortunately, very few, if any, studies have been done on the development of conservation within an ethological perspective. Given the great favor enjoyed at the present time by recently developed methods for systematic observation, methods that are constantly becoming more sophisticated, it is to be hoped that research will be oriented toward discovering the kinds of concrete situations, no doubt quite frequent, where the child is exposed to behaviors of nonconservation and of conservation. In this way, it should be possible to identify more precisely the factors responsible for the transition from nonconservation to conservation. Similarly, there have been numerous efforts expended over a number of years in a number of places to apply Piaget's theory in the elaboration of new teaching methods in schools. In the present context, we shall not be concerned with the question of how well founded or how efficient these methods really are; we simply intend to voice our opinion that conservation, because of its polymorphic character and its essential contribution to each and every concept the child needs to acquire, must of necessity be part of the educational process. Obviously, it would be absurd to think that conservation should be a subject matter to be taught on a par with other subjects. However, it seems to us equally unrealistic and illogical to revive certain no longer accepted forms of the old notion of "school readiness" by claiming that conservation is a kind of prerequisite for school learning, as if it was a notion to be mastered first in one domain, then another, before the corresponding concepts could be taught in school (e.g., wait until the child can conserve number before beginning to teach him arithmetic). All we have tried to indicate—by caricaturing somewhat certain widespread ideas—is that conservation cannot be divorced from academic skill acquisition because it is implicated in the comprehension of concepts that constitute the subject matter of such acquisitions and because it develops concurrently with the progressive mastery of these concepts. This in itself entails no claims concerning the relative efficiency of the various methods that might be invented for teaching these concepts.

The third reason why we believe that conservation has an important place in the study of cognitive development is related to the fact that it is heuristically very rich. The multitude of research produced on the development of conservations, even though of highly variable value and almost consistently limited to certain particular forms of conservation, still has shed a great deal of light on a number of more general problems and has stimulated the creation of new explanatory models as well as the reformulation and extension of currently existing ones. The various methods for evaluating children's level of conservation and the problems of interpretation of the data obtained in these studies have led, for example, and still do today, to a large number of studies on the more general problem of the relationship between language and thinking (e.g., development of nonverbal methods, children's comprehension of the quantitative terms used in these kinds of studies, the relative influence of language and thought). Similarly, conservations provide a privileged domain for theoretical discussions concerning the general notions of developmental stage, structures, décalages, and developmental synchronisms, particularly with respect to the mechanisms of transition from one stage to the next, the sequences of strategies subjects develop for the resolution of a problem, the elusive notion of intermediate stage, and the increasing efforts made to define it in terms other than purely negative ones, etc. One might also mention the contribution afforded by conservation studies carried out in different cultural groups. Such experiments can help assess the relative importance of various factors involved in cognitive development, to the extent that culture is taken as a variable on a par with other variables and to the extent that the research does not limit itself to simply recording the chronological décalages to be found in different cultures but makes an effort to (a) ascertain the reason for a particular décalage; (b) study the décalages within the context of development, as adapted to a particular culture or environment, of the general concept involved in the particular case of conservation studied; and (c) analyze their resistance to change, perhaps by means of training experiments, so as to be able to determine whether these décalages are authentic or artifactual, etc. Finally—to take a last example indicating the heuristic value of studies on conservation—research on conservation can help make more precise the meaning of certain concepts in current usage. Thus, Murray (1976), in order to illustrate the ecological validity of conservation, among other things, refers to his experiments, which showed that confusing the connotative and the denotative aspects of a concept may influence the relative difficulty of certain transformations in the conservation of the weight of objects (e.g., Nummedal & Murray 1969); furthermore, that situational factors, because of that same confusion, may even influence weight conservation with respect to the child's own body (Murray & Johnson 1975; Murray & Tyler 1978), depending on the extent to which a particular situation is connotatively associated with the concept of weight. All these different confusions are well documented in conservation studies, where the child tends to consider as denotative an object property which is only connotative. They appear to bear direct witness to the difficulties experienced by children to resist interference stemming from a failure to distinguish between different physical properties of objects.

Scope and Limits of Experiments on the Learning of Conservation

This second question could be discussed at great length, but discussion of it will be somewhat limited here since the preceding chapter has already called attention to the impasse in which the research tradition on experimentally provoked learning of conservation appears to be caught. Perhaps the most convincing demonstration of why interest has begun to decline for this type of research is that given by Kuhn (1974) in her noteworthy comments on the current model of experimentally induced learning of conservation. One cannot but agree with her statements, for example, about the ambivalence of the criteria customarily applied in evaluating the authenticity of the induced acquisitions: as long as there is no generally accepted definition of the meaning of conservation, the results of different training methods meeting the same criteria (same type of justification, of resistance to countersuggestion, etc.) will be considered authentic or not authentic by different researchers depending on their personal definition of conservation, so that each researcher can only convince himself, but not others, of the efficiency of his methods. Likewise, one cannot but agree with her when she castigates the simplistic conception of Brainerd, which pretends that it is possible to be sure about the authenticity of a conservation judgment on the basis of a simple dichotomous choice of "yes" or "no," explaining, somewhat naively, the decline in interest for experiments of conservation training with reference to the fact that the crucial factor in this kind of learning has now been discovered, that is, reversibility, but without apparently making the distinction between reversibility and revertibility, and without comprehending—to quote the elegant formulation used by Kuhn—that "it is the reversibility of operations, not, as commonly misinterpreted, the operation of reversibility, which constitutes concrete operations" (p. 597). As a way out of the actual impasse, Kuhn proposes recasting the experimental model usually employed in the research on the provoked learning of logical structures. In its outlines, this recast model includes two main elements. The first is a *longitudinal analysis of the spontaneous development* of the notion to be taught experimentally, as well as of the notions that are closely related to this target notion so that one would know the time it normally takes for these notions to become constructed and the relations of synchrony and asynchrony obtaining between these notions. A preliminary analysis of this kind would first of all be a source of inspiration for the elaboration of training methods that are well adapted to the conditions governing the child's spontaneous development; but, more important, it would furnish "an unambiguous criterion" (p. 599) to evaluate the efficacy of the experimental methods, such that the subjects having undergone the training should, in principle, following the training sessions, produce the same behaviors (type of explanation, level of generalization, etc.) as those subjects who attain the analogous level of development spontaneously. The second element of the recast model proposed by Kuhn is a stipulation that the *experimental manipulations should be distributed,* in principle, over a series of experiments following the whole period of normal development, so that its essential characteristics would be respected. In sum, the research strategy advocated is one in which one aims at finding out not the extent to which natural development can be accelerated but, rather, how it can be studied in slow motion. This alternative model proposed by Kuhn, with its ingenuity and breadth of perspective, is likely to introduce a current of fresh air into the heavily scented atmosphere surrounding the overwhelming quantity of researches on induced conservation learning. However, even if we assume

that the repeated experimental interventions and their distribution over the entire period of the corresponding spontaneous development of a whole set of related notions do not offer some
insurmountable problems (e.g., controlling the effects of repetition in the case of certain notions where the transition from preoperational to operational level occurs almost abruptly; separating the effects due to experimental learning from those due to
natural development in the experimental group, which may be
quite heterogeneous as to natural developmental rhythm), it still
does not in any way seem evident to us that the problem of the
ambiguity of the usual criteria of logicality (type of explanation,
level of generalization, etc.) could really be eliminated by a preliminary longitudinal study. In fact, the possibility cannot be
excluded that the problem would simply be pushed back onto the
level of interpretation of the data collected in the preliminary
study itself. As anyone having done normative research (either
cross-sectional or longitudinal) or systematic research on horizontal décalages and developmental synchrony will be able to
testify, the real meaning and logical authenticity of children's
explanations and the analysis of the many factors liable to influence the range of developmental synchronies and asynchronies
raise some problems that are very difficult to solve. For this reason, the suggestion to evaluate the efficacity of the experimental
interventions by means of a comparison between the experimental and the "natural" subjects of equivalent levels is anything
but a magical solution: as a number of authors have already had
opportunity to suspect when, in their experimental studies of
conservation learning or of the learning of other logical concepts,
they thought to include a group of "natural" conservers (e.g.,
Halford 1971; Lasry & Laurendeau 1969; Morin 1974; Pagé 1967),
the ambiguity of the criteria for logicality in the observed progress
cannot be removed in this way, unless one supposes a priori that
the problem is definitely taken care of in normative studies and
that one could be sure from the start of the logicality of the subjects classed as conservers.

Given this state of affairs, and assuming that the principal aim
pursued by the research on the induced learning of certain logical
structures in not so much to accelerate spontaneous development
or even to discover—to paraphrase one of Kuhn's suggestions—
the minimum of acceleration possible but to come to be able to

specify the factors responsible for spontaneous development, and particularly to identify the process mediating the transition from preoperational to operational logic, it is our guess that such a research goal requires absolutely a normative study, ideally longitudinal, of the spontaneous development of the logical structures involved. In this, I am in perfect agreement with Kuhn, but with two important caveats on which depends apparently the true possibility to get rid of all ambiguity in the usual criteria for logicality. The first underscores the necessity to widen the scope of normative studies of the natural development of a given target notion (e.g., conservation of quantities) to be taught subjects in a learning study; but extending not so much to concepts related to the target notion, as Kuhn suggests, assuming that the purpose of this extension is to specify the systematic chronological relations (developmental synchrony and asynchrony) existing between the concepts involved. The analysis of this type of purely extensional generalization from a target to analogous concepts (e.g., different types of conservation) would run into the familiar problems of interpretation of children's justifications; it would be better to proceed to an independent analysis of the construction of the target concept such as, for example, a systematic analysis of the development of the notion of logical necessity in the child, or of the notion of vicariance and of commutability of parts constituting a whole. It is our opinion that this type of generalization would best serve the need for a clarification of the problem of the authenticity of children's justifications in a conservation task and of the crucial problem of the transition from preoperational to operational logic. The second proviso, more positive and more general in scope, is to indicate the danger of confining oneself, in evaluating children's level of conservation, to using only the kind of standardized task most frequently employed. Particularly when, out of concern for rigor or precision and out of a certain distrust of children's verbal explanations, the authors of such tests try to cleanse them of all verbal contamination and to shun systematically anything that might resemble the methods of critical questioning of the kind used by Piaget, there is indeed reason to question more and more seriously the ecological relevance of such tasks and the true significance of the behaviors observed. In accordance with the new ethological approaches (e.g., Strayer 1980; Charlesworth 1978; Wohlwill 1973), it seems increasingly necessary to resort also, in complementary fashion, to systematic observation of children in their natural environment, using observation schedules as inclusive and objective as possible. However, this is by no means to be seen as an invitation to abandon the experimental approach. In this respect, it seems that Bronfenbrenner (1977) speaks the language of reason when, after having justifiably expressed his concern that contemporary developmental psychology has become, to a large extent, "the science of the strange behavior of children in strange situations with strange adults, for the briefest possible periods of time" (p. 513), he also rejects a certain simplistic notion of ecological validity, which claims that only research done in naturalistic situations is scientifically legitimate. What he advocates is rather an expansion and a convergence of the "naturalistic" and experimental approaches, introducing the notion of ecological experiment, which systematically varies environmental conditions, leading both to the discovery and to the testing of hypotheses.

Thus, it is within this kind of a perspective of convergence and complementarity that it seems necessary, for an understanding of the spontaneous acquisition of conservations, to resort to the methods of systematic observation of children in their natural environment. In this way, it should, at least in principle, be easier to evaluate the degree of necessity underlying children's beliefs, when these appear as integrated parts of everyday behavior, and to specify the nature and interaction of the various factors implicated in the spontaneous development of conservations (conflict, imitation, social interaction, etc.). If, then, one decides to proceed to experimental learning studies—a line of research one might consider necessary following the old adage that, in order to understand a phenomenon, one has to try to change it—one might expect that the kind of extended normative study of the kind we have tried to specify, one that is based as much on systematic observation in the natural environment as on laboratory methods, could furnish at least the criteria of logicality necessary for estimating the authenticity of conservation behaviors resulting from the experimental interventions. Only under this condition will it be possible for the research on experimentally induced learning of conservation to emerge from the impasse in which it is presently caught. The data to be obtained in such an extended study of spontaneous development of conservation skills, espe-

cially data concerning the development of the notions of necessity, vicariance, and commutability, would lend themselves well
to a more direct exploration of the nature of the progress made *in
the course of a learning experiment*, perhaps by criterion tests to
be administered at certain intervals during the course of the
learning exercises, instead of restricting the comparisons to the
usual, global pre- and posttest differences. More than one Piagetian researcher would have a great deal to learn, in this respect,
for the experimental techniques (e.g., task analysis, identification
of strategies or rules adopted successively by the subjects) developed by researchers in the information-processing approach (e.g.,
Simon 1962, 1972, 1979; Klahr & Wallace 1976; Siegler 1976,
1978, 1979; Pascual-Leone 1970, 1980; Case 1974, 1978).

Confronting the Cognitivist and Behaviorist Perspectives

In her penetrating analysis of current models of cognitive and
social development and their mechanisms, Kuhn (1978) evokes
the opposition, rather old to be sure but becoming more and more
crystallized, between what she designates as the behaviorist (or
mechanistic) and the organismic perspectives in the study of children's cognitive development. She points out that the analyses
done following the former perspective are essentially oriented
toward observed or observable behavior. The elementary units of
behavior, moreover, are seen as discrete and independent entities
that are basically shaped by reinforcement contingencies con-
sequent upon the subject's acting on the environment. According
to the opposite perspective, the analyses are directed instead
upon internal processes, and its behaviorial units tend progressively toward the formation of integrated structures, the principal
role in this acquisition being assigned to the subject's own selective activation of his interactions with the environment. It is easy
to see that most of the models and theories proposed in the past
and even today to describe or explain child development, particularly when presented in such general terms, can be related to
one or the other of these two general perspectives, which we shall
designate as behaviorist and cognitivist, respectively. We shall
take the term "cognitivism" to refer to the class of theories or
systems which, in order to describe or explain cognitive functions, invoke internal processes inferred from observable behaviors, instead of simply analyzing the behavior itself through which

are expressed the so-called internal processes. Thus, the term encompasses not only the structuralist type of approaches including Piaget's constructivism, but also all the different approaches derived from cybernetic theories of information processing (artificial intelligence, simulation of cognitive processes, analysis of strategies or rules governing behavior, etc.). In a recent article, Cellérier (1979, pp. 89 ff.) reserves the term ''cognitivism'' to the second type of approach, which is essentially directed at studying what he calls ''pragmatic transformations of knowledge into action'' as opposed to ''constructivism'' which is characteristic of developmental psychology, a type of approach directed rather at studying ''epistemic transformations'' of action into knowledge. But in spite of this difference, the two types of approach remain complementary with respect to each other, both being concerned with the relations between knowledge and action, instead of reducing one to the other as in the behaviorist perspective.

Given the decidedly cognitivist perspective with which the problem of conservations has been approached here, it appears necessary to briefly analyze the points of convergence and of divergence between the cognitivist and the behaviorist perspectives; but before proceeding to this analysis, it may be of interest to call attention to a number of current orientations with regard to psychological theories and models, irrespective of the general perspective (cognitivist or behaviorist) to which each theory may be related.

Various Attitudes with Regard to Psychological Theories

This is not the place to offer even a summary presentation of such theories and models or of the sometimes quite virulent controversies opposing one to the other. Our goal is simply to call attention to certain attitudes one is liable to entertain with regard to psychological theories in general.

One attitude we will not bother to discuss is one which one might call that of the *nihilists* or anarchists; these, out of a laudable concern to distrust premature theorizing, show a superior disdain for any kind of theory, devoting themselves wisely to a scrupulous accumulation of facts that are more and more well controlled. As much as one has to recognize that a rich harvest of facts is essential to the construction of any theory, as much has it become self-evident to recall the "caveats," to which Guthrie (1946) called attention 35 years ago in discussing the relations between facts and psychological theories:

> Collections of facts are not science.... They are only the raw material of science and sometimes they are not even that. (P. 2)

> Unless the beads of fact can be strung in order and pattern on the threads of a theory, there is a strict limitation upon imparting psychological knowledge to others.... Theories are the basis of working concepts. They enable men to confront new facts and deal with them successfully.... Theories are required to direct the search for relevant facts. It is theories that endure, not facts.... Facts are likely to be local and temporary. (Pp. 3–4)

About 20 years later, in a study concerned with the epistemology of psychology, Gréco (1967) expressed approximately the same idea but insisted that the possibility of being proved wrong by the facts is a necessary requirement in any scientific endeavor.

> A fact cannot prove anything, to be sure, and a thousand facts only make a chronicle; but a fact can disprove, and any assertion not being capable of being disproved by facts is not a scientific statement. (P. 985)

In sum, although it is necessary to collect facts in order to construct and to test theories, it is just as essential to go beyond facts: science cannot be reduced to a series of facts anymore than history can be reduced to a collection of events.

Aside from these nihilists who despise theories, we find a multitude of *eclectics* who, out of a natural (or acquired) disdain against enrolling themselves under some particular banner, adopt one or the other of the following two attitudes, which are more reassuring: (*a*) either an abstentionist attitude of theory sampling (the academic equivalent of the popular window shopping), with which one glides from one theory to the next with the sole purpose of finding in it an opportunity to research a new fact or to control an old one, but without having any noticeable effect on the theory, by either weakening, proving, or modifying it; (*b*) or a more positive attitude of concordism, inspired by a generous concern with trying to conciliate opposing theories, but which is potentially fruitful only to the extent that these efforts at conciliation can go beyond a simple move to bring the parties together or beyond a superficial mixing (as in a badly tossed salad), to arrive at a real integration, the possible source of a new, more comprehensive theory.

At the other extreme from these eclectic attitudes, one must mention the determined *followers* and *partisans* of a specific system or theory, who possess varying degress of enthusiasm or devotion which may at times take the form of outright sectarianism and even fanaticism.[1] The apologetic zeal with which they defend their cult can make them completely inaccessible to any kind of opposition, to the extent that they become incapable of perceiving contrary facts or theories, if not to try to reduce or transpose them into their own language; because of this, they may even become past-oriented at the risk of not seeing their own theory or system evolve, the system of which they have made themselves exegetes, and so they lock themselves in a closed circle. The natural reaction to these forms of dogmatism is one of systematic distrust, which may in turn pave the way for all kinds of counterattitudes, which, again, can be more or less enlightened or dogmatic: there are the professional skeptics, who take it as a point of honor to question any theory or system perceived as too encroaching or too monolithic; there are the iconoclasts who embark upon a crusade against the cult of idols, dedicating an enormous amount of time and often talent to the demolition of a theory without really substituting another one; there are the Don Quixotes, endowed with a fighting spirit that is somewhat more chivalrous than perceptive, who tend to deform and caricature unconsciously the theory or system to be attacked, after which they blissfully go about demolishing windmills, stab their enemy straw man, or run in open gates; etc. These different martial adventures, stimulating as they may be, seem to us at once too simple, too ambiguous, and not necessarily progressive; often they do not fit the theory, as it is usually possible to find facts that are difficult to reconcile with an existing theory. After all, a theory is never a static system but an open one that is in constant evolution and that has to meet ever new challenges in the form of facts becoming accessible that are contrary to the predictions made by the theory or otherwise novel-demanding integration and consequently a reformulation of the theory.

1. It does not take a great deal of shrewdness to discern the position reserved for the present author in this gallery.

Our gallery would certainly be incomplete if we neglect to re-serve at least a small place to those one might call the *prophets of death* and the *surgeons*. The former have a habit of announcing or predicting with fanfare the imminent death of a theory they con-sider the victim of an unrelenting disease, a diagnosis often based on extremely debatable interpretations of the target theory; thus, they tend to overlook the fact that a theory is in a constant state of elaboration, that a fact or several facts can disconfirm it without necessarily killing it and, most important, that a theory cannot be replaced except by another one. If the diagnosis appears as less pessimistic and somewhat more discriminating, the prophet of death will readily change into a plastic surgeon, who goes im-mediately ahead with amputating the organ (concept, postulate, etc.) seen as beyond cure, not heeding the risk of defiguring the theory or of leaving it forever infirm; or else, he proceeds to selective transplants designed to save the patient. These grafts can be and often are quite beneficial, under the condition that they do not replace the excised part by one that is even more vulnerable.

Divergence and Convergence of the Cognitivist and the Behaviorist Perspectives

The somewhat caricaturistic description just given, purpose-fully limited to certain extreme, but current attitudes—and also purposefully sketched in anonymous terms to leave it to the sym-pathetic reader to have the freedom and perhaps the pleasure to personalize it—should in no way arouse any kind of pessimism. No doubt it is correct to see in this diversity an expression of a normal process instrumental in the development of psychological theories and the price to be paid for progress in science. One should guard even more strongly against the idea that the less than shiny image just conveyed is more appropriate to either one of the two general perspectives (cognitivism and behaviorism) present today: both have led to the development of a great variety of theories and models toward which all and any of the attitudes just described remain possible.

Next, consider the two general perspectives, not to establish their respective validity but to try to recall the various attempts made in the past to reconcile the two approaches in spite of what inevitably sets them apart.

The Necessary Clash. The opposition between what I have chosen to call "behaviorism" and "cognitivism" is inevitable, since the two perspectives refer, in fact, to two different ways to view reality, or, if you wish, to two different paradigms, which radically determine—irrespective of the particular theories that might or might not be constructed or adopted—the methods to be used in the observation of facts, the type of definition used to describe its concepts and constructs, and the level of explication at which one situates one's interpretations and theoretical elaborations. To the extent that one remains exclusively within a single paradigm, it is obvious that the internal processes and the mental structures invoked by the cognitivist are considered superfluous and tautological by the behaviorist as long as the former is unable to demonstrate their existence to the satisfaction of the latter (i.e., independent of the observable behavior), particularly if the latter believes, correctly or incorrectly, that the former invests these processes with the power to "generate" or to "cause" the behavior. Hence the inevitable clash between the two, where the interchanges easily turn into conversations between deaf-mutes, where each caricatures the other as best he can, and where, in the end, one winds up with massive mutual condemnations; to cite the amusing expression of Richelle's (1976, p. 293), Piaget gladly relegates Skinner to "the limbo of empiricism," while Skinner, in turn, leaves Piaget to the "hell of mentalism."

As an example, one might take Skinner's recent (1977a) anticognitivist declaration of faith, in which he systematically accuses the cognitivists (*a*) of having internalized the reinforcement contingencies in the form of cognitive processes, such as associations, abstraction, etc., which he calls useless inventions with no more explanatory power than the reinforcement contingencies after which these processes are modeled; (*b*) of having invented cognitive causes for behavior in the form of cognitive or mentalistic entities and terms, such as thought, volition, sentiments, free will, intentions, etc., which are nothing more than synonyms for behavior (overt or covert) having no more causative value than the history of reinforcements which shaped these behaviors; and (*c*) of having internalized the environment itself in the form of internal substitutes of the external world such as mental representation (instead of sticking to behavior itself in the real world), knowledge acquired by the processes of encoding, storing and retrieval of information (to designate simply the repertory of behaviors, the modification performed upon the control exercised by stimuli, etc.), rules or strategies governing behavior (to designate the effects observable and directly caused by the reinforcement contingencies), etc. For Skinner, who manipulates Occam's razor with utmost but somewhat dangerous dexterity, the "mental apparatus invented" by the cognitivists is nothing but a useless metaphor, since, although no one will doubt that behavior involves internal processes,[2] these processes cannot be known by themselves but only through behavior (overt or covert), upon which they are traced and through which they are expressed. It is hardly surprising that a scientific approach as radical as this—where the economy with respect to inferences is perhaps analogous to the minimal art movement in contemporary painting—should have aroused open controversies that were sometimes quite animated. Let us only mention Chomsky's virulent attacks (e.g., 1959, 1972), Koch's (1976) extremely sharp criticism of Skinner's book (1974) on behaviorism, and the somewhat less emotional but no less significant dispute recently engaged between Skinner and Herrnstein, his former student and present colleague, concerning the evolution of behaviorism (Herrnstein 1977a, 1977b; Skinner 1977b).

In the absence of the royal match Piaget-Skinner, which one might have been able to witness if the two had not decided to ignore one another, we can at least report on a few debates between cognitivists and behaviorists which are perhaps somewhat less spectacular but still very instructive. One exchange is that between Newell (1969) responding as a cognitivist to Bourne's (1969) radically behaviorist stance on the conceptualization of thought and concept learning. As the reader will certainly recall, Bourne vigorously guards against any interpretation postulating underlying internal processes (e.g., intermediate stimuli and responses, symbolic analogues, hypotheses) said to precede observable behavior and whose function it is to generate, regulate, and to determine this behavior.[3] For Bourne—as for any more or

2. "No one doubts that behavior involves internal processes; the question is how well they can be known by introspection" (Skinner 1977a, pp. 9–10).

3. Bourne (1969) admits that he does "not deny the reality of certain private experiences or events such as subvocal speech and visual images" (p. 172); to the extent that thinking is limited to this kind of latent activity, it becomes for him a behavior on a par with other kinds of behavior. And, obviously, he denies that such activities, or any other hypothetical internal action, could direct or regulate behavior.

less stubborn behaviorist[4]—any theory making reference to such internal processes can be contested on the grounds that the only definition one could, and in fact does, give to these processes is in terms of behavior, which reduces them to behaviors (explicit or implicit) which can be observed from the outside, except for the fact that they have presumably passed "underground." One can easily, if one is so inclined, construct theoretical models capable of exact descriptions of behaviors and even capable of predicting them by deriving from them systems of rules or strategies which they follow; but nothing is gained by then asking oneself by which "psychological processes" or by what internal mechanisms the subject comes to adopt such rules and strategies. It is one thing to describe behavior in terms of processes, it is quite another thing to describe processes that presumably control behavior. Thus, it is behavior itself that should be considered a process following certain rules.[5] In sum, Bourne concludes, there are internal physiological processes one might hope to eventually relate to the external processes of behavior; but if there is no good reason to think that the former cause the latter, there is even less justification to think that there are additional internal, psychological processes mediating between the others, so long as one has not been able to demonstrate their existence by observations independent of the behavior itself. Newell's reply to this tightly argued case is not without cleverness. First, he notes certain concessions made by Bourne (e.g., that he grants "permission" to translate behavior into a system of complex rules), and he grants to any behaviorist the right—given that any theoretical explanation is always incomplete, since the elements introduced at one level for the sake of explaining phenomena observed at a lower level always need to be explained independently of those phenomena—to stick to the most obvious level by simply describing observed behaviors without pushing further the search for explanatory factors. Next, using examples taken from the history of the physical and biological sciences, Newell attempts to show that it is advantageous

4. See the excellent document written by Bélanger (1978) on the image and the reality of behaviorism.

5. "The rules are principles of behavior, not principles of a mechanism which in turn produces behavior" (Bourne 1969, p. 175). "*It is a process description of behavior, rather than a description of a process* presumed to control behavior" (p. 190).

not to limit oneself to observe and then describe the regularity of phenomena observed but to search for the mechanisms underlying this regularity. There is no reason to think that it should be otherwise in psychology. Just as the search for mechanisms or physiological processes was able to contribute toward an explanation of certain complex aspects of behavior—which one also might have chosen to simply note—in the same way the search for a theoretical model including a structured set of internal processes underlying a certain behavior presents the undeniable advantage not only of proposing a sufficient explanation—if not a necessary one—of certain (sometimes unexpected) particularities of behavior but also of leading eventually to an increasingly comprehensive theory of behavior, through generalizing certain components of the model to novel experimental situations, or through systematic attempts to verify certain deductions made from the model. Newell rightly fears that his arguments and examples are insufficient to convince Bourne, and he concludes by evoking the distinction between two kinds of theory: those that postulate processes ("process theories"), and those that do without. According to the distinction, which seems much less verbalistic than that made by Bourne in describing behavior in terms of processes (which he accepts), and describing processes that control behavior (which he rejects), Newell thinks that the process theories, in contrast to the other kind such as operant conditioning, aim at describing what happens between stimulus and the behavior following it by invoking psychological processes attributed to the subject (such as the processes of encoding, etc., invoked by information theory). At the same time, he specifies that such models and theories, whose heuristic value seems to me to be indisputable, (1) do not require measuring anything other than behavior itself, on the basis of which the processes can then be inferred; (2) are, strictly speaking, unnecessary, since it is always possible to simply stop at the observation of behavioral regularities, even though it is Newell's opinion that a contemporary use of Occam's razor would rather lead us to consider this rejection of all internal processes itself as excess baggage; and (3) may one day become a simple mirror image of physiological mechanisms, if the progress made in the accumulation of physiological knowledge comes to confirm the theoretical models or demands their completion or reformulation. This last remark evokes in some way the particular form of parallelism or isomorphism that Piaget (1950c, 1957, [1967b] 1968) has chosen to adopt, but in the interest of "prudence and maximal reduction of hypotheses" (1950c, p. 161) between the physiological and the consciousness domains, rejecting, however, any kind of interactionist interpretation and recognizing that "the genetic psychology of behaviors proposes nothing less than to relate the two extreme terms, between which psychology oscillates, that is, biology and logic" (1950c, p. 161). But this form of parallelism, which asserts a fundamental difference between two modes of connections—one that is based on physical *causality* for interrelating physiological processes, and another based on psychological *implication* to interrelate the processes of consciousness—is distinct at once from the simple kind of parallelism between physiology and behavior which most behaviorists (including Bourne, it seems) would be prepared to accept while also denying any kind of intermediate psychological process, and different also from the kind of parallelism between physiological and psychological processes, which most cognitivists (including Newell, it seems) would be prepared to accept as parallelism, in which the latter are only a simple reflection of the former. However that may be, it is obvious that the interchange between Bourne and Newell has left each holding to his positions as far as the question of the reality, the nature, the role, and the autonomy of internal psychological processes invoked by cognitivism is concerned.

A Problematical Conciliation. Even though the ideological clashes, of which we just saw a topical example, sometimes produce the effect of hardening the positions involved, they may also be quite useful sometimes by forcing the antagonists to better define and to introduce more precision into their respective positions. For example, radical behaviorism may often be led to enlarge its perspective to include phenomena previously swept under the rug, and to put greater emphasis on the subject's activity as such in order to fend off accusations of empiricism of which it is frequently made the target. Cognitivism, in turn, makes efforts to define its internal psychological processes (that are not directly observable) in terms of behavior to guard against accusations of mentalism, of which it is often the target, and to make its methods of observation and experimenting more objective, in order to avoid getting lost in the maze of interpretations based on doubtful data of introspection, no longer acceptable, or based upon fragile inferences from facts collected by methods that are no less fragile. In spite of these mutual benefits that sometimes result from their antagonism, the cognitivism and the behaviorism remain basically unchanged and incommensurable. They fiercely resist all efforts at conciliation or integration, as might have been attempted in the past and are still being attempted from time to time. Even if these efforts are not all equally promising, it is clear that they are at once preferable to the mutual ignorance, vitriolic attacks, or the dialogues of deaf-mutes to which we have become accustomed.

It is not our aim, in this place, to present the entire range of such attempts at conciliation; however, we can at least stop to show, by means of a variety of examples, the illusory character and the relative sterility of some of these efforts. The most obvious cases are those where the concessions made on either side boil down to nothing but verbal tributes without any real atter¡pt at conciliation. For example, if it does happen that Piaget makes use of, or reference to, terms currently employed by behaviorists (e.g., stimulus, response, association, reinforcement), he does so mostly to deprive them of their original significance and scope by reinterpreting them within the context of his cognitivist position, where of necessity internal processes such as assimilation, accommodation, equilibration, etc. come up. Once, he even went so far as to utter a curious declaration of "behaviorist" faith, paradoxical as that may be, when he wrote:

A developmental psychology of intelligence . . . cannot be other than behaviorist, for two reasons. From the point of view of interpretation . . . it is constantly forced to translate thought into operational terms and to think of these operations as internalized actions . . . so that it finds itself in the best tradition of pragmatic behaviorism. But, in addition, the developmental psychology of intelligence cannot be but behaviorist by its very method, because, if it is true that adults' introspections yield rather questionable results, when compared to those obtained by an analysis of their actual behaviors in problem solving, then it is even more true in the case of children: practically no confidence at all can be placed in child intro- or retrospection. (1957, pp. 77–78)

Piaget would no doubt be the first to recognize that the sense
assigned to the term "behaviorist" in this text is very far removed
from that given to it by radical behaviorists, when they charge
cognitivists with having invented the internal psychological processes and to have made them into the subject matter of their
science. However, when taking the etymological and most currently used sense of the word "behaviorist," one will hardly find
anyone today who would dispute that psychology is the science of
behavior; no one today, or practically no one, believes that internal psychological processes are directly observable or that introspection is the method par excellence in psychology, unless
one is an enthusiastic supporter of phenomenology, or even of
solipsism or clairvoyance. In all justice to Piaget, it must be added
that this form of verbal tribute sometimes gets paid back. When
Skinner (1977a), for example, states that "no one doubts that
behavior involves internal processes; the question is how well
they can be known through introspection" (pp. 9–10), he makes a
concession to cognitivism that is more verbal than real and, actually, quite trivial: more verbal than real, since this concession
does not prevent Skinner from declaring that the "mental apparatus" of the cognitivists is only a "metaphor" and that cognitivists "invent internal surrogates, which become the subject
matter of their science" (p. 1); rather trivial, too, since Piaget (as
much as any cognitivist) never believed that physiological processes can be open to introspection, and he is the first to acknowledge that internal cognitive processes must be inferred
from behavior and that the awareness one may have of these
cognitive schemata is only possible through actions one performs
on objects (see discussion of this point in Chap. 3).

These purely verbal attempts at narrowing the gap just discussed can be compared to certain efforts deployed by some cognitivists or behaviorists in order to translate into terms more acceptable to their position the concepts and processes invoked in
the other perspective. It hardly seems necessary, for example, to
remind the reader of the exercises regularly performed by Skinner
(e.g., 1974, 1977a) to provide systematic reinterpretations in
terms of the behaviorist perspective, that is, to divest them of all
reference to internal processes apt to explain or control external
behavior, reinterpretations of such notions and constructs as attention, decision, intention, abstraction, inference, etc., which

are habitually invoked by cognitivists. For those interested in narrowing the gap between cognitivism and behaviorism, these kinds of exercises are not without interest, at least for the sake of the greater precision and detail they require each side to contribute to his own position, but they appear just as sterile as the verbal concessions mentioned above. This form of reductionism, where it is not itself reduced to simple verbal behaviors—as Koch (1976) somewhat mischievously suggests—or where it is not assimilated to the legendary bed of Procrustes upon which one strives to force, by all means, processes that are extremely heterogeneous both as to content and as to functioning, cannot but harden the opponent positions instead of bringing them closer together, and really succeeds in convincing no one aside from the followers and believers already won to behaviorism. Another illustration of the utter vanity of these retranslations is finely given in the opposite exercise already performed by Brewer (1974), when he tried to show that behaviorism cannot explain even a very "simple behavior" (p. 1) such as conditioning (classical or operant) in human subjects. From an exhaustive review of the literature on experiments designed to dissociate "conditioning theory" from "cognitive theory" in the domain of conditioning of autonomous responses, motor responses, complex responses (semantic generalization, semantic conditioning, verbal operant conditioning), Brewer derives (p. 27) the following conclusions: (1) "conditioning in the human learning literature is due to the operation of higher mental processes," that is, the subject becomes aware of the relation between the conditioned and the unconditioned stimulus, in the case of classical conditioning, and begins to understand the reinforcement contingencies in the case of operant conditioning; (2) in spite of certain indications in favor of automatic and unconscious processes in the older literature, the more recent methodological advances in this field suggest rather that "there is not and never has been any convincing evidence for unconscious, automatic mechanisms in the conditioning of adult human beings." Dulany (1974), himself a cognitivist, comments on Brewer's thesis with remarkable finesse and intelligent criticism. Dulany argues that the experiments cited by Brewer do not furnish any crucial support in favor of cognitivism against behaviorism but only show that the cognitivist perspective is just as plausible as the behaviorist, and not less plausible, as was always assumed. In justification of his position, Dulany then executes a counterexercise, in which—without changing the nature of conditioning theory and without disputing cognitive methods—he retranslates into behaviorist terms the interpretations made by Brewer in his critical review, adding some auxiliary postulates (internal conditioning, facilitation and inhibition of conditioning, conditioning of verbal report, etc.) no less explicit or plausible than the postulates of the cognitivist variety. Finally, Dulany concludes (1) that the two theories are incommensurable and can each predict and explain the same phenomena; (2) that the explanations offered by cognitivist theory rest on only one hypothetical state, that of awareness, which hardly endows it with greater competitiveness and credibility; and (3) that cognitive theory will not be competitive as long as it does not have at its disposal a rich variety of cognitive variables, and as long as it does not devise experimental models that are sufficiently complex to be able to test an equally rich network of predictions concerning these variables. Such pessimistic conclusions may perhaps be justified in the particular case examined by Brewer and Dulany; but one should not overlook the fact that cognitivism has already inspired, and continues to do so, several theoretical and experimental models of considerable complexity. However this may be, it remains true that it is always possible to translate behaviorism into cognitivism and vice versa, but that attempts at conciliation based on such retranslations always turn out to be rather sterile.

To give an example of a concession made by either cognitivist or behaviorist that is less purely verbal, one might think of Berlyne's (1960, see also 1965) effort to achieve a synthesis, made nearly 20 years ago, between Piaget's and Hull's theories. To be sure, Hull's theory of learning, as well as Berlyne's own position, has little in common with the kind of radical behaviorism just discussed, since it postulates a whole complex arsenal of internal processes in the form of hypothetical constructs; however, it is interesting to cite Berlyne's attempt to reconcile, within a neo-Hullian paradigm, the kind of stimulus-respoonse theory elaborated by Hull and Piaget's theory of cognitive operations. First, Berlyne considers it necessary to apply certain "radical modifications" (p. 46) to Hull's theory for the sake of "achieving a very desirable synthesis that combines the advantages" (p. 45) of

Hull's and Piaget's theories. Specifically, Berlyne suggests the following four additions or innovations: (*a*) "insert between the representations of the stimulus situations representations of transformations that lead from one situation to the next" (p. 46), to account for the fact, suggested by Piaget's theory, that the essential responses of directive thinking are transformations, that is, "responses that effect the change of what has preceded into what follows" (ibid.); (*b*) proceed to a more thorough theoretical and experimental analysis of the notion stimulus-response generalization, mentioned in Hull's theory but not sufficiently exploited, to accommodate the observations deriving from the Gestalt theory concerning the activity of transposition between two situations having the same structure but different content; (*c*) reinterpret Hull's hierarchical habit families by showing that, after the modifications just described in *a* and *b*, one can attribute to the hierarchical habit families the properties that characterize groups and grouping structures, as exploited in Piaget's theory (composition, associativity, inversion, identity); (*d*) integrate within Hull's theory factors of motivation or internal reinforcement (such as attention, curiosity, vigilance, etc., which govern the subject's selective activity in learning and the importance to be attached, in learning, to the conflict aroused by mutually incompatible responses, by uncertainty, surprise, etc.), to account for the fact, many times stressed by Piaget, that behavior is caused not only by physical or social stimulations coming from the environment or by physiological instances. It is easy to see why this form of conciliation was so well received by Piaget (1960), who did not fail to notice the support lent to his own system by the modifications to Hull's theory introduced by Berlyne, but who insisted in qualifying these modifications to make them fit even better with his own positions. For example, he readily accepts the notion of transformational responses, introduced by Berlyne, since this notion evokes directly the internalized actions and operations essential to his own system. But to make sure that the transformations are attributable to the subject (and not to the object itself), he specifies that these transformational responses should not be only copies of external transformations "but responses which relate one response copy to the following one by interposing a transformation that is not a copy, but carried out (in real or internalized action) so that the copy responses become themselves modified'' (p. 110). Similarly, he is pleased to find more attention paid to the notion of stimulus-response generalization, which Hull had only noted but not developed further, because of the fact that this notion and the emphasis placed on it underscore the importance of the processes of assimilation involved in this form of generalization. However, Piaget does not follow the gestaltist interpretation, which Berlyne accepts, of the transposition phenomena illustrating the stimulus-response generalization, because the notion of insight leaves the subject too much in the role of passive spectator rather than that of active assimilator of new situations to a preconstructed schema. Finally, when Berlyne stresses the importance of internal motivation generated by factors such as conflict, curiosity, uncertainty, etc., Piaget at once assimilates this to his own idea of equilibration (and reequilibration) operative in the process of what he calls learning in the wider sense, in which the role of experience implicated in learning in the strict sense is combined with the internal equilibration process. In all, it must be said that the conciliation proposed by Berlyne between Hullian and Piagetian theory, in spite of certain merits, has remained quite unproductive and hardly had any real impact, not only because Hull's theory is becoming less and less current but mainly because what Berlyne achieved is not so much a true synthesis between two different approaches but rather a kind of metamorphosis which radically changes Hull's system into a new one, assuming all the fees of the operation with absolutely no charge to Piaget's system.

To give a somewhat more positive example and a more promising one of a possible conciliation between behaviorism and cognitivism, one where it is at least possible to see the beginnings of a certain integration of perspectives, one might note the current theory of social development in the form it has progressively received by Bandura (1969, 1972, 1974) and Aronfreed (1969a, 1969b, 1972). This theory, as is well known, takes imitation to be the principal mechanism responsible for social learning, with operant conditioning becoming an auxiliary mechanism, even though a necessary one, with respect to imitation. Thus, as is discussed at length by Kuhn (1978) in her remarkable study on the mechanisms of cognitive and social development, Bandura and Aronfreed already had begun 10 years ago to recognize the neces-

sity of having intermediate processes (attending to a model, encoding and storing representations of external stimuli, mental re-
hearsals of these representations, etc.) between external stimuli
and responses in the acquisition of social behaviors. However,
this first real concession to cognitivism is still quite timid and
cautious, since Bandura and Aronfreed take care to specify that
their internal processes are not, strictly speaking, inferred from
behavior but simply related to external stimuli, of which they are,
in the final analysis, only internal copies without exerting any real
influence upon behavior. This limitation imposed explicitly upon
the role of these internal processes has for a long time, as was
underscored by Kuhn, kept these loans taken from cognitive information theory quite void of any real cognitivist content, because of the total absence of a theoretical conception for explaining the selection of stimuli, the mechanism of encoding and
conservation of external stimuli, the nature and mode of functioning of these internal representations, etc. Even though it is
true that Bandura, in a more recent formulation of his views on
social development (1974), has begun to abandon this way of
conceiving internal cognitive processes only in a figurative
mode—to use a distinction made by Piaget between a figurative
and an operative mode of knowing—and no longer is reluctant to
acknowledge that these processes can have a causal, determina-
tive inflluence on behavior (e.g., relating stimuli to responses,
internal self-regulations oriented by personal needs and personal
valuation, selective action upon the environment), Kuhn is right
in estimating that the theory of social learning is not really in a
position to increase its explanatory power, unless it can give itself
a formal structure sufficiently elaborated to define, with some
precision, the mode of organization and functioning of these
intermediate cognitive processes that the theory now accepts. In
spite of these limitations and reservations, it seems that this
theory of social development, derived essentially from a behaviorist perspective, even if it is not in the process of becoming
radically transformed into a cognitivist theory, represents at least
a definite effort at narrowing the distance between the behaviorist
and cognitivist perspectives.

To conclude these rather lengthy considerations concerning the
inevitable confrontation and the problematical reconciliation
between behaviorism and cognitivism, one can note, first, that

cognitivism has less and less reason to fear the positivist inter-
dictions of radical behaviorism. As Haugeland (1978) has been
concerned to show, the contemporary cognitivist perspective is
scientifically no less plausible than the behaviorist perspective: it
has its own credentials (its own explanatory style, an empirically
verifiable method of interpreting cognitive processes, etc.) just
like the behaviorist perspective from which it originated and developed. Thus both can be taken as equally rigorous and experimental.[6] In a systematic comparison between Skinnerian behaviorism and Piagetian constructivism, presented by Richelle
(1976), it is emphasized, and rightly so, that there has always been
a greater tendency to point to the fundamental differences
separating the two systems rather than to certain more general
analogies (e.g., the interest in learning and development, attach-
ing the key concepts to processes and mechanisms of biological
origin, overcoming the dichotomy of innate versus acquired), or
to even more profound commonalities (e.g., the primacy of action
in the analysis of behaviors, the prime importance attributed to
the origins of changes in both ontogenetic and phylogenetic evolution), which are quite easy to perceive, between behaviorism
and constructivism. Yet, it is also obvious that these analogies
and commonalities are not sufficient to mask the fundamental
differences separating the two approaches and upon which we
have dwelled for some time. Aside from the fact that these commonalities may easily invite some form of more or less superficial
concordism—it is certainly not enough to speak of behavior and
experience in order to become behaviorist or empiricist, nor does
it suffice to speak of structures or internal processes in order to
become a structuralist or cognitivist—they appear to us useful in
helping to dissipate certain fundamental ambiguities as well as to
discard many pseudoproblems and sterile discussions. But they

6. "Cognitivism is a natural development from Behaviorism. It retains the same
commitment to publicly observable and verifiable data, the same rejection of
posits and postulates that cannot be treated experimentally, and the same ideal of
psychology as a natural science. Its advantage is having shown, via the system-
aticity and intentional interpretation 'cornerstones,' how to make good empirical
sense of meaningful or rational internal processes—which gives it a much richer
and more powerful explanatory framework. And not surprisingly it has now acquired the institutional earmarks of an advance and thriving science" (Haugeland
1978, p. 225).

cannot provide the ground for any hopes of real integration of two so radically different opposing paradigms.

This settled, one might next ask, What can be predicted and hoped, for the present opposition of behaviorism and cognitivism, for the future of developmental psychology? One might either wish for the arrival of a radically new paradigm that could, so to speak, dissolve the incompatibility inherent in the present ones, or one could admit this incompatibility, while acknowledging that both are legitimate and complementary to each other. It is certainly true that there is nothing sacred and immutable about a paradigm, as was pointed our recently by Haugeland (1978), and the former solution constitutes in principle an exciting possibility; yet the chances for its realization actually appear quite meager. If one takes the creation of a new paradigm to mean the arrival of an entirely novel perspective or way to view reality, that is, an approach that is really revolutionary by its mode of defining and observing behavior, its level of interpretation of reality, its way of conceiving of the problems of interaction between subject and object in development, the antinomy of innate versus empirical, the relations between cognition and affectivity, etc., then this kind of undertaking would still be quite laden with perils, and its realization would be extremely problematical. The history of science in general, and of psychology in particular, indicates persuasively that the advent of a new paradigm is always the fruit of a long maturation, provoked most often by a dissatisfaction with paradigms recognized until then. It is, however, interesting to mention in this connection the attempt made recently by Kuhn (1978) to formulate the elements of a new model in the particular domain of social cognition, in an effort to integrate social and cognitive development in the child. Having shown that neither the "mechanistic" model of the social learning theorists, because of the too-passive role assigned by them to the subject, nor the "organismic" model of developmental theorists of the cognitivist persuasion, because of its lack of information concerning the specific environmental context in which development takes place, are sufficiently well articulated to make up for their respective shortcomings, Kuhn indicates the desire for a new model—a "complete" model—which would incorporate those elements that are valid in each system and would add another dynamic twin element: the constant interaction between cognitive and social influences in the developmental process, and the integration of the structural and the affective or energetic aspects within psychological functioning. Laudable and promising as Kuhn's suggestion may be, it is evident that we are still quite far removed from a new paradigm. Even in the rather vague and general formulation in which it appears, given the limits imposed upon a journal article, Kuhn's model remains largely a prisoner of existing models, by acknowledging that neither model is presently capable of making up for the deficiencies of the other and by adding a highly valuable dynamic parameter. Unfortunately, it is hard to see how, in reality, Kuhn's model can be concretely defined and materialized. The chances of seeing a radically new paradigm make its appearance remain quite small as long as one tries to seek an integration within a single model—with no internal contradiction or superficial varnishing—of two paradigms as diametrically opposed as behaviorism and cognitivism on issues as essential as the question of ontological or mere metaphoric reality of internal psychological processes apt to exercise a determining influence on behavior, the relative contribution, in the formation of behavior, of the subject's active resources as against that of environmental agencies, etc.

For this reason, and while waiting for that prestigious magician who is able to construct a new paradigm capable of rallying the ever-increasing number of researchers that are dissatisfied with the present paradigms, it seems that one will have to settle for the second solution, which consists in accepting the fact that cognitivism and behaviorism—at least in their most radical forms—are two absolutely irreducible and incommensurable models; but then, if one wants the parallel paths followed by the two paradigms to contribute positively to the progress in child development research as both become still better defined and differentiated, it seems obvious that this cannot happen unless each recognizes the other's legitimate status, its truly complementary role, and also recognizes the diversity of theories that each is apt to generate. Such a positive attitude seems to us more fruitful than the reciprocal state of mutual ignorance into which one is apt to retreat, to the more or less virulent controversies one has to witness all too often, and even the superficial mutual conciliations or compromises that tend to be proposed out of an otherwise quite commendable concern for conciliation.

Recognizing the legitimacy of a different paradigm does not mean to indicate one's agreement and, even less, to renounce one's own paradigm. For example, the cognitivist may well consider the behaviorist as being affected by some kind of myopia, as far as his scientific perspective is concerned; but, if he reserves himself the right—to paraphrase Newell (1969)—to push one's research further, the cognitivist may still remain conscious of the fact that such extensions be considered unnecessary. And instead of making idle allegations of automatism, robotologism, etc., against the behaviorist, he might benefit from the admonitions and caveats that the latter never fails to call to his attention, notably with respect to the pitfalls of mentalism, the neglect of environmental factors, the objectivity of his observational techniques, the validity of his inferences, etc. Inversely, the behaviorist may very well be of the opinion that the perspective adopted by the cognitivist suffers from a form of presbyopia; but even if he denies himself the right to go beyond the limits of the observable, he should at least recognize that it is not a ridiculous endeavor to want to pursue one's research beyond those limits that necessarily deserves the massive accusations of mentalism of metaphoricalness often leveled against the cognitivist by the behaviorist, who could only gain by telling himself, in a positive way, that there are dangers in reductionism, verbalism, or passivism, of which the cognitivist is always ready to warn him.

In order to recognize, on the other hand, the true state of complementarity of these two paradigms, it is first necessary to see, as is aptly pointed out by Kuhn (1978), that a paradigm is neither true nor false in itself but rather just a useful means to interpret reality. Further, one has to admit that both cognitivism and behaviorism have, in spite of their deep division, contributed substantially to the science of psychology. But then, we also hope to avoid systematic concordism or eclecticism and, above all, to make the two incommensurable perspectives commensurable; one should recognize, at least, that behaviorism, for one, has greatly contributed, through its systematic rejection of the outdated forms of the introspective method, and by its ingenious and varied techniques of conditioning, to the objectivity of the methods for observing and analyzing behavior and to the efficiency of the methods to control behavior. By applying its principal efforts to factors directly accessible to psychological intervention—that

is, environmental agents and control of external reinforcements—behaviorism has been able to offer to society new kinds
of services or, at least, a much wider range of services than before, particularly in the clinical and educational fields (behavioral
therapy. programmed instruction in the schools, etc.). On the
other hand, it would be unseemly not to recognize that cognitivism—by insisting on the essential role that certain internal cognitive processes play in behavior and by the ingenuity of the
various techniques used to specify, in an empirically verifiable
fashion, the nature and the functioning of these internal
processes—is capable of leading to more extended and more comprehensive explanations of behavior and of the mechanisms involved in behavior than would be the case if one would, in principle, decide to limit oneself to a simple descriptive and functional
analysis of behavior and its modifications.

Finally, even though it is true that neither behaviorism nor
cognitivism are theories in themselves, so that neither can be
either true or false in itself, it is very clear that either one of the
two paradigms—unless one wishes to adopt a stance of systematic distrust against psychological theories in order to stick
scrupulously to the observation of facts—can provide a frame of
reference for a great variety of theories, which are likely to be
opposed to or, in some cases, complement each other. It would
then be up to the individual researcher to examine the validity and
scope of the theories, as long as these satisfy the essential criterion of being empirically testable and falsifiable. Within the cognitivist perspective, for example, there are already quite a variety
of theoretical elaborations (e.g., Piagetian theory and its neo-
Piagetian reformulations, the theories derived from the techniques
of information processing). These are all different from each
other, not only in terms of degree of formalization and generality
but also, and most important, in terms of their particular modes of
conceptualizing the subject's internal representations of the environment (network of stages or schemata, rule systems determining behavior, ordered strategies used in problem solving, etc.).
They also differ in terms of the role assigned to the subject's
constructive activity as against environmental pressures exercised by the physical and the social milieu, and against such factors as hereditary and physiological. Similarly, within the behaviorist perspective, one can easily find a fairly wide range of

theoretical constructions. These may be more or less complex in their composition or their degree of formalization, and they differ from one another in terms of the nature of the mechanisms invoked (conditioning, imitation, etc.) for the development, shaping, and control of behavior, in terms of the way reinforcement contingencies as well as the various types of reinforcement are treated, and even in terms of the degree of radicalism of the behavioral paradigm, with some of the behaviorist theories occasionally admitting certain intervening variables of hypothetical constructs (which have given rise to many controversies concerning the ontological status of these variables and constructs). In sum, to recognize such diversity within each of the two paradigms is one way to gauge the productivity of each, and the confrontation of the theories deriving from each will best serve to reveal their respective insufficiencies and eventually lead the way to the construction of a new paradigm.

Bibliography

Apostel, L.; Jonckeree, A. R.; & Matalon, B. 1959. *Etudes d'épistémologie génétique*. Vol. 8. *Logique, apprentissage et probabilité*. Paris: Presses Universitaires de France.

Apostel, L.; Mandelbrot, B.; & Piaget, J. 1957. *Etudes d'épistémologie génétique*. Vol. 2. *Logique et équilibre*. Paris: Presses Universitaires de France.

Apostel, L.; Mays, W.; Morf, A.; & Piaget, J. 1957. *Etudes d'épistémologie génétique*. Vol. 4. *Les liaisons analytiques et synthétiques dans les comportements du sujet*. Paris: Presses Universitaires de France.

Aronfreed, J. 1969a. The problem of imitation. In L. P. Lipsitt & H. W. Reese (Eds.), *Advances in child development and behavior*. Vol. 4. New York: Academic Press.

Aronfreed, J. 1969b. The concept of internalization. In D. A. Goslin (Ed.), *Handbook of socialization theory and research*. Chicago: Rand McNally.

Aronfreed, J. 1972. A developmental memoir of "social learning theory." In R. D. Parke (Ed.), *Recent trends in social learning theory*. New York: Academic Press.

Bandura, A. 1969. Social learning theory of identificatory processes. In D. A. Goslin (Ed.), *Handbook of socialization theory and research*. Chicago: Rand McNally.

Bandura, A. 1972. Modeling theory. Some traditions, trends and disputes. In R. D. Parke (Ed.), *Recent trends in social learning theory*. New York: Academic Press.

Bandura, A. 1974. Behavior theory and the models of man. *American psychologist*, 29:859–869.

Beilin, H. 1971. The training and acquisition of logical operations. In M. F. Rosskopf, L. P. Streffe, & S. Tabask (Eds.), *Piagetian cognitive developmental research and mathematics education*. Washington: National Council of teachers of mathematics.

Beilin, H. 1978. Inducing conservation through training. In G. Steiner (Ed.), *Psychology of the twentieth century*. Vol. 7. Munich: Kendler. (Published in German only.)

Bélanger, J. 1978. Les images et les réalités du behaviorisme. *Philosophiques* 5 (no. 1):3–110.

Berlyne, D. E. 1960. Les équivalences psychologiques et les notions quantitatives. In D. E. Berlyne & J. Piaget, *Etudes d'épistémologie génétique*. Vol. 12. *Théorie du comportement et operations*. Paris: Presses Universitaires de France.

Berlyne, D. E. 1965. *Structure and direction in thinking*. New York: Wiley.

Berlyne, D. E., & Piaget, J. 1960. *Etudes d'épistémologie génétique*. Vol. 12. *Théorie du comportement et opérations*. Paris: Presses Universitaires de France.

Beth, E. W., & Piaget, J. [1961] 1966. *Mathematical epistemology and psychology*. New York: Gordon & Beach.

Blanchet, A. 1974. La conservation du débit. In J. Piaget, *Etudes d'épistémologie génétique*. Vol. 32. *Recherches sur la contradiction. II. Les relations entre affirmations et négations*. Paris: Presses Universitaires de France.

Botvin, G. J., & Murray, F. B. 1975. The efficacy of peer modeling and social conflict in the acquisition of conservation. *Child development* 46:796–799.

Bourne, L. E., Jr. 1969. Concept learning and thought: behavior, not process. In J. E. Voss (Ed.), *Approaches to thought*. Columbus, Ohio: Merrill.

Bovet, M. 1968. Etudes interculturelles du développement intellectuel et processus d'apprentissage. *Revue suisse de psychologie pure et appliquée* 27:189–199.

Brainerd, C. J. 1972. The age-stage issue in conservation acquisition. *Psychonomic science* 29:115–117.

Brainerd, C. J. 1973a. Judgments and explanations as criteria for the presence of cognitive structures. *Psychological bulletin* 79:172–179.

Brainerd, C. J. 1973b. The stage problem in behavioral development. Unpublished manuscript, University of Alberta.

Brainerd, C. J. 1974. Postmortem on judgments, explanations, and Piagetian cognitive structures. *Psychological bulletin* 81:70–71.

Brainerd, C. J. 1977a. Response criteria in concept development research. *Child development* 48:360–366.

Brainerd, C. J. 1977b. Cognitive development and concept learning: an interpretative review. *Psychological bulletin* 84:919–939.

Brainerd, C. J. 1978a. Un modèle néo-piagétien de l'apprentissage du concept chez l'enfant. *Bulletin de psychologie* 32:509–521.

Brainerd, C. J. 1978b. The stage-question in cognitive-developmental theory. *Behavioral and brain sciences* 2:173–213.

Brainerd, C. J. 1979. Markovian interpretations of conservation learning. *Psychological review* 86: 181–213.

Bresson, F. 1967. Modèles structuraux dans l'étude des comportements cognitifs. In *Les modèles et la formalisation du comportement*. Colloque international du Centre national de la recherche scientifique. Paris: Editions du C.N.R.S.

Bresson, F. 1971. La genèse des propriétés des objets. *Journal de psychologie* 68:143–168.

Brewer, W. F. 1974. There is no evidence for operant or classical conditioning in adult humans. In W. B. Weimer & D. S. Palermo (Eds.), *Cognition and the symbolic processes*. Hillsdale, N.J.: Erlbaum.

Bronfenbrenner, U. 1977. Toward an experimental ecology of human development. *American psychologist* 32:513–531.

Bruner, J. S. 1966. On the conservation of liquids. In J. S. Bruner, R. R. Olver, P. M. Greenfield, et al., *Studies in cognitive growth*. New York: Wiley.

Capon, C., & Kuhn, D. 1979. Logical reasoning in the supermarket: adult females use of a proportional reasoning strategy in an everyday context. *Developmental psychology* 15:450–452.

Case, R. 1974. Mental strategies, mental capacity, and instruction: a neo-Piagetian interpretation. *Journal of experimental child psychology* 18:372–397.

Case, R. 1977. Responsiveness to conservation training as a function of induced subjective uncertainty, M-space and cognitive style. *Canadian journal of behavioral science* 9:12–25.

Case, R. 1978. Intellectual development from birth to adulthood: a neo-Piagetian interpretation. In R. Siegler (Ed.), *Children's thinking: what develops?* Hillsdale, N.J.: Erlbaum.

Cellérier, G. 1979. Structures cognitives et schèmes d'action I. *Archives de psychologie* (Genève) 47:87–106.

Charbonneau, C. 1971. L'influence des aspects figuratifs dans l'acquisition des notions de conservation de substance. Thèse de doctorat inédite, Université de Montréal.

Charbonneau, C., & Robert, M. 1977. Observational learning of quantity conservation in relation to the degree of cognitive conflict. *Psychological reports* 41:975–986.

Charbonneau, C.; Robert, M.; Bourassa, G.; & Gladu-Bissonnette, S. 1976. Observational learning of quantity conservation and Piagetian generalization tasks. *Developmental psychology* 12:211–217.

Charlesworth, W. R. 1978. Ethology: its relevance for observational studies of human adaptation. In G. P. Sackett (Ed.), *Observing behavior*. Vol. 1. *Theory and applications in mental retardation*. Baltimore: University Park Press.

Chomsky, N. 1959. Review of B. F. Skinner, Verbal Behavior. *Language* 25:26–58.

Chomsky, N. 1972. Psychology and ideology. *Cognition* 1:11–46.

Christie, J. F., & Smothergill, D. W. 1970. Discrimination and conservation of length. *Psychonomic science* 21:336–337.

Doré, L. 1979. La dissociation des propriétés physiques de l'objet: son rôle par rapport à la conservation du poids. Thèse de maîtrise inédite, Université de Montréal.

Dulany, D. E. 1974. On the support of cognitive theory in opposition to behavior theory: a methodological problem. In W. B. Weimer & D. S. Palermo (Eds.), *Cognition and the symbolic processes*. Hillsdale, N.J.: Erlbaum.

Elkind, D. 1967. Piaget's conservation problems. *Child development* 38:15–27.

Fortin-Thériault, A. 1977. Comparaison de deux méthodes d'apprentissage par conflit cognitif. Thèse de doctorat inédite, Université de Montréal.

Fortin-Thériault, A., & Laurendeau-Bendavid, M. 1979. Une notion préopératoire de la conservation des quantités. *Bulletin de psychologie* 32:557–564.

Fournier-Chouinard, E. 1967. Un apprentissage de la conservation des quantités par une technique d'exercices opératoires. Thèse de doctorat inédite, Université de Montréal.

Gagné, R. M. 1968. Contributions of learning to human development. *Psychological review* 75:177–191.

Gelman, R. 1969. Conservation acquisition: a problem of learning to attend to relevant attributes. *Journal of experimental child psychology* 7:167–187.

Gelman, R. 1978. Cognitive development. *Annual review of psychology* 29:297–332.

Gillieron, C. 1974. Conservation des longueurs et illusions perceptives. In J. Piaget, *Etudes d'épistémologie génétique*. Vol. 32. *Recherches sur les contradictions. II. les relations entre affirmations et négations*. Paris: Presses Universitaires de France.

Gladstone, R., & Palazzo, R. 1974. Empirical evidence for reversibility by inversion. *Developmental psychology* 10:942–948.

Goustard, M.; Gréco, P.; Matalon, G.; & Piaget, J. 1959. *Etudes d'épistémologie génétique*. Vol. 10. *La logique des apprentissages*. Paris: Presses Universitaires de France.

Gréco, P. 1967. Epistémologie de la psychologie. In J. Piaget (Ed.), *Logique et connaissance scientifique* (Encyclopédie de la Pléiade). Paris: Gallimard.

Gréco, P., & Piaget, J. 1959. *Etudes d'épistémologie génétique*. Vol. 7. *Apprentissage et connaissance*. Paris: Presses Universitaires de France.

Groulx, P. 1974. Apprentissage de la conservation des quantités et apprentissage de la transmission d'égalité des actions de mise en correspondance terme à terme. Thèse de maîtrise inédite, Université de Montréal.

Guthrie, E. R. 1946. Psychological facts and psychological theory. *Psychological bulletin* 43:1–20.

Halford, G. S. 1969. An experimental analysis of the criteria used by children to judge quantities. *Journal of experimental child psychology* 8:314–327.

Halford, G. S. 1970a. A theory of the acquisition of conservation. *Psychological review* 77:302–316.

Halford, G. S. 1970b. A classification learning set which is a possible model for conservation of quantity. *Australian journal of psychology* 22:11–19.

Halford, G.S. 1971. Acquisition of conservation through learning a consistent classificatory system for quantities. *Australian journal of psychology* 23:151–159.

Halford, G. S. 1975. Children's ability to interpret transformations of a quantity. I. An operational system for making judgments based on two witnessed transformations. *Canadian journal of psychology* 29:124–141.

Hauert, C. A. 1980. *Propriétés des objets et propriétés des actions chez l'enfant de deux à cinq ans*. Archives de psychologie (Genève) 48 (monograph no. 7):95–168.

Haugeland, J. 1978. The nature and plausibility of cognitivism. *Behavioral and brain sciences* 2:215–260.

Hebb, D. O. 1968. Concerning imagery. *Psychological review* 75:466–477.

Herrnstein, R. J. 1977a. The evolution of behaviorism. *American psychologist* 32:593–603.

Herrnstein, R. J. 1977b. Doing what comes naturally: a reply to Professor Skinner. *American psychologist* 32:1003–1016.

Hrybyk, M., & Murray, F. B. 1978. Logic in nonconservation: an application of the INRC group. *Genetic epistemologist* 7(no. 2):6.

Inhelder, B., & Piaget, J. [1955] 1958. *The growth of logical thinking from childhood to adolescence: an essay on the construction of formal operational structures*. New York: Basic.

Inhelder, B., & Piaget, J. [1959] 1964. *The early growth of logic in the child: classification and seriation.* New York: Harper & Row.

Inhelder, B., & Piaget, J. 1979. Stratégies. VIII. Procédures et structures. *Archives de psychologie* (Genève) 47:165–176.

Inhelder, B.; Sinclair, H.; & Bovet, M. 1974. *Learning and the development of cognition.* Cambridge: Harvard University Press.

Johnson, P. E., & Murray, F. B. 1970. A note on curriculum models to analyze the child's concept of weight. *Journal of research in science teaching* 7:377–381.

Johnson, W., & Halford, G. S. 1975. Children's ability to interpret transformation of a quantity. II. Judgment and memory for series of one to seven unambiguous transformations. *Canadian journal of psychology* 29:142–150.

Kamii, C., & Derman, L. 1971. Comments on Engelman's paper: the Engelman approach to teaching logical thinking—findings from the administration of some Piagetian tasks. In D. R. Green, M. P. Ford, & G. B. Flamer (Eds.), *Measurement and Piaget.* New York: McGraw-Hill.

Klahr, D., & Wallace, J. G. 1976. *Cognitive development: an information processing view.* Hillsdale, N.J.: Erlbaum.

Koch, S. 1976. More verbal behavior from Dr. Skinner (review of B. F. Skinner's book *About behaviorism,* 1974). *Contemporary psychology* 21:453–457.

Kuhn, D. 1974. Inducing development experimentally: comments on a research paradigm. *Developmental psychology* 10:590–600.

Kuhn, D. 1978. Mechanisms of cognitive and social development: one psychology or two? *Human development* 21:92–118.

Kuhn, D., & Brannock, J. 1977. Development of the isolation of variables schemes in experimental and "natural experiment" contexts. *Developmental psychology* 13:9–14.

Larsen, G. W. 1977. Methodology in developmental psychology: an examination of research on Piagetian theory. *Child development* 48:1160–1166.

Lasry, J. C., & Laurendeau, M. 1969. Apprentissage empirique de la notion d'inclusion. *Human development* 12:141–153.

Laurendeau, M., & Pinard, A. [1962] 1968. *Causal thinking in the child.* New York: International Universities Press.

Laurendeau, M., & Pinard, A. [1968] 1970. *The development of the concept of space in the child.* New York: International Universities Press.

Lefebvre, M. 1973. Influence du niveau initial de développement mental sur l'apprentissage de la conservation par une méthode de conflit cognitif. Thèse de doctorat inédite, Université de Montréal.

Lefebvre, M., & Pinard, A. 1972. Apprentissage de la conservation des quantités liquides par une méthode de conflit cognitif. *Revue canadienne des sciences du comportement* 4:1–12.

Lefebvre, M., & Pinard, A. 1974. Influence du niveau initial de sensibilité au conflit sur l'apprentissage de la conservation des quantités par une méthode de conflit cognitif. *Revue canadienne des sciences du comportement* 6:398–413.

Lebfebvre-Pinard, M. 1976a. Les expériences de Genève sur l'apprentissage: un dossier peu convaincant (même pour un Piagétien). *Psychologie canadienne* 17:103–109.

Lefebvre-Pinard, M. 1976b. A propos des expériences de Genève sur l'apprentissage: note sur la réplique de Pascual-Leone. *Psychologie canadienne* 17:298–299.

Lieberman, D. A. 1979. A (limited) call for a return to introspection. *American psychologist* 34:319–333.

Lunzer, E. 1975. Les co-ordinations et les conservations dans le domaine de la géométrie. In Vinh Bang & E. Lunzer, *Etudes d'épistémologie génétique*. Vol. 19. *Conservations spatiales*. Paris: Presses Universitaires de France.

McCarthy-Gallagher, J., & Kim-Reid, D. 1978. An empirical test of judgments and explanations in Piagetian-type problems of conservation of continuous quantity. *Perceptual and motor skills* 46:363–368.

MacNamara, J. 1976. Stomachs assimilate and accommodate, don't they? *Canadian psychological review* 17:168–173.

MacNamara, J. 1978. Another unaccommodating look at Piaget. *Canadian psychological review* 19:79–81.

Migneron, T. 1969. La genèse des qualités de l'objet chez l'enfant. Thèse de maîtrise inédite. Université de Montréal.

Miller, P. H. 1973. Attention to stimulus dimensions in the conservation of liquid quantity. *Child development* 44:129–136.

Miller, P. H. 1978. Stimulus variables in conservation: an alternative approach to assessment. *Merrill-Palmer quarterly* 24:141–160.

Morf, A.; Smedslund, J.; Vinh-Bang; & Wohlwill, J. F. 1959. *Etudes d'épistémologie génétique*. Vol. 9. *L'apprentissage des structures logiques*. Paris: Presses Universitaires de France.

Morin, T. 1974. Etude de l'apprentissage d'une structure logique concrète (inclusion), III. Mise à l'épreuve des critères de logicité de l'opération. Thèse de maîtrise inédite, Université de Montréal.

Mounoud, P. 1970. *Structuration de l'instrument chez l'enfant.*

Neuchâtel: Delachaux et Niestlé.

Mounoud, P. 1973. Les conservations physiques chez le bébé. *Bulletin de psychologie* 27:722–728.

Mounoud, P. 1977. Nouvelles directions et nouvelles approches dans la théorie piagétienne. Rapport présenté au Septième symposium de la Jean Piaget Society, Philadelphia.

Mounoud, P. 1978. Mémoire et intelligence. In G. Steiner (Ed.), *Psychologie du 20e siècle*. Vol. 7. Munich (Allemagne de l'Ouest): Kendler. (Published in German only.)

Mounoud, P., & Bower, T. G. R. 1974. Conservation of weight in infants. *Cognition* 3:29–40.

Murray, F. B. 1972. Acquisition of conservation through social interaction. *Developmental psychology* 6:1–6.

Murray, F. B. 1976. Conservation deductions and ecological validity. In S. Modgil & C. Modgil, *Piagetian research.* Vol. 7. Windsor, Berks. NFER.

Murray, F. B. 1977. Logic of nonconservation. *Genetic epistemologist* 6:10–11.

Murray, F. B. 1978. The adequacy of conservation reasons. *Genetic epistemologist* 7:5–6.

Murray, F. B., & Armstrong, S. L. 1976. Necessity in conservation and nonconservation. *Developmental psychology* 12:483–484.

Murray, F. B., & Johnson, P. E. 1969. Reversibility in nonconservation of weight. *Psychonomic science* 16:285–287.

Murray, F. B., & Johnson, P. E. 1975. Relevant and some irrelevant factors in the child's concept of weight. *Journal of educational psychology* 67:705–711.

Murray, F. B., & Tyler, S. J. 1978. Semantic characteristics of the conservation transformation. *Psychological reports* 42:1051–1054.

Newell, A. 1969. Thoughts on the concept of process (discussion of Prof. Bourne's paper). In J. F. Voss (Ed.), *Approaches to thought*. Columbus, Ohio: Merrill.

Nummedal, S. G., & Murray, F. B. 1969. Semantic factors in conservation of weight. *Psychonomic science* 16:323–324.

Osiek, C. 1977. Interférences entre différentes propriétés de l'objet chez l'enfant. *Archives de psychologie* (Genève) 45:279–326.

Pagé, M. 1967. Apprentissage de la notion des deux sens de l'orientation I: comparaison de deux types (mixte et homogène) de méthode empirique. Thèse de licence inédite, Université de Montréal.

Paivio, A. 1975. Neo-mentalism. *Canadian journal of psychology* 29:263–291.

Pascual-Leone, J. 1970. A mathematical model for the transition rule in Piaget's developmental stages. *Acta psychologica* 63:301–345.

Pascual-Leone, J. 1980. Constructive problems for constructive theories: the current relevance of Piaget's work and a critique of information-processing simulation psychology. In H. Spada & R. Kluwe, (Eds.), *Developmental models of thinking*. New York: Academic Press.

Piaget, J. [1924] 1976. *Judgment and reasoning in the child*. Totowa, N.J.: Littlefield, Adams.

Piaget, J. 1941. Le mécanisme du développement mental et les lois du groupement des opérations. *Archives de psychologie* (Genève) 28:215–285.

Piaget, J. [1946a] 1970. *The child's conception of time*. New York: Basic.

Piaget, J. [1946b] 1970. *The child's conception of movement and speed*. New York: Basic.

Piaget, J. [1947] 1950. *The psychology of intelligence*. London: Routledge & Kegan Paul.

Piaget, J. 1950a. *Introduction à l'épistémologie génétique*. Vol. 1. *La pensée mathématique*. Paris: Presses Universitaires de France.

Piaget, J. 1950b. *Introduction à l'épistémologie génétique*. Vol. 2. *La pensée physique*. Paris: Presses Universitaires de France.

Piaget, J. 1950c. *Introduction à l'épistémologie génétique*. Vol. 3. *La pensée biologique, la pensée psychologique et la pensée sociologique*. Paris: Presses Universitaires de France.

Piaget, J. 1957. Programme et méthodes de l'épistémologie génétique. In W. E. Beth, W. Mays, & J. Piaget, *Etudes d'épistémologie génétique*. Vol. I. *Epistémologie génétique et recherche psychologique*. Paris: Presses Universitaires de France.

Piaget, J. 1960. La portée psychologique et épistémologique des essais néo-hulliens de D. Berlyne. In D. E. Berlyne & J. Piaget, *Etudes d'épistémologie génétique*. Vol. 12. *Théorie du comportement et opérations*. Paris: Presses Universitaires de France.

Piaget, J. [1964] 1967. *Six psychological studies*. New York: Random House.

Piaget, J. [1967a] 1971. *Biology and knowledge: an essay on the relations between organic regulations and cognitive processes*.

Edinburgh: Edinburgh University Press.

Piaget, J. [1967b] 1968. Explanation in psychology and psycho-physiological parallelism. In P. Fraisse & J. Piaget (Eds.), *Experimental psychology: its scope and method*. Vol. 1. New York: Basic.

Piaget, J. 1967c. Les relations entre le sujet et l'objet dans la connaissance physique. In J. Piaget (Ed.), *Logique et connaissance scientifique* (Encyclopédie de la Pléiade). Paris: Gallimard.

Piaget, J. [1968] 1970. *Structuralism*. New York: Basic.

Piaget, J. [1971] 1974. Causality and operations. In J. Piaget & R. Garcia, *Understanding causality*. New York: Norton.

Piaget, J. 1972a. *Etudes d'épistémologie génétique*. Vol. 27. *La transmission des mouvements*. Paris: Presses Universitaires de France.

Piaget, J. 1972b. *Etudes d'épistémologie génétique*. Vol. 28. *La direction des mobiles lors de chocs et de poussées*. Paris: Presses Universitaires de France.

Piaget, J. 1973a. *Etudes d'épistémologie génétique*. Vol. 29. *La formation de la notion de force*. Paris: Presses Universitaires de France.

Piaget, J. 1973b. *Etudes d'épistémologie génétique*. Vol. 30. *La composition des forces et le problème des vecteurs*. Paris: Presses Universitaires de France.

Piaget, J. 1974a. *Adaptation vitale et psychologie de l'intelligence*. Paris: Hermann. (Trans.: *Vital adaptation and the psychology of intelligence*. Chicago: University of Chicago Press, 1980.)

Piaget, J. [1974b] 1976. *The grasp of consciousness: action and concept in the young child*. Cambridge: Harvard University Press.

Piaget, J. [1974c] 1978. *Success and understanding*. Cambridge: Harvard University Press.

Piaget, J. [1975] 1977. *The development of thought: equilibration of cognitive structures*. New York: Viking.

Piaget, J. 1976. Le possible, l'impossible et le nécessaire. *Archives de psychologie* (Genève) 44:281–299.

Piaget, J. 1977. Essai sur la nécessité. *Archives de psychologie* (Genève) 45:235–251.

Piaget, J. 1979. Correspondences and transformations. In F. B. Murray (Ed.), *The impact of Piagetian theory*. Baltimore: University Park Press.

Piaget, J. & Garcia, R. [1971] 1974. *Understanding causality*. New York: Norton.

Piaget, J., & Inhelder, B. [1966] 1971. *Mental imagery in the child; a study of the development of imaginal representation.* New York: Basic.

Piaget, J. , & Inhelder, B. [1968] 1973. *Memory and Intelligence.* New York: Basic.

Piaget, J. ; Inhelder, B.; & Szeminska, A. [1948] 1960. *The child's conception of geometry.* New York: Basic.

Piaget, J.; Sinclair, H.; & Vinh-Bang. 1968. *Etudes d'épisté-mologie génétique.* Vol. 24. *Epistémologie et psychologie de l'identité.* Paris: Presses Universitaires de France.

Piaget, J., & Voyat, G. 1968. Recherche sur l'identité d'un corps en développement et sur celle du mouvement transitif. In J. Piaget, H. Sinclair, & Vinh-Bang, *Etudes d'épistémologie génétique.* Vol. 24. *Epistémologie et psychologie de l'identité.* Paris: Presses Universitaires de France.

Piaget, J., et al. [1968] 1977. *Epistemology and psychology of functions.* Boston: Reidel.

Piaget, J., et al. 1974a. *Etudes d'épistémologie génétique.* Vol. 31. *Recherches sur la contradiction. I. Les différentes formes de la contradiction.* Paris: Presses Universitaires de France.

Piaget, J., et al. 1974b. *Etudes d'épistémologie génétique.* Vol. 32. *Recherches sur la contradiction. II. Les relations entre affirmations et négations.* Paris: Presses Universitaires de France.

Piaget, J., et al. 1977a. *Etudes d'épistémologie génétique.* Vol. 34. *Recherches sur l'abstraction réfléchissante. I. L'abstrac-tion des relations logico-arithmétiques.* Paris: Presses Universitaires de France.

Piaget, J., et al. 1977b. *Etudes d'épistémologie génétique.* Vol. 35. *Recherches sur l'abstraction réfléchissante. II. L'abstrac-tion de l'ordre des relations spatiales.* Paris: Presses Universitaires de France.

Piaget, J., et al. 1978. *Etudes d'épistémologie génétique.* Vol. 36. *Recherches sur la généralisation.* Paris: Presses Universitaires de France.

Piéraut-Le Bonniec, G. 1977. Développement des capacités d'ab-straction chez le jeune enfant entre 2-0 et 5-0 ans. *Archives de psychologie* (Genève) 45:205–223.

Piéraut-Le Bonniec, G. 1979. Opérations cognitives et sentiment de la nécessité logique. Communication présentée au Congrès international de psychologie de l'enfant, Paris.

Piéraut-Le Bonniec, G., & Jacob, S. 1976–1978. Etude génétique de la construction des propriétés des objets et développement des capacités d'abstraction chez l'enfant de 2 à 7 ans. Travaux du Centre d'étude des processus cognitifs et du langage. Unpublished report issued by Laboratoire de psychologie, Ecole des Hautes Etudes en Sciences sociales (Paris), pp. 53–55.

Piéraut-Le Bonniec, G., & Vurpillot, E. 1976–1978. Etude de la constitution des propriétés concave/convexe/plat et de la relation contenant/contenu chez le bébé de 2 à 12 mois. Travaux du Centre d'étude des processus cognitifs et du langage. Unpublished report issued by Laboratoire de psychologie, Ecole des Hautes Etudes en Sciences sociales (Paris), pp. 53–55.

Pierre-Joly, R. 1974. Influences du processus de dissociation sur le développment de la conservation du poids. Thèse de maîtrise inédite, Université de Montréal.

Pinard, A. 1975. Note sur la compatibilité des notions de stade et de décalage dans la théorie de Piaget. *Psychologie canadienne* 16:255–260.

Pinard, A., & Chassé, G. 1977. Pseudoconservation of the volume and surface of a solid object. *Child development* 48:1559–1566.

Pinard, A., & Laurendeau, M. 1969. "Stage" in Piaget's cognitive development theory: exegesis of a concept. In D. Elkind & J. H. Flavell (Eds.), *Studies in cognitive development: essays in honor of Jean Piaget*. New York: Oxford University Press.

Pinard, A., & Laurendeau, M. 1971. Equilibration et stade dans le système de Piaget. *Contributions à l'étude des sciences de l'homme* 8:7–60.

Pinard, A.; Morin, C.; & Lefebvre, M. 1973. Apprentissage de la conservation des quantités liquides chez des enfants rwandais et canadiens-français. *Journal international de psychologie* 8:15–23.

Pinard, A., & Pierre-Joly, R. 1979. Dissociation des propriétés physiques d'un object et conservation du poids. Rapport présenté au Congrès international de psychologie de l'enfant, Paris.

Reese, H. W., & Schack, M. L. 1974. Comment on Brainerd's criteria for cognitive structures. *Psychological bulletin* 81:67–69.

Richelle, M. 1976. Constructivisme et behaviorisme. *Revue européenne des sciences sociales* 14:291–303.

Rosenthal, T. L., & Zimmerman, B. J. 1978. *Social learning and cognition*. New York: Academic Press.

Siegel, L. S. 1973. The role of spatial arrangement and heterogeneity in the development of numerical equivalence. *Canadian journal of psychology* 27:351–355.

Siegel, L. S. 1974. Development of number concepts: ordering and correspondence operations and the role of length cues. *Developmental psychology* 10:907–912.

Siegel, L. S. 1978. The relationship of language and thought in the preoperational child: a reconsideration of nonverbal alternatives to Piagetian tasks. In L. S. Siegel & C. J. Brainerd (Eds.), *Alternatives to Piaget*. New York: Academic Press.

Siegler, R. S. 1976. Three aspects of cognitive development. *Cognitive psychology* 8:481–520.

Siegler, R. S. 1978. The origins of scientific reasoning. In R. S. Siegler (Ed.), *Children's thinking: what develops?* Hillsdale, N.J.: Erlbaum.

Siegler, R. S. 1979. A rule assessment approach to cognitive development. Paper presented at the meeting of the Society for Research in Child Development, San Francisco.

Simon, H. A. 1962. An information processing theory of intellectual development. In W. Kessen & C. Kuhlman (Eds.), *Thought in the young child. Monographs of the Society for research in child development* 27(2, serial no. 83):150–155.

Simon, H. A. 1972. On the development of the processor. In S. Farnham-Diggory (Ed.), *Information processing in children*. New York: Academic Press.

Simon, H. A. 1979. Information processing models of cognition. *Annual review of psychology* 30:363–396.

Sinclair, H., & Ferreiro, E. 1970. Etude génétique de la compréhension, production et répétition des phrases au mode passif. *Archives de psychologie* (Genève) 40:1–42.

Sinclair Dezwart, H. 1977. Recent developments in genetic epistemology. *Genetic epistemologist* 6 (no. 4):1–4.

Skinner, B. F. 1974. *About behaviorism*. New York: Knopf.

Skinner. B. F. 1977a. Why I am not a cognitivist. *Behavior* 5:1–10.

Skinner, B. F. 1977b. Herrnstein and the evolution of behaviorism. *American psychologist* 32:1006–1012.

Strayer, F. F. 1980. An ethological analysis of preschool social ecology. In W. A. Collins (Ed.), *Minnesota symposia on child psychology*. Vol. 13. Hillsdale, N.J.: Erlbaum.

Szeminska, A., & Piaget, J. 1968. De la copropriété à la conservation: l'égalisation et l'estimation des inégalités. In J. Piaget et al., *Etudes d'épistémologie génétique*. Vol. 23. *Epistémologie et psychologie de la fonction*. Paris: Presses Universitaires de France.

Trabasso, T. 1968. Pay attention. *Psychology today* 2 (October):31–36.

Trabasso, T., & Bower, G. 1968. *Attention in learning: theory and research.* New York: Wiley.

Vadham, V. P., & Smothergill, D. W. 1977. Attention and cognition. *Cognition* 5:251–263.

Van Den Bogaert-Rombouts, N. 1966. Projection spatiale d'une série temporelle. In J. B. Grize et al., *Etudes d'épistémologie génétique.* Vol. 20. *L'épistémologie du temps.* Paris: Presses Universitaires de France.

Wallach, L. 1969. On the basis of conservation. In D. Elkind & J. H. Flavell (Eds.), *Studies in cognitive development: essays in honor of Jean Piaget.* New York: Oxford University Press.

Watson, J. S. 1968. Conservation: an s-r analysis. In I. E. Siegel & F. H. Hooper (Eds.), *Logical thinking in children.* New York: Holt, Rinehart & Winston.

Wohlwill, J. 1973. *The study of behavioral development.* New York: Academic Press.

Index

Index of Names